KOREANS IN THE HOOD

KOREANS in the HOOD

Conflict with African Americans

EDITED BY KWANG CHUNG KIM

THE JOHNS HOPKINS UNIVERSITY PRESS   BALTIMORE AND LONDON

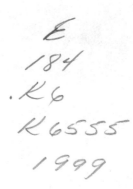

The Johns Hopkins University Press
2715 North Charles Street
Baltimore, Maryland 21218-4363
www.press.jhu.edu

Library of Congress Cataloging-in-Publication Data
will be found at the end of this book.

A catalog record for this book is available from the British Library.

ISBN 0-8018-6103-9
ISBN 0-8018-6104-7 (pbk.)

Contents

KOREANS IN THE HOOD

▮ Introduction

KWANG CHUNG KIM

SOUTH CENTRAL LOS ANGELES ERUPTED ON THE AFTERNOON OF April 29, 1992. For three days, the whole nation was captivated by horrible scenes of fire and violence from America's paradise on the West Coast. The 1992 Los Angeles racial disturbance was a shocking event. The violence that was precipitated by the verdict at the Rodney King trial broke out in South Central Los Angeles and the mayhem that followed destroyed a large proportion of businesses in that area and in nearby Koreatown. As the event unfolded, the mass violence, which had begun as a protest by African Americans against the dominant society, was reconfigured as an interminority group conflict between Koreans and African Americans. During the three days of the disturbance and the subsequent time period, television and other media heavily focused on an incident that had occurred a year earlier, the killing of Latasha Harlins, an African American girl, by a Korean store owner (Chaps. 3, 4, and 5). The media also showed close-ups of armed Korean store owners and their family and friends trying to protect Korean stores during the three days of unrest. Such media coverage created and perpetuated a negative stereotype of Korean entrepreneurs as "heartless merchants," "ruthless exploiters," "gun-toting vigilantes," or "money-crazed people" (Chaps. 3, 5, and 11). Korean merchants unexpectedly endured huge economic losses and suffered from psychological trauma, feeling an anomic sense of helplessness (Chaps. 2, 4, and 5). The violence betrayed their strong belief in the United States as a land of opportunity, where hard work would pay off. Their optimistic (or naive) conviction regarding the strong ties between performance and reward was shattered.

On the whole, the media reported the disturbance as a biracial conflict between Korean store owners and African American residents (Chaps. 3, 4, 5, and 11), dismissing the role the white dominant group plays in generating such interminority group conflict (Chaps. 2, 6, and 8). In this construction of social reality, minority members are blamed for the conflict and its consequences (Chaps. 3, 4, and 5). Thus, along with African Americans' racism, jealousy, and scapegoating, Korean merchants' rude treatment of customers, prejudice, economic exploitation, cultural misunderstandings, limited assimilation, and foreignness were all identified as sources of the conflict (Chaps. 2, 3, 5, 7, and 11). For Korean Americans, this media construction of the event carried a clear message: as the "bad guys," Korean merchants deserved their economic losses and psychological suffering—a plain example of "blaming the victim" logic.

Korean merchants in South Central Los Angeles were doubly victimized: first by their economic loss and the accompanying psychological suffering, then again as they were blamed for their own misfortune. As John Lie and Nancy Abelmann (Chap. 5) stress, the media virtually excluded Korean American voices in the construction of such a social reality. Most first-generation Korean immigrants were frustrated by their inability to articulate their point of view and their criticism of media coverage (Chap. 11). In other words, Korean American perspectives were grossly neglected or misconstrued in the media construction of the event.

In addition to this double victimization of Korean merchants, the national media coverage of the conflict between these two ethnic groups was heavily skewed to the Los Angeles experience. Korean and African American conflict in New York City was relatively obscured, and the Chicago racial experiences remained virtually unknown to outsiders. Unless Korean American experiences of the interracial conflict in these cities are systematically compared, one cannot sufficiently comprehend the diversity and complexity of this conflict. Admittedly, studying the Los Angeles disturbance is essential for understanding Korean merchants' experience of Korean and African American conflict in the United States. Yet, as Jung Sun Park (Chap. 11) argues, the centrality of the Los Angeles disturbance was overemphasized to the extent that it was implicitly or explicitly taken to represent the entire Korean American experience. This position overlooks Korean American experiences of the racial conflict in different cities, which contain both commonalities and differences. Korean Americans' overall experience of the interethnic conflict would be better understood if these were examined through intercity comparison.

The Los Angeles racial disturbance produced numerous scholarly books and articles (Abelmann and Lie 1995; Baldassare 1994; Chang 1993; Light, Har-Chvi, and Kan 1994; Madhubuti 1993; Ong, Park, and Tong 1994; Totten and Schockman 1994; Yu 1994; Yu and Chang 1995). These publications examine the interracial conflict's media coverage, its social structural bases, and various aspects of its overt activities. They suggest numerous ways to reduce the conflict and to promote interracial cooperation. These publications also reveal some limitations to a comprehensive understanding of Korean merchants' experiences of Korean and African American conflict in major cities. First, they are mainly concerned with one form of the interracial conflict that occurred in one city, the 1992 Los Angeles racial disturbance. Second, even the scholarly publications hardly attempt to define the structural position of Korean merchants in urban poor minority communities, which generates and sustains the interracial conflict. Without an understanding of this structural position to serve as a coherent framework of analysis, discussion of Korean and African American conflict would be easily distorted. In this respect, Pyong Gap Min's recent publication, *Caught in the Middle*, presents an insightful analysis of Korean and African American conflict in major American cities. His analysis of the experiences in Los Angeles and New York City and utilization of the middleman minority theory suggest many new ideas about Korean and African American conflict that would have been impossible without intercity comparison and an understanding of the structural position of Korean merchants.

Although many chapters in this book rarely go beyond the stage of exploratory analysis, they offer another opportunity for intercity comparison. This book brings together studies of Korean and African American conflict observed in each of the three major American cities, Los Angeles, New York City, and Chicago. Even though each chapter is about one particular city, assembling them in one book brings out numerous new ideas through the opportunity for intercity comparison. The concluding chapter systematically compares several aspects of Korean and African American conflict across these cities. Nonetheless, the major intent of this book is to present Korean Americans' experiences of the conflict in these three cities for the readers' own interpretation.

In social sciences, our action and inaction reflect our beliefs, interests, and preferences, which in turn shape our perspectives. Our perspectives then generally predefine our selection of research topics, the kind of data collected, methods used and other factors. In this way, our perspectives and factual findings become inseparable; social science findings cannot be considered value-free and disinterested representations of social reality. It is, therefore, imperative to be aware of our own and other available perspectives in the analysis of a social science phenomenon and any factual consequences of these perspectives (Romm 1991). When our values are involved, Max Weber (1949) stresses making the value involvement explicit and examining the implications of such an involvement. This position suggests that members of various racial and ethnic groups who are differentiated by economic position (class) and race or association (ethnicity) are expected to have different perspectives in explaining the common experience of interracial and other intergroup relations. The analysis of Korean American experiences of the interracial conflict presented here is recognized to be a product of such a value involvement—an analysis of the conflict from Korean American perspectives.

As such, the analysis is from the perspectives of Korean Americans' own interests, beliefs, and preferences. Since Korean merchants in urban poor minority communities have emerged as major actors in the interracial conflict and were badly victimized in the Los Angeles mass violence and other events, Korean American perspectives heavily, if not exclusively, reflect those of Korean merchants. This means most of the chapters explicitly or implicitly draw upon Korean merchants' interests and experiences in urban poor minority communities, even though other Korean American perspectives do exist in Korean ethnic communities (Chap. 5).

Since African American residents in urban poor minority communities are those directly involved in the other side of this conflict, their perspectives are recognized as another set of perspectives highly relevant in the analysis of these intergroup relations. Of various African American perspectives, African American nationalistic perspectives were actively and conspicuously utilized in Korean and African American conflict (Chaps. 2, 3, 4, 6, and 11; Min 1996). These perspectives take opposing positions on the two issues of Korean and African American conflict: (1) the presence of Korean merchants in urban poor minority communities and these merchants' business practices and (2) the negative or hostile activities directed at Korean merchants and their businesses by African American residents.

In spite of their middle-class backgrounds, a high proportion of Korean immigrants are excluded from the mainstream occupations in the United States. This forces many Korean immigrants to operate businesses in urban poor minority communities (Chap. 2). From Korean merchants' perspective, operating a small business is an economic necessity for settling in the United States and supporting a family. Korean merchants themselves recognize that some Korean shopkeepers treat African American customers rudely or disrespectfully and that many Korean merchants are prejudiced (Chap. 7; Min 1996). They maintain, however, that the majority of Korean merchants treat African American customers courteously because it is in their economic interests to do so (Chap. 9; Min 1996). They generally reject the charge of economic exploitation and contend that they operate their businesses under heavy competitive pressure from other Korean merchants in the same neighborhoods—creating an environment of intragroup business competition. This competition forces them to lower their prices and to offer goods of a decent quality (Chap. 2). Merchants also stress numerous contributions they have made to urban poor minority communities: the investment in and development of many deteriorated or abandoned neighborhoods, the creation of job opportunities for local youth, the availability of reasonably priced consumer goods to local residents at convenient locations and times, and the implementation of a number of mediation programs (Chaps. 2 and 12). From the perspective of Korean merchants, the major problem facing their business is African American residents' various negative or hostile activities toward them and their businesses. For Korean merchants, these activities are the primary source of Korean and African American conflict.

From an African American nationalistic perspective, the major source of Korean and African American conflict is not these negative or hostile activities toward Korean merchants and Korean businesses but rather the business practices and, indeed, the presence of Korean businesses in African American communities. In the context of African American nationalism, the presence and practices of Korean businesses generate numerous kinds of problems in urban poor minority communities. African Americans' negative or hostile activities are considered necessary in order to express their discontents with Korean businesses. Those with a nationalistic perspective would thus argue that the best way to stop any negative or hostile activities by African American residents would be either to withdraw Korean businesses from African American communities or to change Korean merchants' bad business practices.

As perspectives of minority group members, both Korean merchant and African American nationalistic perspectives reflect grievance or victimization. Nonetheless, the two perspectives point to two different sources for this grievance or victimization. For Korean merchants, the major source of grievance is the negative or hostile activities of African American customers or residents. These activities result in the physical injury or death of store owners, their family members, or their employees, the loss of merchandise, the damage or destruction of their property, and the partial or complete loss of the base of their family livelihood. From the perspective of African American nationalism, the major source of grievance is the presence of Korean businesses, which is seen to inhibit or destroy the African American nationalistic aspiration of community self-control and is regarded as another instance of the historical pattern of outside commercial intrusion into African American communities, exploitation of local residents, expression of contempt for African American residents, and hindrance of African Americans' business development in their own communities. Because of these two opposing perspectives, Korean merchants and many inner-city African American customers or residents are pursuing incompatible goals and interests (Kriesberg 1982).

Moreover, these two contrasting perspectives are aggravated by the delicate relationship of status inconsistency between the two minority groups (Chap. 6). Korean merchants in urban poor minority communities are economically active and powerful as sellers and employers. At the same time, they are politically weak in their ability to prevent or to cope with the local residents' hostilities. In contrast, African American residents in inner cities are more often economically weak, but they are politically stronger than Korean merchants in their ability to organize activities against Korean businesses. This dual inconsistency is an important feature of interminority group conflict—although, when compared with the white dominant group, both Korean merchants and African American residents are weak in both economic and political dimensions.

This book has twelve chapters, arranged according to the city discussed and framed by an introductory and a concluding chapter (Chaps. 1 and 12). The first four chapters (Chaps. 2–5) examine the Korean American experience in Los Angeles. The next three chapters (Chaps. 6–8) discuss the New York City experience. The remaining three (Chaps. 9–11) cover a topic little known to the American public, the Korean American experience of inner-city racial conflict in Chicago. All chapters are concerned with one or two of the three important issues in interracial conflict: (1) defining the structural position of Korean merchants in urban poor minority communities, (2) reviewing the media-constructed social reality of Korean and African American conflict, and (3) analyzing overt forms of such conflict. Together, the chapters represent a concerted effort to analyze Korean Americans' experience of interracial conflict in three major cities.

Three chapters (Chaps. 2, 3, and 8) examine the structural position of Korean store owners. They consider Korean and African American conflict as a conflict between two minority groups in a white dominated society, suggesting that conflict between the two minority groups cannot be understood unless their respective relationship with the dominant group is examined. With this framework, the three chapters contend that Korean store owners in urban poor minority communities are structurally placed as middleman entrepreneurs. As middleman retailers, Korean store owners in urban minority communities stand commercially and racially between their minority customers and those who are involved in the production or wholesale distribution of the goods.

Basing their contribution heavily on data from South Central Los Angeles, Kwang Chung Kim and Shin Kim (Chap. 2) contend that the main cause of Korean and African American conflict stems from the historical and contemporary patterns of African Americans' relationship with the white dominant group. This position requires focusing on the relationship of the two traditional racial groups in the United States, whites and African Americans. The authors also maintain that Korean immigrants' business entry into urban poor communities is a result of their relationship with the white dominant group—demonstrating both a general exclusion of Korean immigrants from mainstream occupations and the availability of inner-city business opportunities avoided by the white dominant group. In such a context of multiracial relations, Korean store owners act as middleman merchants in urban African American and Hispanic American communities.

Edward Chang (Chap. 3) reviews the changing demographics and environment of South Central Los Angeles. The area has been drastically changed by the increasing number of Hispanic immigrants and by the restructuring of the economy through deindustrialization. Race relations in South Central Los Angeles are no longer a biracial relationship between whites and African Americans but a complex set of multiracial relations, which in turn creates multiple sets of interracial conflict. Conflict between Korean store owners and their minority customers intensifies under these tension-filled relations. Chang also regards Korean store owners as middleman minorities and contends that multiple factors (racial, sociocultural, economic, ideological) affect the relationship between Korean store owners and African American residents in South Central Los Angeles. He examines the delicate race relations in terms of

Korean store owners' and African American residents' perceptions of each other. Chang dispels seven common myths about Korean merchants held by many of the urban minority residents.

Drawing on the data from New York City and Los Angeles, Pyong Gap Min and Andrew Kolodny (Chap. 8) note that a high proportion of Korean immigrants are now engaged in self-employed small business, and a substantial proportion of these merchants serve urban African American and Hispanic customers. They characterize these urban merchants as middleman minorities and consider their grocery or liquor retail stores prototype middleman businesses that rely heavily on mainstream, white American producers. They also describe other retail businesses dealing with wigs, handbags, jewelry, clothing, and other goods (mostly imported from Korea, other Asian countries, or Latin American countries) as middleman businesses in a limited sense. Min and Kolodny then examine the recursive nature of Korean intragroup and intergroup relations as a middleman minority. Hostility from inner-city residents enhances the ethnic solidarity and cohesion among Korean merchants, but such ethnic solidarity in turn intensifies negative stereotyping and hostility from inner-city minority residents.

Three chapters in this book (Chaps. 4, 5, and 11) review the mass media, examining what it did and did not do. The core of the media criticism is its negative stereotyping of Korean store owners and its characterization of Korean and African American conflict as only a biracial issue. These chapters also discuss various patterns of Korean American response to the mass media and the impact of media coverage on Korean Americans' ethnic identity.

Kyeyoung Park (Chap. 4) raises the issue of the media's projection of the conflict as biracial. In her study, originally published in *American Anthropologist* 98 (1996) and reprinted here with permission, she asks: What and who are missing here? Where are the white people in this interpretation of the conflict? What kind of racial discourse or structure was the media creating and what role does race play? Park notes that the white-dominated mass media focuses on race, while African American and Korean community leaders explain the tension in terms of culture. In contrast, scholars have stressed the importance of structural forces in race relations. Thus, African American–Korean American conflict is not only about economics but also about meanings. This clash of values and meanings happens within the context of a power relationship.

John Lie and Nancy Abelmann (Chap. 5) examine the media-framed "Black-Korean conflict." This mass media label reflects the influence of dominant ideologies in narrowly constructing the conflict as a biracial issue. Korean Americans expressed their anger and frustration with this media-created social reality and challenged it in some cases. When the mass media articulates a ready-made framework, however, it becomes difficult to challenge the framework's veracity. Lie and Abelmann argue that the media-projected images treated diverse phenomena under the same rubric, homogenizing either group. Such a projection of the interethnic conflict framework reifies each group, thereby eliding significant cleavages and differences between them. Both Koreans and African Americans are differentiated by class and other factors, and thus individual members of each group hold differing views of the interethnic conflict. The authors warn of two negative repercussions of the persistence of the "Black-Korean conflict" frame. First, the very reproduction of the interethnic conflict discourse may serve to heighten individual suspicion and hatred. Second, focusing on the "Black-Korean conflict" averts our gaze from more serious and pressing issues facing South Central Los Angeles in particular and the United States at large.

Jung Sun Park (Chap. 11) focuses not on the general media coverage of Korean Americans but, specifically, the media's transformation and politicization of Korean Americans' collective identity. Park observes that the mainstream media has treated Korean Americans as "foreigners" or "foreign immigrants," signifying their position of marginalization and exclusion from American society. The media has also depicted Korean Americans as helpless people who lack the linguistic ability to articulate their position even in times of crisis, a stereotype that reinforces their foreignness. The media coverage of Korean Americans during the Los Angeles riot shocked Korean Americans in Chicago, who realized that the Korean American population was being portrayed as a powerless and helpless marginalized population without rights. Korean Americans felt the need to find a firm basis for their membership in American society, and they sought such a basis by transforming their collective identity from "Koreans" to "Korean Americans" and politicizing this new ethnic identity. With a new outlook, Korean Americans now claim their full-fledged membership in American society. Their new identity connects them with other Asian groups, changes their perspectives toward African Americans and Hispanic Americans, and keeps intentional distancing from their home country.

As a whole, the chapters in this book provide rich sources of information for an intercity comparison of Korean American experiences. Moving from our review of the Los Angeles experience, we turn to chapters on the two other major cities. Korean American experiences in New York (Chaps. 6 and 7) and Chicago (Chaps. 9 and 10) offer comparisons and contrasts with those in Los Angeles. Uniquely in New York City, many Korean merchants handle fruits and vegetables. Chapters 6 and 7 examine the Korean American experiences of racial conflict at Korean fruit and vegetable stores in New York City. Utilizing resource mobilization theory, Heon Cheol Lee (Chap. 6) analyzes the prolonged African American boycott of Korean stores in New York City. He disputes the common idea that the boycott developed spontaneously out of an interpersonal dispute or incident. Lee argues that such an incident is not a sufficient condition, though it may be a precondition or an opportune event for boycott organizers to call for a prolonged boycott. He defines the New York boycott as an African American boycott of Korean stores in predominantly African American communities within the white dominant society. Although the first few days of the boycott were set up spontaneously by the outraged local residents, the rest of the eighteen-month boycott in New York City was mainly organized and sustained by different African American leaders for their various personal and political interests. The leaders were engaged in an intensive competition for power and recognition—not only with one another but also with white political leaders. As a participant observer, Lee carefully documents the activities of various boycott leaders to mobilize people throughout various stages of the prolonged conflict and to utilize the cultural ideology of African American nationalism to exploit and publicize a perceived inconsistent status between Korean merchants and African American residents.

Korean and African American conflict can also be examined as it occurs at the store level, between individual Korean store workers and individual minority customers. In Chapter 7, Heon Cheol Lee examines this kind of interpersonal dispute. His analysis offers a unique perspective that questions the common idea that cultural misunderstandings and certain behavior patterns of Korean store owners create interpersonal conflict at the store level. He attributes the source of interpersonal tension to what he calls "structural contradictions of Korean businesses" at the store level. Lee concludes that the overall relations between Korean merchants and African American customers were not as bad as presented by boycott leaders and the mass media, stressing that Korean and African American conflict was not the result of ordinary African American customers' explosive dissatisfaction with Korean merchants' so-called disrespectful behavior.

In South Central Los Angeles, Korean liquor stores have been a major target of African American antagonism, while in New York City, fruit and vegetable stores have been a focal point of the interracial conflict. These two types of stores are extremely rare among Korean businesses on the South Side of Chicago, however, where African Americans are heavily concentrated and where Korean and African American conflict has nevertheless occurred. InChul Choi (Chap. 9) chronologically analyzes two forms of Korean and African American conflict observed in Chicago, boycott and mass violence. His analysis of boycott experiences in Chicago confirms Lee's contention that the African American boycotts of Korean stores are often organized and sustained by leaders pursuing personal and political interests. In contrast to Lee's study of the boycott in New York City, Choi's analysis shows that the three recent boycotts in Chicago developed without any concrete sparking incident of interpersonal dispute at the store level. To some extent, Korean store owners in Chicago have successfully contained several attempts at boycott and mass violence. As a major factor in this boycott containment, Choi points to the well-organized merchants' association, under a dedicated leadership with a vision and staffed with members from a community service agency. In contrast with the Los Angeles experience, Choi's chapter also credits the highly responsive and effective Chicago police force with protecting Korean stores when mass violence broke out.

InChul Choi and Shin Kim (Chap. 10) discuss various mediation programs Korean store owners offered to local minority residents and the intensity of Korean store owners' efforts to win the local residents' goodwill. At the same time, they show the limitations of such programs in improving local residents' deprived living conditions. Choi and Kim nevertheless note that as Korean merchants encountered hostility and consumer disputes, they increasingly realized the need to network with African American leaders. According to the authors, this networking must be with legitimate leaders and organizations in African American communities. Any ties, real or perceived, with illegitimate organizations could be detrimental in public relations with the dominant white majority. To illustrate the Chicago networking effort, Choi and Kim have meticulously prepared a chronology of Korean merchants' networking activities.

Overall, three distinct, overt forms of Korean and African American conflict are identified in this book: interpersonal dispute, boycott, and mass violence. As Lee (Chap. 6) suggests, it is necessary to distinguish between interpersonal dispute at particular stores and intergroup conflict. Interpersonal dispute is conflict that occurs between an individual Korean store owner and the store's customers. Intergroup conflict refers to collective conflict between Korean merchants and their supporters, on the one side, and African American local customers or residents and their supporters, on the other. The two forms of collective intergroup conflict observed are boycott and mass violence. These three forms of Korean and African American conflict, interpersonal dispute, boycott, and mass violence, do not exhaust all the possible forms. For example, individual violence is not systematically considered in this book. This form of conflict refers to damage of Korean businesses or physical attacks upon Korean merchants, their employees, or other Koreans, by individual inner-city residents. This form is usually a one-time expression of a particular local resident's hostility toward Korean merchants in general, but it is not necessarily a conflict developed in the process of a business transaction at any certain store.

Intercity comparison of the major forms of intergroup conflict offers an excellent opportunity to better comprehend the Korean and African American conflict. Of the intergroup conflicts that occurred in major cities, the 1992 Los Angeles mass violence has been the most destructive, while the boycott in New York City has been the longest to date.

REFERENCES

Abelmann, Nancy, and John Lie. 1995. *Blue dreams: Korean Americans and the Los Angeles riots*. Cambridge, Mass.: Harvard University Press.

Baldassare, Mark, ed. 1994. *The Los Angeles riot: Lessons for the urban future*. Boulder, Colo.: Westview Press.

Chang, Edward T. 1993. From Chicago to Los Angeles: Changing the site of race relations. *Amerasia Journal* 19:1–3.

Kriesberg, Louis. 1982. *Social conflict*. 2d ed. Englewood Cliffs, N.J.: Prentice-Hall.

Light, Ivan, Hadnas Har-Chvi, and Kenneth Kan. 1994. Black/Korean conflict. In *Managing divided cities*, edited by Seamus Dunn. Keele: University of Keele.

Madhubuti, Haki R., ed. 1993. *Why L.A. happened*. Chicago: Third World Press.

Min, Pyong Gap. 1996. *Caught in the middle*. Berkeley and Los Angeles: University of California Press.

Ong, Paul, Kyeyoung Park, and Yasmin Tong. 1994. The Korean-black conflict and the state. In *The new Asian immigration in Los Angeles and global restructuring*, edited by Edna Bonacich and Lucie Cheng. Philadelphia: Temple University Press.

Romm, Norma R. A. 1991. *The methodologies of positivism and Marxism*. London: Macmillan.

Totten, George O., III, and H. Eric Schockman, eds. 1994. *Community in crisis: The Korean community after the Los Angeles civil unrest of April 1992*. Los Angeles: Center for Multiethnic and Transnational Studies, University of Southern California.

Weber, Max. 1949. *The methodology of the social sciences*, translated and edited by Edward A. Shils and Henry A. Finch. New York: Free Press.

Yu, Eui-Young, ed. 1994. *Black-Korean encounter: Toward understanding and alliance.* Los Angeles: Institute for Asian American and Pacific Asian Studies, California State University.

Yu, Eui-Young, and Edward Chang, eds. 1995. *Multiethnic coalition building in Los Angeles.* Los Angeles: Institute for Asian American and Pacific American Studies, California State University.

Part 1 LOS ANGELES

2 The Multiracial Nature of Los Angeles Unrest in 1992

Kwang Chung Kim and Shin Kim

THE 1965 REVISION OF THE U.S. IMMIGRATION LAW DRASTICALLY IN-creased the number of immigrants from Asian and Latin American countries, ending the historical pattern of numerical dominance by European immigrants (Barringer, Gardner, and Levin 1993; Reimers 1985; U.S. Commission on Civil Rights 1988). The presence of recent non-European immigrants has helped transform the United States into a complex multiracial and multiethnic society, one that goes beyond the traditional biracial relationship between whites and African Americans and the ethnic experiences of European immigrants and their descendants. Such a change in the composition of the U.S. population presents a great challenge to the study of recent racial and ethnic relations.

The Los Angeles racial unrest of 1992 shockingly demonstrated this complex and diverse nature of American society. African American residents in South Central Los Angeles destroyed local businesses as an angry protest against the "not guilty" verdict announced in the case against white policemen charged with beating Rodney King. Hispanic residents took advantage of the opportunity and joined the looting of local businesses (Light, Har-Chvi, and Kan 1994). All the major racial and ethnic groups in the United States were eventually involved: African Americans, whites, Hispanics, and Asian Americans. Korean business owners emerged as the biggest victims of property loss resulting from the riots (Institute for Alternative Journalism 1992).

The Los Angeles unrest has generated numerous debates (Institute for Alternative Journalism 1992). Through these debates, two contrasting positions have emerged, both of which unfortunately regard the unrest as a type of biracial event. One position treats the unrest as a basic conflict between Korean business owners and African American residents in South Central Los Angeles. According to this position, the source of the conflict is the presence of many small Korean businesses in South Central Los Angeles, which has generated a considerable degree of racial tension. African American residents complain that Korean business owners treat African American customers rudely and exploit them economically. Local residents' hostility toward Korean storekeepers was further intensified when a Korean store owner who had shot and killed an African American customer received a lenient sentence from the court (Institute for Alternative Journalism 1992; Madhubuti 1993; *Los Angeles Times* Staff 1992).

A serious problem with this position is that it sees the Los Angeles unrest as an interminority group conflict between two minority groups. This position misses an essential feature of racial and ethnic relations in the United States, namely, that the positions and roles of minority groups in the United States are largely determined by the respective relationship of those groups to the dominant white group. For an adequate analysis of the unrest, therefore, it is necessary to examine the role of the dominant group involved in the interminority group conflict. Charles Simmons alludes to this necessity: "Although there is friction between Black consumers and Korean merchants, this issue was overstated by the media. The Los Angeles problem has much deeper historical and social roots" (1993: 142–43).

Mindful of the powerful role of the dominant group, supporters of the other popular position treat the Los Angeles unrest as a biracial conflict between whites and African Americans. They argue that the conflict originated in the historical and continuing patterns of whites' exploitation and victimization of African Americans. The urban unrest was a way for African American residents in South Central Los Angeles to protest their experience as victims. If exploitation by whites were the main issue, however, one would wonder why Korean business owners turned out to be the biggest victims. This argument does not clearly define the structural position and role of Korean small business owners in the unrest; it instead often treats them merely as bystanders caught between African American rage and white power (Choi 1992).

For a satisfactory analysis of the Los Angeles unrest, it is necessary to recognize the conflict's multiracial nature (E. Kim 1992; Oliver, Johnson, and Grant 1993; Sonenshein 1993; West 1993). We aim, then, to clarify the multiple racial groups involved in the unrest and to examine the nature of their involvement based on their structural positions and roles in the

United States. The diverse factors can undoubtedly be conceptualized in many different ways. For example, Melvin Oliver, James Johnson, and David Grant (1993) define the Los Angeles unrest as a multiethnic rebellion in the sense that African American and Hispanic residents in South Central Los Angeles were involved in the unrest.

We define the Los Angeles unrest as a multiracial event from the perspective of victimization. Several victimized groups are recognizable in the Los Angeles unrest. We focus on the two most severely victimized groups: African American residents in South Central Los Angeles and Korean business owners in South Central Los Angeles and nearby Koreatown. While the victimization experienced by African Americans has been much debated, and feelings of victimization, despair, and anger are said to be the major source of the Los Angeles unrest, little attention has been paid thus far to the victimization of Korean business owners. We therefore put considerable stress on the traumatic experiences of this neglected group, pursuing two questions: Why were Korean businesses in South Central Los Angeles and nearby Koreatown attacked, and What happened to Korean business owners after their businesses were looted or burned? For our analysis, we must also pay attention to the dominant white group's relationship with each of the two victimized groups. The relationship between the two minority groups needs to be examined within this context of the dominant-minority group relationship.

Figure 2.1 illustrates the multiracial currents that fed into the Los Angeles unrest. The basic source is the relationship between whites and African Americans, which has led to African Americans' victimization. A critical issue is the relationship between these two groups, particularly in urban areas during recent American history (A in Figure 2.1). However, African American residents attacked Korean businesses and victimized business owners who had filled delicate socioeconomic roles in South Central Los Angeles (B in Figure 2.1). The Korean immigrants' relationship with the dominant white group encompasses both the Korean immigrants' entry into business in the United States and the middleman minority role some Korean businessmen play in inner-city minority communities (C in Figure 2.1).

For our purposes, the two biracial positions illustrated above treat the role of Hispanic residents as a passive one. Although many Hispanic residents in Koreatown were resentful of Korean storekeepers and landlords and participated in the unrest, they did not initiate the disturbance and instead seem to have simply taken the opportunity to join in (Oliver, Johnson, and Grant 1993; Simmons 1993). Furthermore, most of the His-

FIGURE 2.1 Multiracial Currents Underlying the Los Angeles Unrest

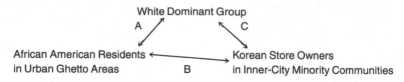

panic residents in South Central Los Angeles and nearby Koreatown were either immigrants or undocumented workers who appeared to be motivated mainly by material gain, looting stores rather than burning them down as an expression of rage, as did African Americans (Light, Har-Chvi, and Kan 1994).

THE CONCEPT OF VICTIMS AND VICTIMIZATION

The concepts of victims and victimization provide important conceptual frameworks necessary for understanding the mass violence in Los Angeles. The term *victims* refers to individuals or a group of individuals who suffer harm inflicted by others, the offenders. The harm may include many kinds of loss or pain: psychological, social, cultural, economic, political, and so on. Victims are not considered responsible (either totally or partially) for this harm. If they were responsible, they could not be considered victims, no matter how enormous their suffering. *Victimization* refers to the victims' suffering, including adverse life conditions that follow from the original harm inflicted by the offenders.

In the discussion of victims and victimization, it is important to examine the nature of the relationship between the victims and offenders, as well as the sociocultural context in which their relationship exists (Elias 1986). The analysis of their relationship often includes the controversial issues of blaming the victim (victims' sharing in the responsibility for their harm) and defending the victim (proclaiming victims' innocence). In order to clarify these issues, Robert Elias (1986) suggests examining the broad social, political, economic, and cultural structures of society. Otherwise, the whole argument of victims and victimization degenerates into a debate over the symptoms of a problem rather than its sources.

AFRICAN AMERIANS' EXPERIENCES OF VICTIMIZATION

African Americans have been mistreated and victimized by the dominant white group in numerous ways throughout American history. For the purpose of our study, the scope of analysis will be limited to African Americans' experiences in the recent industrial and postindustrial eras. As the U.S. economy rapidly industrialized at the end of the nineteenth century, the changing economy demanded a huge number of unskilled workers; this labor demand was initially met by the unprecedented number of immigrants arriving from European countries (Lieberson 1980). After World War I had drastically curtailed the immigration flow from European countries, African Americans in the rural South finally managed to begin a steady flow of migration to major cities, joining the urban labor force there as latecomers. In 1870, according to Douglas Massey and Nancy Denton, 80 percent of African Americans lived in the rural South. A century later, 80 percent of African Americans lived in urban areas; nearly half of them lived in urban areas outside the South (1993: 18).

Owing to the racism of a white majority, these African American migrants and their descendants were forced to live in heavily segregated areas within major cities. Such residential segregation and other types of discrimination are examples of African Americans' experiences of victimization in urban areas. Massey and Denton call this residential segregation "the missing link in prior attempts to understand the plight of the urban poor" (1993: 3). In these congested urban areas, African American residents have watched their job opportunities completely dry up during the steady deindustrialization of the inner city. As a result, a high proportion remain unemployed and poor. This concentrated poverty is the harm that has been inflicted upon African Americans as the victims of white racism throughout the changing context of the U.S. economy.

Massey and Denton point out that at the turn of the twentieth century, only a small number of African Americans were in northern and Midwest or West Coast cities, and they generally lived in racially integrated neighborhoods. But as more African Americans migrated to the major cities during the second decade of the new century, urban whites began to view African American mobility with increasing hostility and alarm. As a result, they started to force the migrant African Americans to live in segregated areas, gradually creating a pattern of residential segregation of major cities.

By the 1930s, the perimeters of African American settlements were well established in most cities, and the level of African American–white residential dissimilarity had stabilized at a very high level. The Great Depression drove more African Americans out of the rural South, which was economically worse off than other parts of the country. From 1930 to 1940, some four hundred thousand African American migrants left the

South for major cities. Massey and Denton note that when these migrants arrived in major cities, they faced unusually bleak residential circumstances. Compounding the problems of segregation, the Great Depression had virtually ended new residential construction after 1929.

World War II further facilitated the migration of African Americans from the rural South into the major cities. After World War II, residential segregation continued to accelerate through the process of suburbanization:

> The suburbanization of America proceeded at a new rapid pace and the white middle class deserted inner cities in massive numbers. Only one-third of U. S. metropolitan residents were suburban residents in 1940, but by 1970 suburbanites constituted a majority within metropolitan America.

> Throughout the United States—in both southern and northern cities—the ghetto had become an enduring, permanent feature of the residential structure of black community life by 1940, and over the next thirty years the spatial isolation of African Americans only increased. (Massey and Denton 1993: 43, 49)

This segregation in the major cities has been accompanied by occupational discrimination against African Americans (Kerner Commission 1968; Lieberson 1980). The two patterns of racial discrimination then reinforced each other, developing the current grim life conditions of inner-city residents. William Wilson (1987) contends that the recent inner-city deterioration also reflects several contemporary forces that operate directly against inner-city African Americans.

One of these forces is the deindustrialization of the inner-city economy. As the U.S. economy shifted from manufacturing to service-oriented industries, numerous inner-city plants were closed and low-skilled manufacturing jobs were eliminated or moved elsewhere. This trend has created a high rate of unemployment in inner-city areas, particularly affecting young male workers. Wilson (1987) stresses that joblessness among these young men is a factor in the current delay in marriage, and both these conditions in turn contribute to the high rate of out-of-wedlock births and single-parent, female-headed households.

Another contemporary force that has severely deteriorated living conditions of inner-city residents is the change in age composition. A greater proportion of young people live in inner-city ghetto areas today than ever before, and their presence contributes to such serious problems as low income, high unemployment rates, and crime. Wilson (1987) observes that inner-city areas are no longer vertical communities in which middle- and working-class African Americans live together with underclass African Americans. The middle- and working-class African Americans, who can afford to move away, have already left ghetto areas, so that only the most disadvantaged segments of the African American community remain (the concentration effect). Wilson maintains that a net result of the concentration effect is social isolation—a lack of contact or of sustained interaction with individuals and institutions that represent the mainstream society. Inner-city ghetto areas are thus plagued with what Wilson calls problems of social dislocation—joblessness, drugs, school dropouts, teenage pregnancies, poverty, out-of-wedlock births, female-headed households, welfare dependency, and serious crime. This deterioration in South Central Los Angeles has also led to an extremely high infant mortality rate there—22 per 1,000 (Hamilton 1992).

Current adverse life conditions of inner-city African American residents, then, stem from a number of historical and contemporary forces, many of which are intricately related to past racial discrimination. For example, because many African Americans have been forced by past residential discrimination to live in inner-city ghetto areas, they are more severely hit than any other racial or ethnic group by the recent deindustrialization of the inner-city economy. The current changes in the age makeup of inner-city residents and the removal of middle- and working-class African Americans from inner cities can both be traced to the bleak inner-city living conditions originally generated by past racial discrimination. The effects of all these forces may then, in part, be considered what Joe and Clairece Feagin (1986) call the side effects, or past-in-present effects, of earlier discrimination. The historical pattern of racism is, therefore, a critical factor in explaining the current victimization of African Americans in inner-city ghetto areas.

RACIAL UNREST IN SOUTH CENTRAL LOS ANGELES

African American residents in South Central Los Angeles have not been excepted from this general pattern of urban degeneration. They have gone through the same kind of concentrated poverty and related victimization. They share their community with another impoverished group, Hispanics, but the two groups live in a highly segregated area as a result of the planned deurbanization of Los Angeles (Cooper 1992). In 1990, only about 6 percent of local residents in South Central Los Angeles had a college degree, and fewer than half of them had completed a high school education (Sonenshein 1993: 173). As many as 230,000 of the community's 630,000 residents live at or below the annual income poverty threshold. While only 18 percent of Los Angeles families live in South Central Los Angeles, 37 percent of the city's impoverished families are found there (Curran 1992).

Large corporations have abandoned South Central and other parts of Los Angeles in recent years, and the resulting job exodus continues to accelerate (Soja, Morales, and Wolff 1983; Oliver, Johnson, and Grant 1993). Living conditions in the community continue to deteriorate, while the underground economy takes over and various forms of vice such as theft, drug trafficking, and prostitution thrive. The whole of South Central Los Angeles has become an explosive mixture of poverty, crime, and drugs (Sonenshein 1993: 163). Under these circumstances, the basic needs in the community are not being met by state, county, or city agencies. Many parts of South Central Los Angeles are physically dismantled, and the area has been written off by banks, corporations, social service agencies, and others (Hamilton 1992).

This accumulation of experiences of victimization and the accompanying sense of despair and anger has been seen as the root cause of the Los Angeles racial unrest. Eui-Young Yu observes that it "was a violent explosion of anger accumulated over years of frustration, helplessness and alienation of people of color, particularly African Americans trapped in the inner-cities of America" (1994: 137). Haki Madhubuti also views the urban unrest as stemming from African Americans' "anger for unfulfilled promises" (1993: xiv). Oliver, Johnson, and Grant (1933) argue that the Los Angeles violence reflects the frustration and alienation built up over the past twenty years among the residents of South Central Los Angeles. Dan Hazen takes the same position in his analysis of the Los Angels racial unrest: "The riots were frightening and tragic, but they gave expression to years of pent-up frustration and anger about decades of forced urban decay, steady increase in poverty, a growing exodus of jobs as corporations have fled South in search of cheap labor, enormous cutbacks in every kind of government support and exponential increase in homelessness and violence" (1992: 10).

The "not guilty" verdict in the trial against officers who were videotaped beating Rodney King was the event that sparked the explosion of

African Americans' anger. This verdict stood as a symbol of whites' racism and their insensitivity to African Americans' suffering, and it was taken as a terrible insult to the dignity of African Americans (Madhubuti 1993). The following reaction by members of an African American church who counseled against the residents' street violence demonstrates the stunned experiences of African American residents in South Central Los Angeles: "The mood at the First A.M.E. Church was somber. One could still see the shocks and disbelief on the faces of the church members and all who gathered to watch as the verdict was read. . . . Pounding his fist into his left hand, Rev. Cecil Murray began to cry, 'They gave no nothing, nothing, not even a bone, dear God, not even a bone' " (*Los Angeles Times* Staff 1992: 59).

When even members of a moderate African American church experienced such intense shock and disbelief, it is not surprising that people on the street responded much more violently. Local residents started to loot and burn local businesses Wednesday evening, April 29, 1992, and their destructive behavior continued, with little police response, until Friday. The local residents' apparent attempts to move into white areas such as Beverly Hills and the Westside were curtailed by police forces, but mobs easily flooded into Koreatown. Along with Hispanic residents there, African Americans looted or burned small Korean businesses (*Los Angeles Times* Staff 1992). Although their anger was directed toward the white dominant group, what residents actually did was to vandalize and destroy local nonwhite businesses and other properties, including a large number of small Korean businesses that were left unprotected by the police force during the three days of unrest. Those reporting on the destruction were taken aback by the lack of police support: "By Thursday evening, Koreatown was besieged by flames and looters. Desperate calls for help to city authorities were not answered. Koreans thought they had many friends in City Hall, as they had given generously to politicians. In times of danger, however, Koreans learned that they had to stand all alone" (Yu 1993: 2).

KOREAN BUSINESS OWNERS' EXPERIENCES OF VICTIMIZATION

As a whole, the Los Angeles unrest turned out to be the most destructive urban riot that has ever occurred in the United States (Oliver, Johnson, and Grant 1993; *Los Angeles Times* Staff 1992). During the Los Angeles violence, 58 persons died, 2,383 were injured, and over 17,000 were arrested (Sonenshein 1993: 223). Total property damage has been estimated to be between $785 million and $1 billion (Oliver, Johnson, and Grant 1993); approximately 4,500 businesses were totally or partially damaged, about half of which (2,300) were Korean businesses in South Central Los Angeles and nearby Koreatown. The total estimated Korean property damage ranged between $350 million and $400 million (KAIAC 1993). Grocery stores (273 stores, with estimated damages of $67 million) and swap meet shops (336 shops, with estimated damages of $55 million) were hardest hit, followed by clothing shops (222 shops, with estimated damages of $34 million) and liquor stores (187 stores, with estimated damages of $42 million). Other types of Korean businesses damaged by the unrest included dry cleaners, electronic shops, gas stations, jewelry shops, restaurants, beauty salons, auto shops, video shops, and furniture shops (Yu 1993: 4).

What adversities are faced by Korean immigrants who lost their businesses in South Central Los Angeles and Koreatown? The most immediate problem is the strong sense of despair, helplessness, and hopelessness felt by Korean business owners and their family members. Their businesses, built up through many years of hard work and sweat, were suddenly reduced to ashes. Most of the destroyed businesses (65%) were uninsured at the time of the rioting, and a survey indicates that ten months after the unrest, only one-quarter of the Korean victims (27.8%) had reopened their businesses (KAIAC 1993). Most of the businesses that reopened were those that had sustained the least amount of damage. Half of the victims (49%) viewed their chances of rebuilding as nil, and only the remaining 29 percent looked at their chances of rebuilding with any optimism (KAIAC 1993).

The victims' other immediate problem is how they can obtain the money necessary for daily living. Many of them were forced to borrow money at high interest rates in order to pay their living expenses and attempt to reopen their businesses. As a result, they could no longer pay their mortgages and many have already lost their houses or are now threatened with eviction. For Korean immigrants, home ownership is a conspicuous symbol of achieving the American dream; for them, the loss of this dream is particularly painful and jarring. The victims in the survey mentioned mortgage and rental assistance as their greatest need (KAIAC 1993).

In addition to financial problems, victims and their family members generally suffer from the psychological and physical symptoms of depression and other severe forms of shock following sudden loss:

The majority of riot victims had portrayed moderate to severe symptoms of post traumatic stress disorder. Many of the victims have stated that they have difficulty of sleeping and continue to have frequent nightmares about their burning and / or looted businesses. Some have developed ulcers and many have not regained their lost appetite and weight. These victims suffer under extreme stress and chronic attacks of depression, anxiety and fear. One victim's daughter became so overwhelmed [that] she attempted suicide. Clearly there is a tremendous amount of anger and guilt that desperately needs to be processed. There is evidence of an increase in family conflict, domestic violence, child abuse and substance abuse. It is also clear that these symptoms and incidents of abuse are directly related to the riot and victim's financial difficulties. Unfortunately, although so many victims suffer from severe anxiety and poor health, a great deal of suspicion and shame attached to mental health related services inhibit them from readily receiving counseling. (KAIAC 1993: 5–6)

As suggested by these observations, a severe form of victimization experienced by Korean immigrants during the rioting is a tense relationship with their immediate family members, kin, friends, and others. With the loss of their livelihood, the victims are placed in a position of desperately needing to seek help from others, while the victims themselves have little ability to help anyone. In this situation, the victims often experience their relationships with others as frustrating, even humiliating, while at the same time they often feel slighted by others. Such an interpersonal difficulty is likely to be accompanied by a drastic change in the victims' self-concept, because they suffer from an enormous loss of self-confidence and respect. Self-doubt and other severe forms of personal deterioration are thus another form of the fallout Korean immigrants suffered following the unrest.

Korean immigrant entrepreneurs came to the United States to pursue the American middle-class dream (Hurh and Kim 1988). In pursuit of this dream, they had an unshakable belief in the American system, trusting that hard work would pay off here. Their faith in the whole American system was badly shaken—leaving in its place a sense of despair and anomie. Their feelings of betrayal have been intensified not just by the original harm inflicted by the minority local residents but also by the subsequent disappointing responses from various federal, state, and local government agencies (KAIAC, 1993). This is another severe loss—an intangible, but extremely devastating, experience of victimization.

The Middleman Minority Role of Korean Immigrant Entrepreneurs

To analyze the experiences of victimization of Korean immigrant entrepreneurs in South Central Los Angeles and nearby Koreatown, it is necessary briefly to review their experiences in the American labor market. Like other recent Asian immigrants, Korean immigrants who came to the United States had generally enjoyed a high preimmigration socioeconomic status. Many had already completed a college education in Korea, and most of those with occupational experience in Korea had been employed either in professional and technical occupations or administrative and managerial occupations prior to immigrating (Hurh and Kim 1988; U.S. Commission on Civil Rights 1988). Like other recent Asian immigrants, their immigration may thus be characterized as a "middle-class migration."

Most Korean immigrants could not, however, utilize their Korean educational and occupational resources in the American labor market. With the exception of those college graduates who had majored in health-related fields, most discovered that their education and occupational experiences were generally not recognized in America. These college graduates were thereby excluded from the mainstream occupations for which they had been trained. The jobs available to them in America were those jobs usually available to all immigrant workers: (1) occupations with a short supply of workers; (2) occupations avoided or disdained by native-born whites; and (3) low-wage, low-skill occupations.

Currently, as in the recent past, health care jobs in the United States fall under the category of occupations with a short supply of workers. So, with the exception of those in health-related fields, immigrating college graduates generally face the stark reality of limited occupational choices. The types of occupations currently available to them are either self-employment in a small business or low-wage, low-skill service or manual occupations. Faced with this limited choice, college graduates naturally prefer self-employment, even though running a small business is probably an occupational step down for most. Even those with no college education view the employment conditions associated with low-wage, low-skill occupations as unfavorable, also preferring self-employment in a small business.

This limited occupational structure in the American labor market has compelled a high proportion of Korean immigrants without any previous business experience in Korea or any systematic business preparation in the United States to open and operate small businesses. Their business can, therefore, be considered a new phenomenon emerging from the unfavorable labor market situation facing Korean immigrants in the United States. The small business opportunities available to them are, however, also limited and tend to be of two types: an inner-city retail or service business or an extremely labor-intensive business (e.g., laundry and dry cleaning services or fruit and vegetable shops). These two types of small business are generally so risky, low-status, or difficult to manage that many native-born whites tend to avoid them.

Consistent with this summary, Ivan Light and Edna Bonacich observe that a large majority of Korean service and retail businesses in Los Angeles are located in nonwhite, low-income areas that have been ignored and underserved by big corporations (1988). Korean immigrants' entry into inner-city minority markets, therefore, stems from the interaction of two features of their relationship with the white dominant group in the United States: (1) the exclusion of Korean immigrants from the mainstream professional and technical occupations or administrative and managerial occupations, which are usually dominated by native-born whites (U.S. Bureau of the Census 1990); and (2) the availability of business opportunities in inner-city minority communities, which are usually avoided by native-born whites (Kim, Hurh, and Fernandez 1989; Light and Bonacich 1988).

Edna Bonacich and her colleagues attempted to characterize Korean small business in the United States in terms of the middleman minority theory, but they have subsequently abandoned this effort (Bonacich, Light, and Wong 1980; Bonacich and Jung 1982; Light and Bonacich, 1988). Light and Bonacich (1988) argue that the middleman minority framework is too restrictive to analyze small Korean business in the United States. They also state that the middleman minority theory stresses sojourning minorities and is oriented toward the Third World context, whereas small Korean business is found in a developed country and Korean immigrants are not generally sojourners (1988: 17–18).

The middleman minority theory is indeed too restrictive a tool for analyzing small Korean business as a whole in the United States, but we find it useful for analyzing a type of small Korean business, namely, those operating in inner-city, low-income African American or Hispanic communities. Relevant here are the social conditions under which middleman minorities are likely to thrive, not their role as sojourners. As Jonathan Turner and Edna Bonacich (1980) stress, middleman minorities tend to thrive in a highly stratified society. If the socioeconomic gap between the elite (the dominant group) and the masses (the minority group) is great in a society, this gap hinders effective interaction between the two groups. The society then needs another distinct group to stand between the two groups and perform an intermediate, or mediating, role. Edna Bonacich and John Modell thus characterize middleman minority entrepreneurs as those who are socially or racially distinguished and "tend to concentrate in trade and commerce—that is, to act as middleman between producers and consumers" (1980: 14).

The racial and socioeconomic gap between the white dominant group and the inner-city African American and Hispanic communities in major American cities offers Korean immigrants just such a middleman business opportunity. As retailers, Korean business owners in inner-city African American and Hispanic communities are at the end of a complex process of production and distribution of the goods needed by inner-city minority residents. Producers of these goods are mostly American corporations or international corporations located in South Korea, Taiwan, and other Third World countries (Illsoo Kim 1981; Light and Bonacich 1988). A high proportion of these two types of corporations are intimately related through the international involvement of American corporations through direct investment, transfer of capital or technology, subcontracting, and so on (Light and Bonacich 1988). The goods produced by these corporations are eventually distributed to Korean retailers through Korean and white wholesalers (Kim and Hurh 1985).

We find no evidence that major American banks, big corporations, or government agencies (white-dominated institutions) have actively helped or assisted Korean immigrants to enter small business in inner-city minority communities (Bonacich, Light, and Wong 1980; Light and Bonacich 1988). Korean immigrants have instead relied heavily on their own resources and those of their ethnic group (Kim and Hurh 1985; Light and Bonacich 1988; Min 1988). By running a business in inner-city ghetto areas and distributing goods purchased from white-dominated corporations and Third World manufacturers, these Koreans are inevitably placing themselves in the position of middleman minority, whether they are aware of it or not. What Korean retailers actually do in inner-city minority markets is "distribute the products of big businesses in hard-to-access central city markets" (Light and Bonacich 1988: 23).

As middleman retailers, Korean business owners in inner-city minority communities share their profits with suppliers (producers and whole-salers). As those who reside and spend their earnings elsewhere, Korean business owners and their suppliers contribute, to some extent, to the draining of local economic resources. They are, therefore, perceived by many inner-city residents as outside invaders who exploit local minority residents and undermine African American communities' economic autonomy by preventing local residents from establishing their own businesses in the community.

Responsibility of Korean Immigrant Entrepreneurs

Were Korean business owners in South Central Los Angeles and nearby Koreatown responsible for their losses? Most of the residents in South Central Los Angeles and in other inner-city, low-income communities are currently too poor to sustain any viable retail business in their neighborhoods. These areas have therefore largely been abandoned by those who would otherwise dominate the markets: white merchants, chain stores, and big corporations. Even those African Americans who are entrepreneurially capable have left the inner-city areas rather than set up shop there (Wilson 1987). As a result, the inner-city ghetto areas contain only the barest rudiments of retail trade (Massey and Denton 1993: 135).

Under these stark conditions, Korean immigrant entrepreneurs stand out as the group that has most actively invested in these areas, which otherwise are wastelands of empty store fronts, burned-out buildings, and vacant lots (Massey and Denton 1993: 137). Korean business owners have thus contributed to the development and revival of many deteriorated or abandoned neighborhoods (Light and Bonacich 1988: 6). Their business has created employment opportunities in areas with high rates of unemployment and generated earnings for local youth.

It is not surprising that Korean merchants in these abandoned markets have encountered little resistance or competition from big corporations or native-born white or African American entrepreneurs. In this respect, their business experiences are quite different from those of prewar Japanese immigrants on the West Coast (Bonacich and Modell 1980). However, because many Korean immigrants enter the same types of retail market and draw upon the same ethnic resources, most experience intense competitive pressure from other Korean business owners (Kim and Hurh 1985).

This intragroup competition forces Korean business owners to keep the prices of their goods relatively low. In order to do so, Korean retailers and their family members must work unusually long hours and maintain a frugal lifestyle. Such difficult measures are necessary to reduce the labor costs of their business and to enable them to survive commercially in the difficult low-income markets whose economy Daniel Fusfeld and Timothy Bates (1984) call "penny capitalism." Light and Bonacich characterize the long hours of Korean business owners and their family members as "a disguised form of cheap labor" (1988: 23) and further explain that "the Korean entrepreneurs and their families worked longer hours to earn a lower return on their human capital than did the non-Korean entrepreneurs" (1988: 176).

Because of their immigrant status, inner-city Korean entrepreneurs and their family members are desperate to secure a socioeconomic base in the United States, so they are strongly motivated to manage their business, however difficult. Furthermore, they have come from a country where the standard of labor and employment conditions are much tougher than in the United States. During the 1970s and 1980s, when most of the Korean entrepreneurs in business today came to the United States, Korea exported large quantities of goods manufactured by workers receiving low wages and working extremely long hours (Light and Bonacich 1988). This background has imbued many Korean immigrant entrepreneurs in the United States with an intense commitment to an Asian version of the Protestant ethic. Korean immigrants, therefore, seem better prepared to manage businesses in inner-city areas than native-born entrepreneurs.

It seems inevitable that the residents in South Central Los Angeles and other inner-city minority areas have come to depend, to a large extent, on outside entrepreneurs for their daily necessities. Most of the local residents are too poor to start their own business or are entrepreneurially unprepared to do so, and the inner-city markets are generally too small or too risky to entice big corporations or chain stores. Of those who are nevertheless interested in these areas, immigrant entrepreneurs seem to offer the local residents a decent retail business. Of these immigrant entrepreneurs, Korean business owners have filled the inner-city niche and created intense intragroup competition among Korean-owned businesses. Korean immigrant entrepreneurs are hardly in a position, then, to exploit local residents by charging unusually high prices, inasmuch as their prices are set by the pressure of this intense competition. Such a business climate actually benefits local consumers enormously, as prices would undoubtedly be higher under the monopolistic or oligopolistic market that might exist in the absence of competing immigrant entrepreneurs.

The concentrated poverty and suffering that led to the Los Angeles unrest already existed long before Korean immigrants started their businesses in South Central Los Angeles (Kerner Commission 1968; Oliver, Johnson, and Grant 1993). Furthermore, these Korean immigrants ran their businesses diligently and frugally under heavy pressure of intragroup competition. So why were Korean businesses attacked in South Central Los Angeles and nearby Koreatown? Two factors seem to answer this question. First, with their history of victimization and their related sense of anger and frustration, African American residents in inner-city areas tend to perceive any outside business owners as part of the established system of exploitation and treat them with hostility and suspicion (Light, Har-Chvi, and Kan 1994). Inner-city residents are then not inclined to perceive the changing roles of various entrepreneurial groups in different socioeconomic contexts, even when undeniable differences are found among these groups, such as the differences observed between Korean and Jewish storekeepers (Chang 1993). For African Americans, all non-African American entrepreneurs in their communities represent the same homogeneous group of exploiters, regardless of their history or their business activities. The following statement demonstrates such a stereotypical judgment of immigrant business owners: "Ethnic groups that have made it into the American Dream have traditionally stepped on the necks of African-American communities on their way up. Jews, Italians, Greeks, Chinese, Arabs and now East Indians and Koreans have all, to greater or lesser degrees, quickly assimilated this Fundamental Law of Immigrant Upward Mobility" (Martin 1993: 32).

Second, some situational elements associated with Korean entrepreneurs' middleman minority position helped facilitate the Los Angeles attacks. As an angry protest against the white establishment, local residents in South Central Los Angeles attempted to attack and destroy the targets nearest to hand; many businesses located in South Central Los Angeles were destroyed regardless of the owners' ethnicity (Institute for Alternative Journalism 1992).

Korean businesses were also somewhat more tempting targets than other businesses, because their culturally and racially different owners made them more visible and they had clearly proliferated in the area (Oliver, Johnson, and Grant 1993; Los Angeles Times Staff 1992). At the same time, Korean businesses located in South Central Los Angeles and Koreatown were easily accessible to African American and Hispanic residents. Furthermore, these businesses had little power to stop local residents' attacks or to retaliate. In this sense, Korean business owners are typical middleman minority entrepreneurs—economically active but politically weak or helpless. Unfortunately, their plight was worsened by the virtual absence of police protection during all three days of rioting (*Los Angeles Times* Staff 1992; Yu 1993). These three characteristics—visibility, accessibility, and vulnerability—explain the disproportionate property loss of Korean entrepreneurs during the Los Angeles unrest. In sharp contrast, white residents in Beverly Hills and other areas were well protected by the Los Angeles police force during the same period (*Los Angeles Times* 1992). Though highly visible, these white residents were neither accessible nor vulnerable.

During the riots, then, Korean businesses were convenient scapegoats upon whom local residents could express their anger. African American residents substituted local Korean businesses as a target of hostility, exaggerating the economic conflict of interest between Korean entrepreneurs and local residents (Light and Bonacich 1988: 323). In this process, Korean business owners paid a heavy toll and ended up shielding the business interests of the white establishment. These Korean store owners were, therefore, the victims of the misdirected anger of African American residents as middleman minority entrepreneurs in ghetto markets. Manning Marable expresses this position eloquently:

> One tragic outcome of this legacy is the rage directed against the Asian American community during the Los Angeles riots, during which 1,800 Korean-owned businesses were damaged or destroyed. Black young people need to understand that it is not the Korean-American small business merchant who denies capital for investment in the black community, controls the banks and financial institutions or commits police brutality against blacks and Latinos. There may be legitimate complaints between the two groups. But such misdirected anger makes a unified response to race and class oppression virtually impossible. (1992: 83)

One specific complaint expressed by local residents against Korean business owners before and during the unrest in South Central Los Angeles and other urban ghetto areas was that Korean business owners treat their minority customers disrespectfully (Shin Kim, 1994). While it is conceivable that some Korean business owners treat their minority customers in such a way, it is equally conceivable that others do not. Unfortunately, the idea of rude treatment by Korean store owners spread, becoming a collective prejudice against all Korean business owners—a simplified, negative view applied to all members of a group. Local residents generally suggest that Korean culture is the source of such rude behavior. This expressed complaint clearly carries a victim-blaming message: Because of their culture, Korean business owners were rude to African American customers. Due to this rude behavior, Korean business owners deserved the property loss inflicted during the Los Angeles riots.

On the issue of the rude treatment of customers, one may wonder, on the one hand, whether Korean business owners are ruder than other business owners in the same areas. A preliminary study shows that a great majority of African American customers do not think that Korean business owners are much different from other business owners (Shin Kim 1994). On the other hand, if Korean culture accounts for the rude treatment of customers, Korean business owners in other areas should also treat their customers disrespectfully. Yet, no evidence has been found that customers (Korean, white, or racially mixed) in other areas single out Korean business owners for their rudeness. Cultural differences do create a definite problem of misunderstanding between Korean business owners and their African American customers, but misunderstandings should be clearly distinguished from the alleged Korean habit of treating customers rudely.

The issue of rudeness should be examined in the context of interaction between storekeepers and customers. Today, Korean business owners are gravely concerned about frequent robbery and shoplifting attempts. Korean business owners pay an extremely high price for these crimes—economically, psychologically, and physically, as many incidents have resulted in the injury or death of business owners and employees (Shin Kim 1994). In such a defensive atmosphere, an owner's behavior may be perceived as rude by African American customers. However, complaints about such rude behavior were exaggerated and were used as part of the victim-blaming logic for looting and burning Korean businesses.

CONCLUSION

The Los Angeles unrest was the most destructive urban riot in American history. One victimized minority group victimized another minority group. A real tragedy in the Los Angeles disturbance is that while the deprived structural conditions associated with African Americans' victimization remain basically the same, their anger has devastated another minority group, Korean immigrant entrepreneurs. As a result, the Los Angeles unrest has intensified minority sufferings as experienced by Koreans in the United States without any prospect of improving the difficult life conditions of either minority. The Los Angeles unrest demonstrates again the meaning of the lesson stressed three decades ago by the Kerner Report: "Violence cannot build a better society" (1968: 2). The tense situation left in the wake of such destruction is very likely to set into motion another cycle of minority unrest in the future.

This unfortunate current state of complex racial relations in Los Angeles and other major American cities calls for a systematic analysis of the structural mechanisms of urban racial unrest. The Los Angeles unrest signals a new era of such racial relations, one that must be conceptualized in terms of multiracial events. This approach calls attention to both the relationship between minority and dominant groups and the interminority group relationships in the United States.

If applied correctly, the middleman minority theory offers a useful and coherent perspective from which to analyze the roles of multiple race and ethnic groups that are distinguished from one another economically (and racially or ethnically) in a hierarchical way. The theory also suggests that, along with other social elements, the two critical factors—race and class—are intertwined. Therefore, it is crucial systematically to examine the influences of these two factors on such multiracial relations. If one factor is stressed at the expense of the other, studies will miss some essential ingredients of these complex relations.

REFERENCES

Barringer, Herbert, Robert W. Gardner, and Michael J. Levin. 1993. *Asians and Pacific Islanders in the United States*. New York: Russell Sage Foundation.
Bonacich, Edna, and Tae Hwan Jung. 1982. A portrait of Korean business in Los Angeles: 1977. Pp. 75–98 in *Koreans in Los Angeles*, edited by Eui-Young Yu, Earl H. Phillips, and Eun Sik Yang. Los Angeles: Koryo Research Institute and Center for Korean-American and Korean Studies, California State University.
Bonacich, Edna, Ivan Light, and Charles Choy Wong. 1980. Korean immigrant small business in Los Angeles. Pp. 167–84 in *Sourcebook on the new immigration*, edited by Roy Simon Bryce-Laporte. New Brunswick, N.J.: Transaction Books.
Bonacich, Edna, and John Modell. 1980. *The economic basis of ethnic solidarity: Small business in the Japanese American community*. Berkeley and Los Angeles: University of California Press.
Chang, Edward T. 1993. From Chicago to Los Angeles: changing the site of race relations. *Amerasia Journal* 19:1–3.
Choi, Laura. 1992. Black rage and white power. In Institute for Alternative Journalism, *Inside the L.A. riots: What really happened and why it will happen again*.
Cooper, Marc. 1992. L.A.'s state of siege: city of angels, cops from hell. Pp. 12–19 in Institute for Alternative Journalsim, *Inside the L.A. riots: What really happened and why it will happen again*.

Curran, Ron. 1992. Malign neglect. Pp. 24–25 in Institute for Alternative Journalism, *Inside the L.A. riots: What really happened and why it will happen again.*

Elias, Robert. 1986. *The politics of victimization: Victims, victimology and human rights.* New York: Oxford University Press.

Feagin, Joe R., and Clairece Booth Feagin. 1986. *Discrimination American style,* 2d ed. Malabar, Florida: Robert E. Krieger Publishing.

Fusfeld, Daniel R., and Timothy Bates. 1984. *The political economy of the urban ghetto.* Carbondale, Ill.: Southern Illinois University Press.

Hamilton, Cynthia. 1992. The making of an American Bantustan. Pp. 19–20 in Institute for Alternative Journalism, *Inside the L.A. riots: What really happened and why it will happen again.*

Hazen, Daniel. 1992. Forward to Institute for Alternative Journalism, *Inside the L.A. riots: What really happened and why it will happen again.*

Hurh, Won Moo, and Kwang Chung Kim. 1988. *Uprooting and adjustment: A sociological study of Korean immigrants' mental health.* Final Report Submitted to National Institute of Mental Health, U.S. Department of Health and Human Services.

Institute for Alternative Journalism. 1992. *Inside the L.A. riots: What really happened and why it will happen again.*

Korean American Inter-Agency Council (KAIAC). 1993. Korean American Inter-Agency Council announces results of a comprehensive survey assessing situation of Korean American victims ten months after the 1992 LA riots. Unpublished report.

Kerner Commission. 1968. *Report on the national advisory commission on civil disorders.* Washington, D.C.: U.S. Government Printing Office.

Kim, Illsoo. 1981. *New urban immigrants: The Korean community in New York.* Princeton, N.J.: Princeton University Press.

——. 1992. *Newsweek,* May 18.

Kim, Kwang Chung, and Won Moo Hurh. 1985. Ethnic resource utilization of Korean immigrant entrepreneurs in the Chicago minority area. *International Migration Review* 19:82–111.

Kim, Kwang Chung, Won Moo Hurh, and Marylin Fernandez. 1989. Intra-group differences in business participation: Three Asian immigrant groups. *International Migration Review* 23: 73–95.

Kim, Shin. 1994. Political economy of Korean–African American conflict. Chap. 13 in *Korean Americans: Conflict and harmony,* edited by Ho-Youn Kwon. Chicago: North Park College and Theological Seminary.

Kwon, Peter, 1992. The first multicultural riots. Pp. 88–93 in Institute for Alternative Journalism, *Inside the L.A. riots: What really happened and why it will happen again.*

Lieberson, Stanley. 1980. *Piece of a pie: Blacks and white immigrants since 1880.* Berkeley and Los Angeles: University of California Press.

Light, Ivan, and Edna Bonacich. 1988. *Immigrant Entrepreneurs: Koreans in Los Angeles, 1965–1982.* Berkeley and Los Angeles: University of California Press.

Light, Ivan, Hadas Har-Chvi, and Kenneth Kan. 1994. Black/Korean conflict in Los Angeles. Chap. 6 in *Managing divided cities,* edited by Seamus Dunn. London: Ryburn Publishing.

Los Angeles Times Staff. 1992. *Understanding the riots: Los Angeles and the aftermath of the Rodney King verdict*. Los Angeles: Los Angeles Times.

Madhubuti, Haki R., ed. 1993. *Why L.A. happened*. Chicago: Third World Press.

Marable, Manning. 1992. L.A. point of view. Pp. 82–83 in Institute for Alternative Journalism, *Inside the L.A. riots: What really happened and why it will happen again*.

Martin, Tony. 1993. From slavery to Rodney King: Continuity and change. Pp. 27–40 in *Why L.A. happened*, edited by Haki R. Madhubuti.

Massey, Douglas, and Nancy A. Denton. 1993. *American apartheid: Segregation and the making of the underclass*. Cambridge, Mass.: Harvard University Press.

Min, Pyong Gap. 1988. *Ethnic business enterprise: Korean small business in Atlanta*. Staten Island, N.Y.: Center for Migration Studies.

Oliver, Melvin, James H. Johnson, and David M. Grant. 1993. Race, urban inequality, and the Los Angeles rebellion. In *Introduction to social problems*, edited by Craig Calhoun and George Ritzer. New York: McGraw-Hill.

Reimers, David M. 1985. *Still the golden door*. New York: Columbia University Press.

Simmons, Charles E. 1993. The Los Angeles rebellion: Class, race and misinformation. Pp. 141–55 in *Why L.A. happened*, edited by Haki R. Madhubuti.

Soja, Edward, Rebecca Morales, and Goetz Wolff. 1983. Urban restructuring: An analysis of social and spatial change in Los Angeles. *Economic Geography* 58:221–35.

Sonenshein, Raphael J. 1993. *Politics in black and white: Race and power in Los Angeles*. Princeton, N.J.: Princeton University Press.

Turner, Jonathan H., and Edna Bonacich. 1980. Toward a composite theory of middleman minorities. *Ethnicity* 7:144–58.

U.S. Bureau of the Census. 1990. *Statistical abstract of the United States*. Washington D.C.: U.S. Government Printing Office.

U.S. Commission on Civil Rights. 1988. *The economic status of Americans of Asian descent: An exploratory investigation*. Washington, D.C.: U.S. Commission on Civil Rights, Clearing House Publication 95.

Waldinger, Roger, Howard Aldrich, Robin Ward, and Associates. 1990. *Ethnic entrepreneurs*. Newbury, Calif.: Sage Publications.

West, Cornel. 1993. *Race matters*. Boston: Beacon Press.

Wilson, William Julius. 1987. *The truly disadvantaged: The inner city, the underclass, and public policy*. Chicago: University of Chicago Press.

Yu, Eui-Young. 1993. SA-I'KU (April 29) riots and the Korean-American community. unpublished paper.

——. 1994. *Black-Korean encounter: Toward understanding and alliance*. Los Angeles: Institute for Asian American and Pacific Asian Studies, California State University.

3 New Urban Crisis: Korean-African American Relations

EDWARD T. CHANG

HISTORICALLY, THE CENTRALITY OF RACE IN THE UNITED STATES, AS Michael Omi and Howard Winant (1986) put it, has been framed in a white-black paradigm. Race problems have simply meant "black" problems. However, the recent development of ethnic tensions between Korean Americans and African Americans challenges this traditional white-black pattern.

To Korean Americans, the question of race took on special meanings as they were forced to play the role of "middlemen" between the white dominant and African American/Latino subordinate populations during the Los Angeles riots of 1992. Los Angeles was especially hostile toward Korean Americans during 1991 and 1992. Such hostility was fueled by several factors: the shooting death of Latasha Harlins and the subsequent probationary sentence imposed on the convicted shooter, Soon Ja Du; the overrepresentation of Korean-owned stores in African American and Latino neighborhoods; and the disgraceful media dissemination of images of Korean Americans as rude, greedy, selfish merchants who refuse to learn the English language (Chang and Oh n.d.). The climax of this hostility, the Los Angeles riot, was an event that deeply affected Korean American identity, survival, and ethnicity.

During the civil rights movement of the 1960s, race occupied the center stage of American politics; the 1970s were years of racial quiescence, when minority movements of the previous period seemed to wane (Omi and Winant 1986). In the 1980s and 1990s, race and class debates again occupied the center stage, but they took a different form. The heightened interethnic tensions between minority groups (i.e., Korean–African American or African American–Latino) during the 1980s and 1990s began to expose the complexity of race relations. With the resurgence of neoconservative ideologies, "color-blind" policies attempted to silence any discussion of "race." Massive attacks against the poor, uneducated, underclass and minority populations polarized American society along racial and class lines.

The demographic shifts in larger urban cities such as Los Angeles, New York, Chicago, and the Washington, D.C., area created new sets of economic, political, social, and racial issues. The phenomenal growth of the Asian Pacific American population over the last three decades has created a vastly diverse population, both ethnically and economically (Ong 1994). Not only has the new Asian immigration aggravated relations between Asians and whites, but it has also increased tensions between Asians and African Americans, particularly between Korean merchants and African American customers. In Los Angeles, the restructuring of the economy—in the form of plant shutdowns, relocated industry operations, and foreign investments—has deepened racial and class inequality in the city, adding fuel to the Korean–African American conflict.

Since the mid-1980s, Korean–African American conflicts have surfaced in many urban areas in the United States. Amid economic despair, many inner-city African Americans have perceived Korean merchants as "aliens" who have "taken over" their community. Thus, the Korean–African American conflict has emerged as one of the most explosive issues of urban America.[1] During the Los Angeles civil unrest, the media portrayed the 1992 riots as an extension of the on-going conflict between Korean American merchants and African American residents, although nearly half of the looters arrested were Latinos.[2] Indeed, the Los Angeles rioting was the first multiethnic civil disorder in America that clearly reflected the population changes during the past three decades (Chang 1994a).

This chapter examines the economic, cultural, and ideological factors of the Korean–African American conflict. The purpose is to understand how Korean Americans and African Americans perceive each other and to discern the roles of race and class in the conflict. How do we look at interminority conflict in relation to the declining number of whites, whose power remains dominant but is being transformed?

Methodology

The data came from interviews, participant observation, and content analysis. A significant portion of the data was collected from in-depth interviews, each usually lasting two to three hours, with thirty-four Korean merchants (twenty-four men and ten women) in South Central Los Angeles. Since the objective of the interviews was to collect information about the equality of life, the individual perceptions, and the racial ideology of immigrant entrepreneurs, I placed an emphasis on establishing a rapport with interviewees. Most Korean merchants were reluctant to be interviewed unless I was referred by someone they knew, respected, and trusted; some refused to be interviewed. Often, the Korean informants began the interview session by saying, "I am telling you this because you are a Korean." Once a rapport had been established, I was able to observe interactions between Korean merchants and African American customers. Sometimes I was left in charge of the store while the merchants were away, and on one occasion a Korean merchant asked me to run the store for an entire day while she took a vacation. Finally, I was able to obtain valuable primary research data on African American values and attitudes toward other groups from Professor Byron Jackson (formerly of the California State University at Los Angeles). His data provided insights into the general attitudes and political behaviors of African American residents in the greater Los Angeles area.

South Central Los Angeles

The Los Angeles riots were a short but expressive symptom of a violent frustration at the heart of urban America. And while South Central Los Angeles has been the single most concentrated focus of the crisis, similar conditions recur persistently in many other parts of Southern California and the United States at large (Scott and Brown 1993). South Central Los Angeles covers a broad geographical area whose boundaries can roughly be defined as Santa Monica Freeway, on the north, to the Imperial Highway, on the south, and from Van Ness/Arlington on the west to Alameda on the east.

The demographic changes have been more dramatic in South Central Los Angeles than in any other part of the city. The face of South Central Los Angeles changed as the "black flight" to the suburbs accelerated during the 1980s. The African American population in South Central Los

Angeles declined from 369,504 to 295,312 between 1980 and 1990. This suggests that what was once primarily an African American area has increasingly become a Latino community; Latinos now make up nearly half of the residents of South Central Los Angeles.

Such demographic changes have increased tensions and polarized different ethnic and racial groups. In the aftermath of the Los Angeles riots, hostility has continued to grow between Korean Americans and African Americans, between Latinos and African Americans, and between whites and African Americans. African Americans feel that they are being attacked—squeezed out—by the increasing numbers of immigrants from Latin America and Asia. Latin Americans often compete with African American residents for affordable housing, jobs, education, health, and social welfare programs (Navarro 1993). An article in the *Los Angeles Times* on July 22, 1992, detailed one such confrontation over employment opportunities in South Central Los Angeles. During the summer months of 1992, Danny Bakewell of the Brotherhood Crusade initiated a highly publicized campaign to close down Los Angeles construction sites that did not employ African Americans. Xavier Hermosillo, chairman of the Latino organization North East West South of America (NEWS), responded by organizing sting teams of undercover construction workers with video cameras, who monitored work sites and recorded Bakewell's efforts to replace Latino workers with African Americans.

As South Central Los Angeles has been transformed into a multiethnic community, African Americans have become concerned that they are losing influence and control in what used to be their exclusive domain. Many African Americans are suspicious of the rapidly growing numbers of Latino residents and Korean American store owners in "their neighborhoods." Latino and African American political interests also clashed over the issue of redistricting for the city council, assembly, and congressional seats in Los Angeles. Latinos demand proportional representation to reflect population changes, while African Americans argue that they are entitled to retain their share of gains to compensate for past injustices.

Racial and economic inequalities have produced a pattern of geographical segregation among the minorities that reside in the high-poverty areas of South Central Los Angeles. These impoverished areas house only 18.4 percent of the total population of Los Angeles County, but they are home to 38 percent of the county's poor (Ong et al. 1993). South Central Los Angeles also suffers from chronic joblessness, low skills, low wages, overcrowding, high rents, limited access to mortgage financing, poor public health, and a breakdown of the educational system. These conditions have produced social ills such as family breakdown, illiteracy, drugs, violence, and crime (Scott and Brown 1993). Against this background, we can begin to understand the nature and causes of Korean–African American conflicts.

KOREAN AMERICAN PERCEPTIONS
OF AFRICAN AMERICAN RESIDENTS

Regardless of their educational and occupational background, many Korean immigrants have been exposed to the American values of democracy, Christianity, meritocracy, and individualism before their arrival in the United States. During the past thirty years, as a result of Korea's rapid industrialization and modernization, Korean society has undergone a tremendous economic, social, and cultural transformation. As Korean society has modernized, Western (particularly American) values have become a part of Korean culture and national identity. Most Korean immigrants have prepared themselves for immigration to the United States by retaining traditional Korean values while becoming accustomed to, or at least exposed to, American culture.[3] The influence of Christianity and Western values on Korean society is quite substantial and affects all aspects of Korean life.

In the course of this presocialization, some Korean immigrants have also been exposed to negative images of African Americans as criminals, welfare recipients, alcoholics, drug addicts, or simply lazy—stereotypes portrayed in many American movies, television shows, and American Forces Korea Network (AFKN) programs in Korea.[4] As a result, many Korean immigrants arrive in the United States with ready-made negative views of African Americans. On the other hand, some Korean immigrants had no images of African Americans prior to their arrival in the United States.

Because the majority of Korean immigrants held professional or managerial positions in Korea, operating a small business in the United States represents underemployment and a loss of status (Min 1988; Yu 1982). Thus, a goal of Korean immigrant shopkeepers is to quickly regain their middle-class status, possibly by operating bigger stores. Having been exposed to positive images of America as the land of opportunity, many Korean immigrants truly believe in the notion of a meritocracy in which one can rise as high as one's talents and abilities permit. This ideology is consistent with Confucian values. Specifically, one's social ranking is determined by one's educational background. So, given the relatively lower educational level of African American residents in South Central Los Angeles, many Korean immigrants tend to look down on them.

In the past, the Korean-language media in America has also contributed to the negative images of African Americans by printing inflammatory articles about their alleged violence and criminal activities against Korean immigrants.[5] An African American male is often singled out as the criminal, although a careful reader will find that the accusations reported against African Americans in such news stories are often without concrete proof.

Korean Americans often express a fear of African Americans, who are seen as violent and physically stronger than they are. This fear often stems from personal experience as victims of African American assailants. When Korean merchants are robbed, mugged, burglarized, and murdered in their establishments, such negative stereotypes are reinforced. Losses from these crimes are not merely economic but psychological as well. Although merchants are fully aware of the risks of operating a small business in high-crime areas such as South Central Los Angeles, they are still devastated when their loved ones are put in danger, injured, or murdered. In a *Korea Times* article on January 20, 1988, reporting on the death of his brother, storekeeper Tong Kim lamented, "My brother Thomas wanted to live an American dream and he never got it."

AFRICAN AMERICAN PERCEPTIONS OF KOREAN AMERICANS

Historically, non–African American merchants have dominated the economy of African American communities. Many African American leaders have advocated self-help or economic development as a way to improve the quality of life for urban African Americans. However, many African American economic developments and business ventures have failed due to lack of capital or skills, redlining, institutional discrimination, and racism.

There is a widespread sense of abandonment and displacement among residents of South Central Los Angeles. African Americans are disillusioned by the paradox of the civil rights movement, which opened the doors to all minorities and to women, but not to the majority of African Americans. They are asking themselves why they are still shut off from the promise of prosperity and upward mobility. African Americans are still perceived as a liability rather than an asset by the dominant white

TABLE 3.1 Feelings of Los Angeles African Americans toward Various
Ethnic Groups

	Close (%)	Not Close (%)
Whites	84.7	13.1
Jewish	69.9	25.1
Hispanic	83.7	· 14.8
Asian	62.4	32.7

Source: Jackson 1988.

society. With such pent up rage, it is not surprising to see scapegoating of
Korean merchants in South Central Los Angeles, who, because of their
proximity, are easy targets of this African American frustration and anger.

According to the Jackson Survey, Asians are the ethnic group least
liked by African Americans in Los Angeles. Conducted in June 1988, the
survey was part of the research project "Los Angeles Racial Group Consciousness and Political Behavior Survey." As shown in Table 3.1, African
Americans in Los Angeles feel closer to whites, Hispanics, and Jews than
to Asians. Almost one-third (32.7%) of the African American respondents
had negative feelings towards Asians. This percentage is much higher
than that for whites (13.1%), Jews (25.1%), and Hispanics (14.8%).

The Jackson survey also found that the African American residents of
the affluent middle-class community of Inglewood had a greater percentage of negative attitudes toward Asians (38.9%) than the residents of
South Central Los Angeles (34.3%). Although this represents a difference
of only 4.6 percent, it is still significant because residents of Inglewood
usually do not interact with Korean merchants on a daily basis. This suggests that African Americans' negative attitudes toward Asians do not
necessarily arise only from direct contact (i.e., as customer and merchant).

The survey data also indicate a direct correlation between racial consciousness, class, educational background, and historical experiences.
Racial consciousness may be the most important contributing factor in
determining the degree of antagonism toward Asians and other racial
groups. Although 50 percent of the residents of South Central Los Angeles agreed with the statement "African American people don't do well
in life because they don't work hard," only 38.6 percent of the residents of
Inglewood agreed. More South Central Los Angeles residents (54.9%)
than Inglewood residents (43.7%) disagreed with the statement "African
American people do not get a good education or job because they do not
have the same opportunity" (Jackson 1988). In other words, African

TABLE 3.2 Customer Base of Korean-Owned Businesses

	Los Angeles (%)[1]	Dallas (%)[2]	New York (%)[2]
African Americans	10	34	39
Asian Americans	22	5	3
Latinos	17	40	37
Whites	48	21	19
Others	0	9	2

1. Yu, 1990:10.
2. National Korean American Grocer (KAGRO) Journal. Vol 3, no. 4 (July / August) 1994:32–33.

American residents in Inglewood tend to blame institutionalized racial discrimination for holding back African American progress in the United States, whereas more residents of South Central Los Angeles tend to blame themselves. This difference may explain why more residents of Inglewood harbored negative feelings toward Asians.

Regardless of class background, however, an overwhelming percentage (91.9%) of African Americans in Los Angeles want more African American–owned business in their neighborhoods. African Americans have voiced anger and frustration toward the overrepresentation of Korean-owned stores in their neighborhoods. Korean Americans are often accused of "planning to take over African American neighborhoods and extract maximum profits" (Cleaver 1983). Many African Americans believe that Korean immigrants are doing business only in their neighborhoods. Contrary to this popular belief, the majority of Korean business in the United States is not located in African American neighborhoods. As table 3.2 shows, the proportion of Korean businesses that do cater primarily to African American customers is as follows: 10 percent in Los Angeles, 34 percent in Dallas and 39 percent in New York.

CONFRONTATION: RACIAL OR ECONOMIC?

While tensions between Korean merchants and African American customers have escalated, members of the African American community repeatedly deny that race is the key factor. When four Korean merchants were shot and killed in April 1986 in Los Angeles, some suggested the possibility that these shootings were racially motivated crimes. However, it is extremely difficult, if not impossible, to prove that these African American assailants shot and killed the Korean merchants because of their hatred toward Korean immigrants. South Central Los Angeles and other large urban cities suffer from high crime rates. Crimes involving drugs and violence affect African American residents more than they do Korean merchants, in fact, as African American residents are more often than not the victims. For example, in Los Angeles, African American victims constituted 45.1 percent of the total homicide rate in 1987, while Asians comprised only 2.2 percent of the total (Los Angeles County Health Department 1987).

Many Korean businesses in African American neighborhoods have to bear the burden of crimes because they are located in high risk neighborhoods. However, many Korean-owned businesses were specifically targeted and destroyed by African Americans during the 1992 Los Angeles riots. Joe Hicks of the Southern Christian Leadership Conference commented: "There is no doubt that in the violence following the verdict Korean merchants were, in fact, targeted for destruction. There was a nasty anti-Asian, anti-Korean mood circulating throughout the streets of L.A. We can't deny it and we have to deal [with] that, straight up" (Hicks 1994). Larry Aubry of the Los Angeles County Human Relations Commission also recognized this anti-Korean sentiment during the civil unrest. "It was clear to me that they [Korean stores] were targeted" (Aubry 1994: 57).

Rising anti-immigrant and anti-Asian sentiment also contributed to the tension between the Korean and African American communities. Anti-Asian sentiment had risen sharply as the United States consistently posted trade deficits with Asian countries (particularly Japan). The African American community has been particularly affected by plant closures, relocations, and the restructuring of the American economy (Ong 1993; Blueston and Harrison 1982).

An example of this backlash against Asian immigrants is evidenced by Los Angeles City Councilman Nate Holden's proposal "STOP SELLING AMERICA," which attempted to prohibit non–U.S. citizens from purchasing property in the city of Los Angeles. Holden argues that "we are watching our precious land, a finite resource, being sold to foreigners to satisfy the greed of a few and our founding fathers never had intentions of selling our country to foreigners" (*Los Angeles Herald* June 30, 1989).

ECONOMIC FACTORS: UNDERLYING ETHNIC TENSIONS

Since the Korean–African American relationship involves immigrant minority merchants and native minority customers, the unique conditions and circumstances of each community must be examined. The middleman minority theory (Blalock 1967: 79–84; Bonacich 1973; Bonacich and Jung 1982; Loewen 1971; Zenner 1982) suggests that "because of their economic niche, immigrant groups [e.g., Koreans] are likely to experience friction with at least three important segments of the population: clientele, competitors, and labor unions" (Bonacich 1973). In other words, the middleman minority theory predicts that Korean merchants cannot avoid friction with the African American community because of the built-in conflicting relationship with their African American customers. Korean merchants face hostility from African American merchants, who charge that they are driving them out of business by undercutting prices. It is easy to see how the problem can be exacerbated when the sellers are immigrants and the buyers are poor. The middleman minority thesis provides a very pessimistic future for Korean-African American relations. The theory suggests that Korean immigrants must get out of African American areas, leave the occupation of shopkeeper altogether, or work with the African American community to achieve reconciliation.

In a related study of the Los Angeles African American community, Ronald Tsukashima (1986) suggests that economic inequalities are the most important factor determining the relationship between African Americans and Jews. "African American anti-Semitism resulted from the perceived or real economic inequality between African Americans and Jews, especially those economic exchanges in which there has developed a collective perception on the part of a less powerful, poorer minority that another minority has tended to make undue profit out of it" (Tsukashima 1986).

Indeed, the root cause of the interethnic conflict between Koreans and African Americans appears to be economic survival. African American complaints against Korean merchants often focus on the following economic issues: (1) "they [Korean merchants] do not hire African American workers"; (2) "they overcharge African American customers for inferior products"; (3) "they do not contribute their profits back to the African American community" (Chang 1994). In other words, many African Americans perceive Korean merchants as a threat to their own economic survival, sometimes seeing them as part of a long line of "outsiders" who have traditionally exploited the African American community. However, a majority of African American customers do indicate that "it does not matter who serves them as long as they receive good service" (Stewart 1989: 9). Mindful of these complaints from the African American community, many Korean businesses have begun to contribute to African American civic and voluntary organizations.

The economic factor in the merchant-client relationship is, no doubt, one of the main sources of the problems between Korean Americans and African Americans. However, it does not appear to be the sole, or even the most important, factor behind Korean–African American conflict. If the targeting of Korean merchants is indeed the direct result of a double standard, then the issue of interethnic conflict has racial implications as well as economic ones.

SOCIAL AND CULTURAL FACTORS: UNDERLYING CONFLICTS

Cultural misunderstanding between the two groups plays an important role in fueling and sometimes escalating the confrontations. African American customers complain that Korean merchants treat them with disrespect and say the merchants can't communicate with them. "Mono-cultural people [i.e., Koreans] doing business in a multi-cultural society is potentially problematic. Particularly, South Central Los Angeles is probably the worst place Koreans can come into," declared Larry Aubry of the Los Angeles County Human Relations Commission, adding that "Koreans don't know how to interact with customers."[6] Melanie Lomax, vice president of the NAACP observes, "It is clear these [Korean immigrants] are hard-working and industrious. But there's a high degree of resentment being bred against them in the African American community." Lomax claims that cultural differences account for the majority of the disputes between Korean merchants and African American customers: "We've identified it as cultural differences—both groups are not particularly educated about the other's cultural heritage" (Los Angeles Times April 15, 1985).

According to Ella Stewart (1989), Koreans and African Americans have different sets of rules concerning proper attitudes and behaviors in the business setting. If the rules are violated, a negative reaction should be expected. Stewart found that Korean merchants most frequently mentioned loudness, bad language, and shoplifting as inappropriate behaviors by African American patrons, stating that they should show respect and courtesy and should apologize more frequently. African American patrons most frequently mentioned Korean merchants' or employees' negative attitude—either ignoring patrons or watching them constantly, as well as throwing their change on the counter—as inappropriate behaviors (Stewart 1989).

Often, showing no shame or guilt is more difficult for Korean merchants to comprehend than the criminal act itself. As one merchant explained, "I can live with losing a six pack of beer. If I catch the thief, he still comes back to my store ten minutes later." Shaking his head, he added, "I don't understand it." Incidents of shoplifting aside, however, Koreans generally want their African American customers to be more courteous, polite, and respectful.

When Korean merchants encounter what they consider an inappropriate act, they basically react in two ways: by ignoring the customer or by getting angry and confronting him or her. Korean merchants believe that ignoring an African American patron is often a rational and appropriate response to an "inappropriate behavior." The underlying assumption is that a person who shows no respect for them is not worth paying much attention to. Because Korean merchants place such a high priority on appropriate and inappropriate behavior, sometimes they even forget that they are businessmen. Instead, they engage in direct confrontations with customers. "How can I smile at the customer who uses bad language and shows no respect for me?" declared one merchant.

Being totally ignored by a merchant is an especially sensitive issue for many African American patrons. There is a strong sense of victimization among residents of South Central Los Angeles. Being ignored by others, especially by merchants, is a direct insult to one's humanity, regardless of one's nationality or ethnicity (Stewart 1989). "I patronize the gas station because a Korean lady always greets me with 'hello' and never forgets to say have a nice day," said one African American man. "Across from that gas station, there is an African American–owned gas station. But he has never said hello or been friendly to me, so I patronize the Korean-owned gas station."[7] African American protesters at a Korean store held picket signs stating, "Cultural Difference? A Smile Is Universal," "Your Pride Is More Valuable than a Free Clock," and "They Call Us 'Nigger' in There."[8]

A "typical" Korean merchant response (or lack of response) to a customer often escalates from a potentially volatile situation into a direct confrontation. The following is an example of how a conflict begins. This example is just one of many conflicts from my participant observational study.

An African American woman approaches the Korean merchant and demands a refund for clothes she bought three days ago.

AFRICAN AMERICAN PATRON: The color of these pants and blouse does not match.

KOREAN MERCHANT: I don't sell this kind of clothing. Did you bring a receipt with you? [*carefully examining the clothes*] This clothing has been washed already anyway. I cannot exchange it even if you bought this from my store.

AFRICAN AMERICAN PATRON: [*angrily*] I bought this clothing at this store three days ago. [*grabs another item of clothing inside the store*] Look! This one is the same.

KOREAN MERCHANT: I told you that this clothing is not from my store. [*He walks away and gestures for her to leave the store*]

AFRICAN AMERICAN PATRON: [*upset by the Korean merchant's attitude of ignoring her, she becomes even more demanding*] I want a complete refund right now!

This confrontation goes on for a few more minutes. Security guards come to the store and take the woman to the office to try to resolve the conflict.

The Korean merchant thought that the best way to resolve the situation was simply to avoid the confrontation by ignoring the woman. His underlying assumption was that he did not want to waste his time arguing with her because he had no respect for her. The underlying assumption of the African American patron was that this was a "typical" Korean merchant's behavior. These assumptions gave rise to an unusually hostile exchange between merchant and patron.

These mutual negative perceptions and the encounters between Korean American merchants and African American customers often perpetuate a vicious cycle. A common complaint of Korean merchants is that they feel they "cannot afford not to keep eyes on the African American customers because they steal goods if you don't watch them carefully." "Sometimes, you know they stole something, but there is no proof, even if I searched them. I have to take the loss" (from author's interviews). For these reasons, some Korean merchants may show very little sympathy toward African American customers because they are preoccupied with their own economic status and security. Yet, at the same time, "being watched while shopping was the most frequently mentioned rule violation by African American patrons."[9] "They are always watching you. They treat you like a criminal or 'dirt' by watching you all the time. When I go in their stores I know I am going to be watched so I go in with an attitude" (Stewart 1989: 11). These behaviors reinforce the stereotypical perceptions of "rude" Korean American merchants and African Americans as "criminals."

Korean merchants usually have no historical understanding or awareness of the American civil rights movement and U.S. race relations in general.[10] However, ignorance and cultural misunderstandings alone are not the only causes of this conflict. The preexisting volatile and conflicting relationship between the two groups must be examined more closely. As noted by Stewart, "Like social interaction, then, the content or quality of interaction is more important in predicting anti-Koreanism than the mere exposure to either social or economic contact." This content or quality of interaction plays a critical role in either minimizing or exacerbating tension.

KOREAN AMERICAN MERCHANTS: MYTHS AND REALITIES

The absence of accurate information and lack of adequate education to inform each other has often created myths or rumors among African Americans and Korean merchants. Politicians, media, and community leaders have exploited the issue by endorsing such myths and stereotypes. In order to reconcile and begin the reconstruction process, we must separate myths from realities; such myths have played an important role in exacerbating confrontation between Koreans and the African American community. A "demythification" process must begin now to clear up any misunderstandings and myths about Korean merchants.

Myth 1. Korean American merchants are receiving special loans and assistance from the government. This is absolutely false. Korean Americans do not receive any special loans or assistance from the government.

Myth 2. Korean American merchants only do business in the African American community. The clientele of Korean-owned businesses in Southern California breaks down as follows: 48 percent whites, 22 percent Korean Americans, 17 percent Latinos and only 10 percent African Americans (Yu 1990: 9–10).

Myth 3. Korean merchants are foreigners who do not have a right to be in this country. Contrary to this popular myth, most Korean Americans are here legally and are either permanent residents or American citizens. According to the 1990 census, 67.6 percent of Korean Americans are American citizens by birth or naturalization.[11]

Myth 4. Korean American merchants do not hire African American employees. Korean American merchants are in a very difficult position in regards to hiring African American workers—damned if they do; damned if they don't. During the 1960s, Jewish shopkeepers were accused of operating a "slave market" for underpaying African American employees. On the other hand, Korean American merchants are being accused of *not* hiring African American youths. Even if most Korean-owned mom-and-pop stores hire one or two African American employees, it would have very little economic impact on the African American community. Many Korean stores do, in fact, hire African American workers, but minimum wage jobs are not going to solve the inner city's economic problems.

Myth 5. Korean American merchants do not contribute to the African American community and take profits away from the community. It is unfair to stereotype all Korean American merchants like this. Some Korean American merchants have contributed to local baseball teams, schools, and nonprofit organizations. On the other hand, others have not done so. Korean American merchants do have an obligation to participate in community affairs and contribute more to the African American community.

Myth 6. Korean merchants often sell inferior products for a higher price. A slightly higher price is normal for all small neighborhood convenience stores, and this practice is certainly not limited to Korean merchants. In exchange, the consumer gets the time-saving convenience of shopping close to home. Overall, mom-and-pop stores can neither compete with the volume of sales at large chains nor bypass the wholesalers and bargain directly with the manufacturers. A rudimentary understanding of supply and demand should make this situation clear.

Myth 7. Korean merchants are rude and disrespectful to their customers. Indeed, some merchants are rude and disrespectful to their customers. However, cultural differences between Korean and African Americans are sometimes misinterpreted as rudeness and disrespect. Korean and African Americans have different sets of rules concerning what are appropriate attitudes and behaviors. For example, Koreans are taught not to make eye contact while talking to elders and strangers. If you make eye contact with an elder, in Korean culture you are being rude and disrespectful to that person. In American culture, however, appropriate etiquette requires one to make eye contact.

CLASH OF IDEOLOGIES

The "immigrant theory" (Glazer 1975; Glazer and Moynihan 1963; Sowell 1980) predicts that recent immigrants from Asia and Latin America will follow the examples of European immigrants who have successfully entered mainstream American society through hard work and assimilation. The immigrant theory places emphasis on individual social and economic upward mobility through discipline, hard work, education, and the willingness to work long hours.

Most Korean immigrants have adopted the immigrant ideology and regard themselves as middle-class people in the process of succeeding in America, while many African Americans instead believe in a version of "internal colonial ideology." The internal colonial theory (Blauner 1972) views the pattern of American race relations in terms of the continual oppression of Third World peoples. It rejects the notion that European immigrants and non-European immigrants have had the same chances to succeed in American society. People of color are seen as having been placed in a subordinate position by economic exploitation, political subjugation, and racism.

Unaware of the history of oppression and exploitation of minority groups by white America, most Korean immigrants believe that America is a "land of opportunities." In this context, then, Korean immigrants often show no respect toward African American customers who are unemployed and dependent upon government programs, believing that African Americans in such situations should not blame anyone except themselves for their misery and misfortune. Many Korean immigrants have no awareness that the development of the African American slums was a direct outcome of racial discrimination in employment, housing, education, and politics.

Since the majority of Korean immigrants came to America after the civil rights movement, they are often not cognizant of the long history of racial discrimination and African American struggles toward equality, freedom, and civil rights. African Americans are, in turn, angry because Korean immigrants do not show any respect toward their struggle. Ironically, Korean immigrants are among the many beneficiaries of the civil rights movement. Indeed, the passage of the 1965 Immigration and Nationality amendments, which opened the door for Korean immigration, was partly a result of the civil rights movement.

More importantly, the two groups have different perceptions about success in America. Becoming an independent entrepreneur represents "success" to many African Americans, while it is nothing more than an avenue for "making a living" to many Korean immigrants (Bonacich 1988; Light and Bonacich 1988; Min 1988, 1989). Although Korean immigrants move into small business in search of the American dream, they often face the cold reality that they cannot make much money as shopkeepers. "I know that I can't make much money in this business," said one merchant. Although some businesses have become successful, the majority of Korean-owned small stores are struggling to make ends meet.

Confrontations derive from the different historical, economic, and ideological experiences of the two groups. Victimized African Americans in the inner cities, who have learned to stand up for their rights because of historical persecution and oppression, will not tolerate attacks on the most important thing they have left—their dignity.

CONCLUSION

The demographic shift and restructuring of the American economy has increased racial and class polarization. The recent growth of Asian American and Latino populations has aggravated relations between Koreans and African Americans, Latinos and African Americans, and whites and African Americans. The heightened interethnic tensions between minority groups not only challenges the traditional white-black race relations paradigm but also demands new visions and institutional reforms in our society.

Despite the ongoing efforts of the Black-Korean Alliance (BKA) and Korean and African American churches to improve relations between the two communities, the situation has continued to worsen—as we have witnessed during the 1992 Los Angeles riots, in which many Korean-owned stores were targeted and destroyed by African American rioters. The BKA, established in 1986 to improve Korean–African American relations, was disbanded in November 1992. The breakup of such coalitions was due to a combination of the structural makeup of the coalitions themselves (e.g. membership), the nature of the larger communities involved, and the assumptions underlying the formation of the coalitions.[12]

The role of government must be evaluated and fundamentally challenged. Existing institutions and organizations have not been able to effectively deal with the newly emerging problem of interminority disputes. In order to resolve or reduce tensions between minority communities, existing institutions must change or new institutions must be created to effectively deal with conflicts between minority groups. The lack of sufficient human and financial resources was the most crucial deficit that contributed to the dissolution of coalitions in Los Angeles. This lack of resources is symbolic of the fact that interminority relations are not a priority among the city and county administrations.

The need for making human relations an integral aspect of our lives must be clearly understood. In order to solve many of the existing problems between the Korean American and African American communities, coalition building based on economic and political interests and commonalities is a necessity. Latinos have also emerged as a major force to reckon with in Los Angeles as well as in other parts of the United States. In Los Angeles, labeling the interethnic issue as Korean–African American tension excludes the Latino community from the dialogue. Interethnic tension cannot be adequately addressed without including the Latino voice. The success or failure of building coalitions will depend upon how well these interested communities are able to minimize their differences while maximizing similarities.

NOTES

1. For more details, see Edward T. Chang, "New Urban Crisis: Korean-Black Conflicts in Los Angeles," (Ph.d. diss., Department of Ethnic Studies, University of California, Berkeley, 1990). In addition, there have been numerous newspaper reports concerning the increasing tensions between Korean merchants and African American residents: James Cleaver, "Asian Businesses in Black Community Cause Stir," *Los Angeles Sentinel*, August 11–September 1, 1983; *Metro News*, (Chicago), May 12, 1984; *Philadelphia Daily News*, December 15, 1986; *New York Times*. January 19, 1985, May 7, 1990, May 14, 1990, August 31, 1990; *New York Newsday*, December 22, 1988, February 13, 1990, May 10, 1990, January 4, 1991; *Los Angeles Times*, May 18, 1986, May 20, 1990; *Rice Magazine*, April 15, 1985; *Insight*, February 9, 1987.

2. According to the arrest record of the Los Angeles County Sheriff's Department, 12,545 arrests were made between 6 P.M., April 29, and 5 A.M., May 5, 1992—the period of civil disorder. The racial breakdown of those who were arrested is as follows: 45.2 percent Latino, 41 percent African American, and 11.5 percent white (Pastor 1993). The Rose Institute data states that Latinos comprised 51 percent of those arrested and 30 percent of those who died, and up to 40 percent of the damaged businesses were Latino owned. For more details about the role of Latinos in the Los Angeles civil unrest, see Navarro 1993.

3. Post-1965 Korean immigrants are known as new urban immigrants because they tend to be highly educated, family-oriented, and middle class or urban professional. See Kim 1981; Won Moo Hurh and Kwang Chung Kim, "Adhesive Sociocultural Adaptation of Korean Immigrants in the U.S.: An Alternative Strategy of Minority Adaptation," *International Migration Review* 18, no. 2 (1984): 188–216; Yu 1983; Min 1988.

4. Fifty African American high school and college students were invited to visit South Korea from July 16 to August 10, 1994. One student recalled his encounter with a Korean: "The Korean host asked if I wanted to smoke or drink. When I said 'no,' he was shocked. [The] Korean host said, 'I thought all blacks were heavy smokers and drinkers'" (from author's interview).

5. The Korean-language media play an important role in shaping the opinions of the Korean-American community because a majority of Korean immigrants subscribe to Korean-language newspapers, watch Korean-language television, and listen to Korean-language radio programs daily. Due to language barriers, most immigrants rely heavily on this media as their only source of information and news.

6. Author's interview with Larry Aubry on September 22, 1988. Aubry also

made the same statement on a public television documentary, "Clash of Cultures," January 17, 1987, KCET channel 28 (Los Angeles).

7. Author's interview with one of the African American residents of South Central Los Angeles.

8. From a demonstration during the boycott of the Slauson Indoor Swap Meet, which began on November 18, 1989.

9. Indoor Swap Meet merchants seem to be more conscious of African American customers' sensitivity and behavior. One merchant said, "If I don't pay attention to the customer or do not greet him or her (can I help you?), he or she will simply walk away to another store."

10. I wrote a Korean-language book titled *Who African Americans Are*. Within three months of publication, it went into its third printing. This market demand shows the degree of willingness of Korean immigrants to learn about African American history and culture.

11. See the *Korea Times*, January 7, 1994: A1. According to the article 67.6 percent Korean Americans are citizens of the United States.

12. For a detailed discussion about the breakup of the BKA, see Jeannettee Diaz-Viadezes and Edward T. Chang, "Building Cross-Cultural Coalitions: A Case Study of the Black-Korean Alliance and the Latino-Black Roundtable" *Ethnic and Racial Studies* 19, no. 3 (July 1996): 680–700.

REFERENCES

Aubry, Larry. 1994. Why are Koreans targeted? In *Black-Korean encounter: Toward understanding and alliance*, edited by Eui-Young Yu. Los Angeles: Institute for Asian American and Pacific Asian Studies.

Blalock, H. M. 1967. *Toward a theory of minority group relations*. New York: John Wiley.

Blauner, Robert. 1972. *Racial oppression in America*. New York: Harper and Row.

Blueston, Barry, and Bennett Harrison, eds. 1982. *The deindustrialization of America*. New York: Basic Books.

Bonacich, Edna. 1973. A theory of middleman minorities. *American Sociological Review* 37:547–59.

——. 1988. The social costs of immigrant entrepreneurship. *Amerasia Journal* 14 (1).

——. 1989. The role of the petite bourgeoisie within capitalism: A response to Pyong Gap Min. *Amerasia Journal* 15 (2): 195–203.

Bonacich, Edna, and Tae Hwan Jung. 1982. A portrait of Korean small business in Los Angeles: 1977. Pp. 75–98 in *Koreans in Los Angeles: Prospects and promises*, edited by Eui-Young Yu, Earl H. Phillips, and Eun Sik Yang. Los Angeles: Koryo Research Institute and Center for Korean-American and Korean Studies, California State University.

Chang, Edward T. 1992. Building minority coalitions: A case study of Korean and African Americans. *Korea Journal of Population and Development* 21 (1): 37–56.

——. 1993. Jewish and Korean merchants in African American neighborhoods: A comparative perspective. *Amerasia Journal* 19 (2): 5–22.

——. 1994a. America's first multiethnic riots. In *The state of Asian America: Activism and resistance in the 1990s*, edited by Karin Aguilar-San Juan. Boston: South End Press.

——. 1994b. Myths and realities of Korean-Black American relations. Pp. 83–89 in *Black-Korean encounter: Toward understanding and alliance*, edited by Eui-Young Yu.

——, ed. 1993. Special Issue of *Amerasia Journal: Los Angeles—Struggles toward Multi-ethnic Community* 19 (2): 69–85.

Chang, Edward T., and Eunjin Angela Oh. Korean American dilemma: Violence, vengeance, vision. Unpublished manuscript.

Chang, Edward T., and Eui-Young Yu. 1994. Chronology of Black-Korean encounter. In *Black-Korean encounter: Toward understanding and alliance*, edited by Eui-Young Yu.

Cleaver, James H. 1983. Asian businesses in black community cause stir. *Los Angeles Sentinel*, August 11: A1.

Glazer, Nathan. 1975. *Ethnicity: Theory and experience*. Cambridge, Mass.: Harvard University Press.

Glazer, Nathan, and Daniel Moynihan. 1963. *Beyond the melting pot: Negroes, Puerto Ricans, Jews, Italians, and Irish of New York City*. Cambridge, Mass.: Massachusetts Institute of Technology Press.

Hicks, Joe. 1994. Rebuilding in the wake of rebellion: The need for economic conversion. Pp. 79–82 in *Black-Korean encounter: Toward understanding and alliance*, edited by Eui-Young Yu.

Hurh, Won Moo, and Kwang Chung Kim. 1984. *Korean immigrants in America: A structural analysis of ethnic confinement and adhesive adaptation*. Madison, Wis.: Fairleigh Dickinson University Press.

Jackson, Byron O. 1988. Los Angeles racial group consciousness and political behavior survey. California State University, Los Angeles.

Kim, Illsoo 1981. *New urban immigrants: The Korean community in New York*. Princeton, N.J.: Princeton University Press.

Light, Ivan, and Edna Bonacich. 1988. *Immigrant entrepreneurs: Koreans in Los Angeles*. Berkeley and Los Angeles: University of California Press.

Loewen, James. 1971. *The Mississippi Chinese: Between black and white*. Cambridge, Mass.: Harvard University Press.

Los Angeles County Health Department. 1987. Annual report.

Min, Pyong Gap. 1988. *Minority business enterprise: Korean small business in Atlanta*. Staten Island, N.Y.: The Center for Migration Studies.

——. 1989. The social costs of immigrant entrepreneurship: A response to Edna Bonacich. *Amerasia Journal* 15 (2): 187–94.

——. 1990. Problems of Korean immigrant entrepreneurs. *International Migration Review* 24 (fall): 436–55.

Navarro, Armando. 1993. South Central Los Angeles eruption: A Latino perspective. In (Special Issue) *Amerasia Journal: Los Angeles—Struggles toward Multiethnic Community*, edited by Edward T. Chang, 19 (2): 69–85.

Omi, Michael, and Howard Winant. 1986. *Racial formation in the United States: From the 1960s to the 1980s*. New York and London: Routledge and Kegan Paul.

Ong, Paul, et al. 1993. Poverty and employment issues in the inner urban core. In *South Central Los Angeles: Anatomy of an urban crisis*, edited by A. J. Scott and E. R. Brown.

——, ed. 1994. *The state of Asian Pacific America: Economic diversity, issues, and politics*.

Public Policy Report. Los Angeles: The LEAP Asian Pacific American Public Policy Institute and the UCLA Asian American Studies Center.

Pastor, Manuel. 1993. *Latinos and the Los Angeles uprising: The economic context.* Claremont, Calif.: Thomas Rivera Center.

Scott, A. J., and E. R. Brown, eds. 1993. *South Central Los Angeles: Anatomy of an urban crisis.* Los Angeles: The Lewis Center for Regional Policy Studies, University of California, Los Angeles.

Sonenshein, Raphael J. 1993. *Politics in black and white: Race and power in Los Angeles.* Princeton, N.J.: Princeton University Press.

Sowell, Thomas. 1980. *Ethnic America.* New York: Basic Books.

Stewart, Ella. 1989. Ethnic cultural diversity: Ethnographic study of cultural study of cultural differences and communication styles between Korean merchants and African American patrons in South Central Los Angeles. M. A. thesis, Department of Communications, California State University, Los Angeles.

Terkel, Studs. 1993. *Race: How blacks and whites think and feel about the American obsession.* New York: Anchor Books.

Totten, George O., III, and H. Eric Schockman, eds. 1994. *Community in crisis: The Korean American community after the Los Angeles civil unrest of April 1992.* Los Angeles: Center for Multiethnic and Transnational Studies, University of Southern California.

Tsukashima, Ronald. 1986. A test of competing contact hypothesis in the study of black anti-Semitic beliefs. In *Contemporary Jewry*, Vol. 7, edited by Arnold Dashefsky. New Brunswick, N.J.: Transaction Books.

Wilson, William Julius. 1978. *The declining significance of race.* Chicago: University of Chicago Press.

Young, Philip K. Y. 1983. Family labor, sacrifice, and competition: Korean greengrocers in New York City. *Amerasia Journal* 10 (2): 53–72.

Yu, Eui-Young. 1983. Korean communities in America: Past, present, and future. *Amerasia Journal* 10 (2): 23–51.

———. 1990. *Korean community profile: Life and consumer patterns.* Los Angeles: The Korea Times/Hankook Ilbo.

———, ed. 1994. *Black-Korean encounter: Toward understanding and alliance.* Los Angeles: Institute for Asian American and Pacific Asian Studies.

Zenner, W. 1982. Arabic-speaking immigrants in North America as middleman minorities. *Ethnic and Racial Studies* 5:457–77.

4 Use and Abuse of Race and Culture: Black-Korean Tension in America

Kyeyoung Park

With lyrics such as "Don't follow me up and down your market / Or your little chop-suey ass will be a target," and "Pay respect to the Black fist / Or we'll burn down your store, right down to a crisp," Ice Cube's 1991 album, *Death Certificate*, turned out to be a warning. In South Central Los Angeles, on March 18, 1991, a black teenager, Latasha Harlins, was shot and killed by a Korean grocer, Soon Ja Du, in a dispute over a $1.79 bottle of orange juice. Superior Court judge Joyce Karlin fined Du $500, put her on probation, and ordered her to perform 400 hours of community service. While few killers are granted such a light sentence, there was no reason to send Du to jail, said the judge. She was not a menace to society. The African American community of Compton rose up in anger. "You shoot a dog," my African American interviewees said, "and you go to jail. You shoot a black kid and you get probation." Committees were formed and rallies held.

The media described this Los Angeles controversy as a racial confrontation between blacks and Koreans. Headlines in the *Los Angeles Times* announced: "Boycott: Business Has Plummeted in a Store where Korean American Owner Killed a Black Man"; "Korean Stores Firebombed; 2 of 3 Hit Have Seen Black Boycott"; "Blacks Won't End Korean Store Boycott" (*Los Angeles Times* 1991a, 1991b, 1991d). An editorial stated that protesters may feel they have a legitimate gripe, "but in the long run, boycotts rarely address the real, core problem and only add to community tension" (1991c).

In this portrayal of the controversy, one needs to ask what and who are missing here. Where, for example, are white people in this interpretation of the conflict? Are Koreans simply another "white" group? What kind of racial discourse or structure is the media creating, and what role does race play in this conflict?

In contrast to the media's focus on race, black and Korean community leaders explain tensions in terms of culture. They claim that cultural differences account for the majority of the disputes involving merchants and customers. Addressing a boycott in New York, a Korean Human Relations staff member testified:

> Korean merchants' seeming attitudes toward their customers are the source of many tensions. . . . It is their frustration . . . they appear arrogant and rude. . . . Western culture is very open. It is kind, always smiling, that is the tradition. But we are very different. If a Korean woman smiles at an unknown man we would think she is a prostitute. Even if they don't smile it is not their intention to be rude or arrogant . . . they are not trained to smile.[1]

While there are some real cultural differences between Korean merchants and African American residents, it is questionable whether these differences are the root of the problem.[2]

Whereas community leaders emphasize culture and the media focus on race, scholars have stressed the importance of structural forces in race relations—for instance, the commercial role of minority middlemen (Bonacich and Jung 1982; Chang 1990; Light and Bonacich 1988). Korean merchants, when they operate outlets that serve as the intermediary between a local population and individuals in economic and political power, play a role similar to that of other ethnic minorities in third-world colonies. The middleman theory orients us toward the conflict-ridden relationships between customers and merchants of different ethnic backgrounds. Although the middleman minority concept is a useful starting point for understanding the role of Korean merchants, the situation is far more complex.

The emergence of conflict among nonwhite minority groups has been explained as the direct consequence of increasing immigration and major changes in the social, economic, and demographic structure of American society that place minority groups in competition for scarce and valuable resources (Johnson and Oliver 1989). Although economics may be at the base of potential conflicts, the problems between Korean merchants and black buyers are also social; these conflicting roles are defined along racial-ethnic lines (Ong, Park, and Tong 1994). This conflict is further heightened by racially based and racially distinct perceptions and misperceptions (Stewart 1991) and by sharp cultural and linguistic differences, all of which produce a gulf of misunderstanding.

Black-Korean conflict is not only about economics but also about meanings. The clash of values and meanings happens in the context of a power relationship. "Inequality and hierarchy come already embedded in symbolic systems as well as elaborated through contextualized material practice" (Yanagisako and Delaney 1995: ix–x).[3] Douglas Massey and Nancy Denton's *American Apartheid* (1993) shows how whites develop a tangible stake in their whiteness through residential segregation. More recently, David Palumbo-Liu (1994) examined the white media construction of race relations in the aftermath of the Los Angeles uprising, showing how Koreans are seen as "surrogate whites" in black-white conflicts. Here, I want to explore how white racism is reconstructed in the context of black-Korean tension.[4]

BLACK RESIDENTS AND KOREAN AMERICANS IN SOUTH CENTRAL LOS ANGELES

Tensions between Koreans and black residents have developed in inner-city neighborhoods during the past two decades. Tensions between white, especially Jewish, merchants and black residents in New York City have existed since the 1920s and came to the fore during the riots of the 1960s. However, the circumstances of conflict now are different from conditions during the 1920s and even the 1960s. The increasing numbers of Asian and Latin American immigrants living or working in inner cities as a result of the Immigration and Nationality amendments of 1965 complicate the political situation in ghetto areas.[5]

Race has shaped and been shaped by U.S. politics (Omi and Winant 1986), but the changes in South Central Los Angeles have occurred in the context of post–civil-rights racial politics. Although race continues to be important in America, racial oppression has declined over the last half-century. However, this waning of oppression is not a linear, irreversible process (Espiritu and Ong 1994: 297). With the restructuring of the global order and the recurring economic crises in the United States, racially motivated state policies and hate crimes are once again on the rise. In the 1980s the Reagan administration attempted to reverse the political gains of the racial minority movements of the 1960s. The current attacks on affirmative action have also had effects on South Central Los Angeles.

Disinvestment has occurred not only in the private sector but also in the public sector (Johnson et al. 1992; Ong, Park, and Tong 1994: 269). Under successive Republican administrations, federal and state governments withdrew funds for community-based organizations, undermining key institutions in the community. As in many other inner-city communities throughout the nation, the state abandoned its "War on Poverty" in South Central long before poverty was eliminated. The combination of New Federalism and declining dollars for community action led to increasingly scarce funds for social programs in depressed neighborhoods (Logan and Harvey 1987). The deindustrialization of America, accompanied by the flight of American capital, plant closings, and further transnationalization of capital flow and labor migration, has intensified the suffering of the urban poor (Bluestone and Harrison 1982; Ong and the Research Group on the Los Angeles Economy 1989).

Analyses of the political economy of South Central Los Angeles show a community that has been increasingly isolated, politically and economically, from mainstream society. As the traditional industrial core of the city, South Central bore the brunt of the decline in manufacturing employment, losing 70,000 high-wage, stable jobs between 1978 and 1982. Major companies such as General Motors, Goodyear, Firestone, and Bethlehem Steel closed plants in or around the area (Johnson et al. 1992). According to a study by the United Way, a total of 321 plants or industries left the area over a fifteen-year period. The 1990 census reported that approximately one in three South Central residents lived in a household with an income below the official poverty line, a rate over twice that for the county as a whole. In 1990, only 59 percent of adults (ages 20–64) in South Central worked, a figure 16 percent lower than the rate for the county (Ong 1993).

It was during this period of growing poverty and oppression of inner-city blacks that Korean immigrant merchants entered urban neighborhoods, where the cost of starting or purchasing a business was relatively low (Light and Bonacich 1988; Park 1997). Korean Americans opened small businesses by relying on various sources of sociocultural capital, the Korean traditional financial system based on the *kye* (a rotating credit association), and, to some extent, capital brought from Korea, as well as family labor and educational resources. As new immigrants they experienced downward mobility, from employment as white-collar professionals in Korea to owning and operating small businesses in America. This was due to a combination of language and cultural barriers, nontransferable professional credentials, and discrimination in workplaces.

In Los Angeles, one in three Korean immigrants operates a small family business with few or no employees. According to a study by the Korean-American Grocers Association (KAGRO), there are 3,320 Korean American–owned liquor stores and markets in southern California, with annual sales totaling $1.8 billion. In South Central Los Angeles, a predominantly black and Latino community, the NAACP estimates that up to 70 percent of the area's gas stations are now owned by Koreans. Korean business leaders report that as many as one-third of the community's small markets and liquor stores are Korean-owned. However, in the county of Los Angeles, the proportion of Korean business ownership in black neighborhoods accounts for only 10 percent of all Korean businesses.[6] This means that the majority of Korean Americans run businesses in other low- or lower-middle-class neighborhoods in Los Angeles, including Koreatown. Despite their volume of business ownership in South Central, most Korean American merchants reside outside the area. In addition, despite the popular portrayal of Korean Americans as a model minority, they have little political power or wealth.

CONSTRUCTION OF RACE AND ETHNICITY AMONG KOREAN IMMIGRANTS

Koreans believe themselves to be more civilized than any other people except the Chinese. Jeongduk Yi (1993: 20) reports that Koreans dismissed whites as *yangi*, Western barbarians, until the late nineteenth century, when Korea was confronted by the military power of the supposedly inferior *yangi* and *waenom* (a derogatory term for the Japanese). After the turn of the century, whites occupied a higher position in the Korean conception of the world racial hierarchy because of their superior economic, military, and political power. Since 1945, the predominance in government and business of Koreans educated in the United States and the presence of the U.S. Army in South Korea have further contributed to this conception of whites, specifically white Americans (Yi 1993: 21). The pervasive American cultural presence in South Korea, especially since the Korean War, has also influenced Korean immigrants' racial attitudes. After Korean Americans have lived in the United States for a time, their experiences of running small business enterprises helps structure their emergent ideologies of race and ethnicity. While some develop elaborate conceptualizations of the United States as a multiethnic society, others develop simpler notions—for example, the lighter one's skin, the better one should be treated.

For Koreans operating small businesses, interethnic encounters arise in their day-to-day operations. Korean business proprietors become aware of their subordinate position to whites in the American system of ethnic stratification. They recognize their role in replacing white American small business proprietors via "ethnic succession" and understand that whites are aware of this as well. In the United States, many Koreans experience discrimination as an ethnic minority for the first time, and some unfortunately reapply the treatment they receive to other minorities.[7]

During this current urban turmoil, black residents have picketed and boycotted Korean merchants in South Central and complained about being overcharged and not treated with respect. In 1991, the Brotherhood Crusade, a vocal black organization headed by the charismatic Danny Bakewell, organized a boycott against Chung's Liquor Mart. Earlier, Tae Sam Park, the owner, had killed Lee Arthur Mitchell during an attempted robbery. What prompted the protest was a belief that the killing was unwarranted because Mitchell had been unarmed. There were further deaths on both sides as violence surrounding the issue continued, and eventually tensions culminated in the looting and burning of Korean businesses during the Los Angeles crisis of 1992.[8]

THE INSTIGATING ROLE OF WHITENESS IN BLACK-KOREAN CONFLICT

The black-Korean American discourse is a triadic relation, not a dyadic one. It begins with the respective relationships of the two minorities to whites, and it puts Asians, in particular Koreans, in a paradoxical position in U.S. race relations. The triad is exemplified by the court's lenient sentencing of Soon Ja Du, the Korean immigrant shopkeeper convicted of shooting Latasha Harlins. Judge Karlin, a white woman, argued that the rules against probation should not apply in the Harlins-Du case. The judge stated three reasons that this was an unusual case, justifying Du's lenient sentence:

> First, although the basis for the presumption against probation is technically present, that is, a gun was used, I find that it does not apply. The statute [Pen. Code 1203, subdivision (e)(2)] is aimed at criminals who arm themselves and go out and commit crimes. *It is not aimed at shopkeepers who lawfully possess firearms for their own protection.* Secondly, the defendant has no recent record, in fact, no record

at all of committing similar crimes or crimes of violence. Third, I find that the defendant participated in the crime under circumstances of great provocation, coercion, and duress (*Los Angeles Daily Appellate Report* April 23, 1992: 5315; emphasis added).

Racial inequality is routinely played out in judicial sentencing, usually in favor of whites and against blacks. Blacks know that whites who kill blacks get less rigorous sentences, while blacks who kill whites get the most stringent sentences. Given this racialized formula, black community members could see that Du was judicially treated as a white because she killed a black. They could also surmise that she would have been sentenced as a black had she dared to kill a white. Among those I interviewed, a black male, a 26-year-old United Parcel Service carrier, explained:

Soon Ja Du should not have shot Latasha. If Latasha was another race, such as white, I do not think Soon Ja Du would have received a light sentence. I believe that Soon Ja Du thought that she could get away with it. Tension exists between the two groups because the Koreans have their stores in the black neighborhoods and do not employ blacks. Blacks have to shop at the Korean stores because they are in their neighborhoods. Members of Korean descent are different. Koreans have stereotypes of blacks from television.

A black female graduate student interviewee states:

The role of race is high. The tensions have always been there and the last straw has broken the camel's back. The judge was unfair. A black postal carrier received six months in jail for beating a dog, but this woman receives probation for killing a human. The police and government officials have a code among themselves: Cover each other's ass. They avoid accountability and do not like to take responsibility for their actions. I do not trust cops.

These comments contrast with Korean merchants' evaluation of the role of race. Several of them indicated that race was not a real factor in relations between shopkeeper and customer, and they felt that the media had injected race into a situation where it was not relevant. A fifty-two-year-old grocery market owner and former pharmacist in Korea, Mr. Kim, maintains that:

This Du Soon Ja incident has nothing to do with race. This is not so much a racial confrontation but rather a problem between merchants and customers. I see cultural differences as contributing to similar conflicts. I find fault with the American media. They keep spreading a message along racial lines and exaggerated the incident in order to satisfy themselves, which is often their job. It is like doctors who keep warning you that you are ill.

Similarly, many Korean merchants believe that for years the mainstream media has inflamed the impassioned rage black people feel toward Koreans through superficial, insensitive, and unbalanced coverage of incidents involving customers and shopkeepers. Kapson Lee, editor of the English edition of the *Korea Times*, writes: "First, the media unduly emphasized the Korean ancestry of Du, thus, indirectly and perhaps inadvertently, contributing toward a negative image of Korean Americans in the eyes of Black people. Second, it played into the hands of those whose vested interest it was, and is, to exploit such fallacious images" (Lee 1994: 255).

Unraveling "Culture"

Korean merchants attribute the main causes of these incidents to social and cultural differences—difficulties with merchant-customer communication, poverty in black communities, situational or psychological factors, or the media. Black residents do not agree with this assessment although they do acknowledge cultural differences. In such conflicts, the role of culture emerges in four different ways: (1) Korean Americans' approach toward business, (2) blacks' and Korean Americans' perceptions of each other's cultures, (3) the impact of the dominant society's discourse on black and Korean relations, and (4) the social construction of race by both Koreans and blacks, mediated by the dominant cultural discourse. Here I present Korean shopkeepers' views first, then I will move on to those of the black community.

Mr. Kim actually had known the Du family before the incident. His assessment of the shooting implicates the cultural traditions informing Korean Americans' approach to business. Their reliance on family labor means that individuals work long hours, a stressful situation that leads to fatigue and can sometimes contribute to irrational responses.

That shooting occurred as they were overworked and under lots of stress. They might be too tired to control themselves even over very trivial things. Like other Korean immigrant families, Mr. Du relied upon family labor, especially [that of] his wife, Du Soon Ja. I find it problematic to rely on family labor heavily. You might save some money on wages, but you do not realize that family members force themselves to work beyond their capability. I know it from my own experience with running a drugstore in Korea. That's why I do not allow my wife to work here. Mr. Du used to be showy, and always went to the bank and took part in other activities in the Korean community. Therefore, it was always Mrs. Du who ran the store. They own another store. In this context, I really want fellow Koreans to reflect on the way they operate their stores. Even a small store should hire at least part-time local help, if possible African Americans, instead of just exploiting family labor.

Another grocer I interviewed, Mrs. Song, feels overwhelmed by the difficulties of running a small business in a poor urban neighborhood. She also tells us that the dominant society, through mass media, can amplify interracial tension in a shopkeeper's store by focusing on shootings and boycotts involving Korean merchants and black customers: "Even this morning a customer threatened us, mentioning a possible boycott. I am very scared. I do not want to cause trouble. If they do damage to goods, it is hard for me to be pleasant toward them. We try to treat and serve our customers, but sometimes they just expect us to serve them better. However, too much has been reported, and the media aggravated the whole matter."

In exploring the issue of culture, I asked my interviewees to describe themselves and their culture, and to show how their culture is similar to and different from other cultures. The shared—and yet problematic—opinion was that Koreans have more culture than blacks. References to "more culture" or "less culture" or "no culture" revealed that popular notions of the term *culture* differ from anthropological ones. Reflecting these popular notions, Mrs. Song compares Korean American culture with black culture: "We are enlightened not to steal, unlike African Americans in this neighborhood. Their parents do not pay attention to their children's education. Especially, since doing business in this south central L.A., I found that they do not have jobs. Lack of employment—they usually do not work."

Mr. Pai, another grocer, differs from others in that he has some structural understanding of African American history:

I try to understand them better. Thanks to their civil rights movement, we Koreans, as *yakso minjok* [a lesser nation], are able to live now in America. As blacks have been oppressed for a long time, they have accumulated their hostility toward others, including us.

Both Koreans and blacks are the same. However, our social background and way of thought are drastically different from theirs. For example, as far as children's education is concerned, it is common for Korean parents to sacrifice themselves to educate their children, which you cannot find either among whites or blacks.[9] White parents do their duty to a certain extent but not fully like Korean parents, and black parents seem to ignore their children's education. For example, I raised my children to go to graduate school. In addition, strong family ties and respect for their parents are virtues, which one cannot find in America due to its welfare system.

While sharing some sentiments expressed by Korean shopkeepers, a black woman I interviewed named Jennifer explains cultural differences by saying that Koreans "have more of a culture than Americans. They are not yet Westernized. They have rituals. They believe in Buddha. They have Buddhas in their stores and offer food to the Buddhas. I went into a nail salon. It freaked me out when I saw the Koreans worshiping Buddhas in the store. Koreans have a culture. We do not. I cannot speak African or Jamaican." Here, *culture* is taken to mean something foreign to America.

RACIAL AND CULTURAL DISCOURSES

Through their assumptions and ongoing constructions of race and culture, blacks, Koreans, and white institutions all interpret black-Korean conflict in different ways. Blacks attribute problems to racist exploitation and discrimination, Koreans focus on business practices and communication, and the white establishment reflects the biases of capitalism (property owners over customers) and a white-Asian-black racial hierarchy.

Meanwhile, the media-led discourse portrays black-Korean conflict as a racial confrontation yet describes the details largely in terms of cultural differences, seldom mentioning the lack of public policy to deal with urban problems such as racism and poverty. Whether the media blame the conflict on race or culture, their coverage is ahistorical. They further racialize black-Korean tension by conveying black intolerance of Koreans, which fuels the biases of Korean merchants, and they further contribute to Koreans' negative portrayal of blacks through their use of stereotypical images. The media reify and misrepresent the nature of interethnic tension by ignoring the historically situated social process that lies behind it.

The mass media portrayal is interpreted differently by Koreans and blacks. In the views of many Korean Americans, the media's frequent replaying of the videotape coverage of the Harlins killing and their constant refrain of "the Korean-born grocer killing a black teenager" sowed the seeds of social conflict. They wondered whether there was a conspiracy among the white-dominated media to pit one ethnic group against another and then sit back and watch the groups destroy each other. For many black viewers, the same videotape was a continual reminder that the criminal justice system is grossly unjust to the black community. In the Harlins-Du case, as in countless others, the judicial system applied a racialized formula. As a consequence, black-Korean tension was more drastically intensified by state intervention and media coverage than by the actions of blacks or Koreans.

In addition to the white media and judiciary, educational institutions also construct an exclusionary public sphere. Korean merchants lack an understanding of the alienation of inner-city blacks from public education. Although Korean merchants have become skeptical of the way the media handle black-Korean conflict, they have not expanded this insight into an understanding of the judicial or educational system, nor do they seem to understand the structural links between such establishments and the white media.

State agents, such as Judge Karlin in the Harlins-Du case, are major players in the development of racial tension. As David Goldberg (1993: 11) argues, the state articulates, legitimizes, elaborates upon, and transforms racialized expression and racist exclusion, and by doing so it helps render them acceptable. One result is that racial discourse has been confused with, and replaced by, cultural discourses. A new definition of race has emerged, replacing old concepts based on biology: "Race is coded as culture, what has been called 'the new racism,' making no reference to claims of biology or superiority . . . [this is] a style of cultural self-construction that is not just nostalgic but future oriented, not simply static but transformative, concerned not only with similarity and continuity but also with difference and rupture" (Goldberg 1993: 73). Since neither blacks nor Koreans want to be criticized for racial bigotry, they attribute their conflicts to cultural differences. Korean community leaders can ignore their own responsibilities by emphasizing the right to private property. Black community leaders can ignore broader issues by emphasizing maltreatment by Korean merchants.

Anthropological conceptualizations of culture give insufficient attention to problems of power and social conflict (Wolf 1982). My interviewees' cultural conceptions are along the line of Antonio Gramsci's proposition that "cultural processes unfold within a sharply divided society, a hierarchy of class domination backed by political power. Culture becomes part of the process of domination" (Alexander and Seidman 1990: 6).

Rudeness, lack of smiles, and other bad manners of Korean merchants have been explained as "cultural baggage" from Korea. Do Koreans have such elements in their culture? Let us take the example of the smile. All of my Korean merchant interviewees worked seven days a week and often sixteen hours a day—112 hours per week. Some said, "We are too tired to smile and be nice to our customers." Nonetheless, smiling must be studied in relation to the gender, class, and historical backgrounds of Koreans. For instance, a woman from the countryside tends not to smile in encounters with strangers. Given the fact that most new immigrants are from the cities and have professional backgrounds, however, this argument cannot be applied. I contend that if these shopkeepers ran businesses in middle- or upper-income neighborhoods in America, they might smile lest they offend affluent white customers. Most likely they do not smile because they operate in ghettos.

Koreans take pride in themselves and explain their successes in terms of having "more culture" (family unity, ethnic solidarity, education) than blacks. Blacks also describe Koreans as having more culture than themselves. Nevertheless, as Eric Wolf (1994: 7) reminds us, culture is changing and manifold, not a fixed and unitary entity. As in the case of black-Korean conflict, cultural differentiation produces a politics of meaning. Though there is some grudging respect, there is also the implication that people with strange rituals and unfamiliar Asian beliefs are in some sense not like "us" Americans. It would seem that the more "American" you are, the less culture you ought to have. Is the assumption that being deculturated is what being American is all about, and that therefore Koreans, with their cultural richness, have fewer claims to belong in American society?

At the same time, the continuing black-Korean conflict contributes to the creation of a new racial discourse: race as culture. This conflict focuses on relations between blacks and Korean immigrant merchants, but it evokes larger issues: the reproduction of capitalist relations in contemporary America and the redefinition of race and culture in today's multiethnic society.

NOTES

This chapter was originally published, in slightly different form, in *American Anthropologist* 98, no. 3 (1996). Reprinted with permission.
1. Meeting, November 1989, Community Conciliation Center, New York.

2. Ella Stewart (1991) documented the communication problems that Korean merchants and employees and black patrons have with one another: "Korean respondents most frequently mentioned loudness, bad / false language, and shoplifting as inappropriate behaviors exhibited by Black patrons. . . . By comparison, Black patrons most frequently described Korean merchants / employees' negative attitude and being watched constantly, as well as throwing money on the counter as inappropriate behaviors" (Stewart 1991: 16–17).

3. I draw on recent historical scholarship that has focused on the role of white racism as a hidden element in creating an exclusionary public sphere. Works such as David Roediger's *The Wages of Whiteness* (1991), Alexander Saxton's *The Rise and Fall of the White Republic* (1990), and Michael Rogin's article "Blackface, White Noise: the Jewish Jazz Singer Finds His Voice" (1992), along with Michael Omi and Howard Winant's *Racial Formation in the United States* (1986), examine the roots of racism and its different manifestations in different time periods.

4. For my ethnographic research, I focus on the geographical area bordered by Figueroa Street to the east, Western Avenue to the west, the University of Southern California to the north, and Ninetieth Street to the south. A total of thirty black residents and nineteen Korean American small-business proprietors were interviewed. Most of the interviews focused on the 1991 Soon Ja Du–Latasha Harlins incident. Most interviews with black participants were obtained at African American–run businesses such as hair salons and barber shops, and most Korean American interviews were collected at Korean American–run stores, mainly liquor stores and grocery markets.

Korean merchants were receptive, with certain exceptions, toward the Korean American researcher. As expected, black residents showed various responses. Some were glad to talk to a multiracial group of researchers. While one researcher interviewed a black woman, the other people in the hair salon became very curious about the research and began to ask questions; soon others wanted to be interviewed as well. Another man was interviewed while he styled a patron's hair. The place was filled with excitement and laughter. Everyone had something to say, and it became difficult to interview just one person. Others whom I met on the street were quick to show their anger. A lady shouted to me, "Yeah, that's the treatment for a colored woman's death. Bullshit! I already sent a letter to request the judge's recall. That's all I can say." However, it was remarkable to see many others respond very calmly, with a historical view of this tragic incident.

5. For the case of Harlem, see Yi 1993; on the tensions between Jewish merchants and black residents in New York City, see Naison 1984 and Malcolm X 1989 [1964]: 283. The immigration amendments of 1965 abolished immigration restrictions based on "national origins" and the allocation of quotas to various countries, finally placing Asian countries on equal footing with other nations.

6. According to Professor Eui-Young Yu, the customer base of Korean-owned businesses throughout Los Angeles is 48 percent white, 22 percent Korean, 17 percent Latino, and only 10 percent African American (quoted in *L.A. Weekly* 1992).

7. Koreans in Japan have experienced severe discrimination; however, the Korean experience in Japan is not often mentioned in relation to the Korean American experience. Perhaps Korean Americans tend to view the Korean experience in Japan in terms of Japanese colonialism, a different context than the Korean American experience.

8. Between January 1, 1990, and April 1992, at least twenty-five Korean American merchants were killed by non-Korean gunmen (*Los Angeles Times* 1992). However, I argue that these statistics rhetorically serve activists and leaders in both communities, and they have little to do with race per se. Because many merchants in South Central are Koreans doing business in a black community, any urban violence, including murder, usually automatically involves both groups.

9. I suspect this isolated view is held mainly by Koreans.

REFERENCES

Alexander, Jeffrey C., and Steven Seidman, eds. 1990. *Culture and society: Contemporary debates.* Cambridge: Cambridge University Press.

Bluestone, Barry, and Bennett Harrison. 1982. *The deindustrialization of America: Plant closings, community abandonment, and the dismantling of basic industries.* New York: Basic Books.

Bonacich, Edna, and Tae Hwan Jung. 1982. A portrait of Korean small business in Los Angeles: 1977. Pp. 75–98 in *Koreans in Los Angeles: Prospects and promises*, edited by Eui-Young Yu, Earl H. Phillips, and Eun Sik Yang. Los Angeles: Koryo Research Institute and Center for Korean American and Korean Studies, California State University.

Chang, Edward. 1990. New urban crisis: Korean-black conflicts in Los Angeles. Ph.D. diss., Department of Ethnic Studies, University of California at Berkeley.

Espiritu, Yen, and Paul Ong. 1994. Class constraints on racial solidarity among Asian Americans. Chap. 10 in *The new Asian immigration in Los Angeles and global restructuring*, edited by Paul Ong, Edna Bonacich, and Lucy Cheng. Philadelphia: Temple University Press.

Goldberg, David Theo. 1993. *Racist culture: Philosophy and the politics of meaning.* Oxford: Blackwell.

Johnson, James H., Jr., and Melvin L. Oliver. 1989. Interethnic minority conflict in urban America: The effects of economic and social dislocations. *Urban Geography* 10:449–63.

Johnson, James H., Jr., Cloyzelle K. Jones, Walter C. Farrell, and Melvin L. Oliver. 1992. The Los Angeles crises: A retrospective view. *Economic Development Quarterly* 6:356–72.

Lee, Kapson Yim. 1994. Portrayal of Korean Americans in the media. Pp. 251–56 in *Community in crisis: the Korean American community after the Los Angeles civil unrest of April 1992*, edited by George O. Totten III and H. Eric Schockman. Los Angeles: Center for Multiethnic and Transnational Studies, University of Southern California.

Light, Ivan, and Edna Bonacich. 1988. *Immigrant entrepreneurs: Koreans in Los Angeles 1965–1982.* Berkeley and Los Angeles: University of California Press.

Logan, John, and David Harvey. 1987. *Urban fortunes.* Berkeley and Los Angeles: University of California Press.

Los Angeles Times. 1991a. Blacks won't end Korean store boycott. August 31: B1.

———. 1991b. Boycott: Business has plummeted in a store where Korean American owner killed a black man. July 2: A1.

———. 1991c. Editorial. October 25: B6.

——. 1991d. Korean stores firebombed: 2 of 3 hit have seen black boycott. August 19: B1.

——. 1992. We saw our dreams burned for no reason. May 5: B7.

L.A. Weekly. 1992. Korean Americans in L.A. January 3–9: 15–16.

Malcolm X, with Alex Haley. 1989 [1964]. *The autobiography of Malcolm X.* New York: Ballantine Books.

Massey, Douglas S., and Nancy A. Denton. 1993. *American apartheid: Segregation and the making of the underclass.* Cambridge, Mass.: Harvard University Press.

Naison, Mark. 1984. *Communists in Harlem during the depression.* New York: Grove Press.

Omi, Michael, and Howard Winant. 1986. *Racial formation in the United States: From the 1960s to the 1980s.* New York: Routledge.

Ong, Paul. 1993. The economic base of South Central Los Angeles. Unpublished report. Department of Urban Planning, School of Public Policy and Social Research, University of California, Los Angeles.

Ong, Paul, Kyeyoung Park, and Yasmin Tong. 1994. The Korean-black conflict and the state. Pp. 264–94 in *The new Asian immigration in Los Angeles and global restructuring,* edited by Paul Ong, Edna Bonacich, and Lucy Cheng. Philadelphia: Temple University Press.

Ong, Paul, and the Research Group on the Los Angeles Economy. 1989. *The widening divide: Income inequality and poverty in Los Angeles.* Los Angeles: the Research Group on the Los Angeles Economy, the University of California, Los Angeles.

Palumbo-Liu, David. 1994. Los Angeles, Asians, and perverse ventriloquisms: On the functions of Asian America in the recent American imaginary. *Public Culture* 6:365–81.

Park, Kyeyoung. 1997. The Korean American dream: Immigrants and small business in New York City. Ithaca, N.Y.: Cornell University Press.

Roediger, David R. 1991. *The wages of whiteness: Race and the making of the American working class.* London: Verso.

Rogin, Michael. 1992. Blackface, white noise: The Jewish Jazz Singer finds his voice. *Critical Inquiry* 18:417–53.

Saxton, Alexander. 1990. *The rise and fall of the white republic: Class politics and mass culture in nineteenth-century America.* London: Verso.

Stewart, Ella. 1991. Ethnic cultural diversity: Perceptions of intercultural communication rules for interaction between Korean merchants/employees and black patrons in South Los Angeles. Paper presented to the 19th Annual Conference of the National Association for Ethnic Studies, Pomona, Calif.

Wolf, Eric. 1982. *Europe and the people without history.* Berkeley and Los Angeles: University of California Press.

Wolf, Eric. 1994. Perilous ideas: Race, culture, people. *Current Anthropology* 35:1–12.

Yanagisako, Sylvia, and Carol Delaney, eds. 1995. *Naturalizing power: Essays in feminist cultural analysis.* New York: Routledge.

Yi, Jeongduk. 1993. *Social order and contest in meanings and power: Black boycotts against Korean shopkeepers in poor New York City neighborhoods.* Ph.D. diss., Department of Anthropology, City University of New York.

5 The 1992 Los Angeles Riots and the "Black-Korean Conflict"

JOHN LIE AND NANCY ABELMANN

ONLY THE 1994 SOUTHERN CALIFORNIA EARTHQUAKE SEEMED TO shake the public amnesia regarding the 1992 Los Angeles riots. Although it was the most destructive U.S. civil disturbance of the twentieth century, the events have receded from popular discourse and entered the realm of history. Yet, one legacy of the 1992 Los Angeles riots is the widespread belief in the existence of a sustained interethnic conflict between African Americans and Korean Americans.[1]

As journalists and pundits came to recognize the 1992 riots as a multiethnic riot, rather than a reprise of the 1965 "black race riots" in Watts, many seized on the "Black-Korean conflict" as its crucial subtext. Richard Rodriguez (1992) wrote, "One of the most important conflicts [of the Los Angeles riots] was the tension between Koreans and African Americans." In this line of reasoning, the light sentence meted to Soon Ja Du for killing a young African American, Latasha Harlins, in a shop quarrel, was seen to be the proximate source of African American anger. This anger escalated and later exploded when innocent verdicts were given to four police officers standing trial for the beating of Rodney King. As Mike Davis (1992: 5) observed, "Latasha Harlins. A name that was scarcely mentioned on television was the key to the catastrophic collapse of relations between L.A.'s black and Korean communities." Latasha Harlins soon became virtually synonymous with the "Black-Korean conflict."

Here, we analyze Los Angeles Korean Americans' responses to the Black-Korean conflict and question the conflict's salience. Our argument is based on in-depth interviews with Los Angeles Korean Americans within one year of the *Sa-i-gu p'oktong* (the April 29 riot). In brief, most Korean Americans challenge the Black-Korean conflict frame. While few altogether deny problems between African Americans and Korean Americans, most people we interviewed were steadfast in downplaying either the significance of the conflict itself or its relevance for explaining the Los Angeles riots. We take up three diverse groups of Korean Americans: progressives, workers, and merchants. We then criticize the Black-Korean conflict framework, which explains diverse phenomena under the same rubric while homogenizing ethnic groups. We argue that the Black-Korean conflict is beside the point for most Korean American merchants in pursuit of their American dreams.

RESISTING THE "BLACK-KOREAN CONFLICT"

Korean Americans in Los Angeles resisted and rejected various media representations of the Los Angeles riots, from the individual images of gun-toting vigilantes to the overall focus on the Black-Korean conflict. In many conversations, Korean Americans, particularly first-generation immigrants, expressed their anger and frustration with television and newspaper coverage of the riots and of Korean Americans. Although capable of understanding media discourses and frames, many were incapable of articulating their criticisms and interpretations. Language barriers often proved insurmountable for first-generation Korean Americans. Indeed, their frustration with the media and the pleasure of speaking unfettered in Korean led to many effusive interview sessions. Most Korean Americans minimized, if not outright denied, the existence of the Black-Korean conflict. One former Korean marine's vehement denial was not unique: "This [the Los Angeles riots] has *nothing* to do with the Korean-Black conflict [*hanhûk kaltûng*]; there is no such thing."

Let us survey three groups: progressives, workers, and merchants. In spite of their different standpoints, they all converge in challenging the media-disseminated interethnic conflict frame.

Perhaps no group was more insistent in rejecting the regnant media frame than Korean Americans with progressive political views. To them, the Black-Korean conflict was largely, if not entirely, a media construction. It served to foster intraminority conflict—the classic "divide and conquer" strategy of the American power elites—and to maintain the racial and economic status quo. A second-generation Korean American man committed to progressive politics argued that the media anaesthetized people to accept the vision of an interethnic conflict. Similarly, Roy Hong of the Korean Immigrant Workers' Advocates suggested that the power elite and the media had manufactured the Black-Korean conflict.

The arrival of South Korean officials after the riots, meanwhile, projected a distorted image of the powerful Los Angeles establishment's favoring Korean Americans over other minority groups. Hong (1992: 11) observed, "I believe the South Korean government's involvement doesn't help us in any way. But when these people come the mayor greets them, gives them the key to the city and so on, and the Black and Latino communities understandably feel something is going on. Well, all the sucker got is a key!" In this account, the city authorities and the mass media were complicitous in projecting a favored image of the Korean American victims: "The politicians are again exploiting the Koreans by appearing to favor us" (Hong 1992: 11). In fact, most Korean Americans felt riot relief efforts and the U.S. government's response to the riots were woefully inadequate (Abelmann and Lie 1995: Chap. 2).

The working-class Korean Americans we interviewed also minimized the existence of an interethnic conflict. Furthermore, what they said undermined the common assumption of Korean American homogeneity, presenting instead class differences within the group. At a demonstration of unemployed workers seeking compensation for riot damage, a newly laid-off worker repeated several times: "Blacks did well." He suggested that African Americans would have been squeezed out of South Central Los Angeles had they not rose up in the riots. Having worked side by side with African Americans for many years, he was angry that African American and Korean American employees had been excluded from government aid and other disbursements.

Another worker offered a different interpretation of African American rioting, saying "Blacks felt ignored." He continued, "You have to look at their long history of being put down, hundreds of years—they have been put down by every single ethnic group. Fifty years ago they rose up, they rose up in the [1992] riots, and they will rise again in fifty years." His cycle of African American insurgence—riots every fifty years—expressed his empathy for African Americans' plight. The saddest moment of the riots for him came when a young African American coworker, who for years had called him "Daddy," left saying that he was not willing to die protecting the store. This Korean worker had been deeply disturbed to see the interethnic solidarity he had known evaporate in the riot's flames. He had been left alone in the store, unable to contact the absent Korean

American owner living in the suburbs, and for all his commitment to the store, he had been laid-off after the store burned down during the riots. In spite of worrying about sustaining a livelihood for his family, he waxed optimistic that Korean American, Latino, and African American employees who had lost their jobs in the wake of the riots would fight together for government aid. Class, then, remains an important element of his world view, even as he identifies himself unproblematically as a "Korean."

These and other working-class reactions suggest that there are deep rifts in the Korean American community; there exists no simple ethnic homogeneity among Los Angeles Korean Americans. The assertion of an interethnic conflict breaks down against the recalcitrant reality of class divides within ethnic groups.

Some Korean American merchants were no less insistent on downplaying the significance of the Black-Korean conflict. Several college-educated Korean American merchants discussed the causes of the 1992 riots in light of the perceived interethnic conflict. Their extended narratives approximate political-economic explanations of the riots: they spoke of deindustrialization and its impact on South Central Los Angeles, the niche for Korean Americans' entrepreneurship created by the exit of white ethnic merchants and of supermarket and large retail chains, and so on. The political economy of late-twentieth-century Los Angeles, indeed of the global economy, explained both Korean Americans' entrepreneurship in South Central Los Angeles and the impoverishment of their African American customers. In effect, then, some Korean American merchants explained the riots and African Americans' frustration by emphasizing political and economic factors (cf. Davis 1993).

While Korean American merchants' interpretations took a variety of idiomatic forms, they all undermined the dominant media prism. The political-economic narratives were told as if to say, "Don't people know what is going on in this country?" Many merchants' views were punctuated by their familiarity with the context and current reality of South Central Los Angeles. Several Korean American merchants spoke of African American history not as a strange or distant story but as one they knew, in some cases, through decades of contact. In some Korean American merchants' narratives, then, the Black-Korean conflict is beside the point; the real story of the riots, as well as the trajectories of both ethnic groups, must be sought elsewhere.

Many Korean Americans in the Los Angeles area, then, directly challenge the dominant portrait of the raging Black-Korean conflict. Their counterstories cast considerable doubt on the significance of such a frame. Yet, why did the Black-Korean conflict become virtually an article of faith in many reports on the 1992 Los Angeles riots?

FRAMING THE "BLACK-KOREAN CONFLICT"

The power of the media frame establishes the "truths" of social reality. The capacity of the mainstream media establishment to articulate a ready-made format makes it difficult to challenge that format's veracity and legitimacy. Television and newspaper reports, recognizing the "reality" of the Black-Korean conflict, assiduously sought to illustrate it and perpetuate it. In this discursive formation, disparate individual events—altercations, bickering, and conflicts—found a ready-made explanation.

The power of the dominant frame squelched efforts to undermine its legitimacy. For example, Angela Oh, who stressed that Korean American merchants were simply in the wrong place at the wrong time—and hence challenged the Black-Korean conflict media frame—was given media attention only to have her message undermined before she spoke a word. In May 1992, she appeared on *Nightline* to challenge the dominant media's interpretation. However, before the camera turned to her, a voice-over surveyed the riot destruction and narrated: "Korean American businesses were targeted for annihilation because of high animosity by African Americans." Later, she described how she was often pigeonholed by the media: "The producer will call you up and say, we are going to talk about where we go from here, and they interview you and do this whole little prep, and when you go to the station—and this literally happened to me on a national network station—the issue becomes 'Black-Korean conflict,' the reason for the riots in L.A." (Hicks, Villaraigosa, and Oh 1992: 47).

The mainstream media, furthermore, virtually excluded Korean American voices. Here, the inability of many first-generation Korean American merchants to articulate their media criticisms and to advance alternative interpretations proved fatal. Language barriers played an important role in silencing Korean American voices.[2]

The Black-Korean conflict, once lodged in public discourse, offered a powerful absorbent for concrete and individual instances of anger. The juxtaposition of statements made in the heat of the riots as Korean American merchants defended their stores and mourned their losses and African American rioters expressed their frustration and anger produces a compelling portrait of two groups in conflict. As we have elaborated (Abelmann and Lie 1995: Chap. 6), the interethnic conflict frame resonates with underlying American ideological currents, which pit Asian

Americans, as a model minority, against African Americans, as an urban underclass. Dominant ideologies, then, facilitated the construction of the interethnic conflict framework.

Further, the Black-Korean conflict framework makes sense, retrospectively, of the various altercations and tensions between the two groups and projects a generalized image of burning interethnic tensions. Reporters resurrected the 1991 Flatbush boycott in New York as one more instance of the Black-Korean conflict. Yet, in such a presentation, one of the chief weaknesses of this interethnic conflict explanation emerges. As the Flatbush case suggests, the presumption of the interethnic conflict brings together distinct instances under a single rubric. The Flatbush boycott against a Korean American merchant was largely staged by recent Haitian immigrants (Rieder 1990). While "black" in the U.S. racial framework, Haitian blacks are not synonymous with African American blacks. Consider, for instance, reports on the "Black-Haitian conflict" in Miami (Portes and Stepick 1993: 54–56). It is inaccurate to render African Americans in South Central Los Angeles and recent Haitian immigrants in Queens as members of a homogeneous group.

The interethnic conflict framework reifies each ethnic group and thereby elides significant cleavages and differences in each group. As we have seen, class differences constitute a significant feature of Los Angeles Korean Americans. The same can be said for African Americans. In spite of the presumption of ethnic homogeneity, there are significant differences of opinion on the Black-Korean conflict among African Americans (see, e.g., Alan-Williams 1994; Madhubuti 1993; Reed 1993). While black nationalists may condemn Korean American merchants as "exploiters," other African Americans welcome the Korean American mercantile presence in South Central Los Angeles. The assumption of ethnic homogeneity cannot be sustained against a highly diverse population.

Finally, we should recall that the well-known facts of the Los Angeles riots do not square with the assumed significance of the Black-Korean conflict. It was not the Black-Korean conflict, for example, that sparked the 1992 Los Angeles riots, but rather the anger and frustration over the "not guilty" verdict following the Rodney King beating. In other words, African American anger was directed at the "white" establishment and the miscarriage of justice, not at Korean American merchants. The majority of the people arrested for rioting and looting, moreover, were Latinos, not African Americans. In this regard, Ishmael Reed (1993: 44) remarked, "If the looting of the Korean south central district by black youth indicates an anti-Korean bias among blacks, then why doesn't the looting and burning of Korean stores by whites in Koreatown . . . indicate a bias of whites toward Koreans?"

In summary, then, the Black-Korean conflict reifies the conflict and the groups. We should neither lump disparate ethnicities under the same category nor should we overlook the significant diversity within each ethnic group. Korean Americans we surveyed suggest that the presumption of ethnic homogeneity is highly questionable. The Black-Korean conflict frame, then, is problematic not only empirically but conceptually as well.

BLAMING CLASS OTHERS AND RACIST ELDERS

Nonetheless, we heard scattered comments from Korean Americans who blamed other Korean Americans for generating or sustaining the Black-Korean conflict. There were two major sources: wealthy Korean Americans who blamed class "others," and second-generation Korean Americans who criticized their parents and other first-generation Korean Americans for their racism toward African Americans.

Some affluent Korean Americans pinned part of the blame for the Los Angeles riots on Korean American shopkeepers. An upper-middle-class suburban housewife suggested that some Korean American shopkeepers' attitudes and actions justified the anger of African Americans. According to her, swap meet stall owners, who came from "lower level" backgrounds, often voiced racist remarks about African American and Latino customers and treated them rudely. Simultaneously, she was equally scornful of the nouveau riche Koreans, who flaunt their wealth ostentatiously and incur the wrath of less affluent African Americans and others. Although she claimed to harbor no racial prejudices—she said that she had treated her customers courteously when she used to work—she felt that was not the case for class "others," whether upper-class snobs or lower-class racists.

In a similar vein, a millionaire Korean American import-export tycoon asserted that Koreatown is full of "failures" who care little about the United States, desiring only to "show" people back home. Hence, he claimed, they were unconcerned about non-Korean Americans and the United States in general. In his view, Korean American shopkeepers who were only concerned about South Korea generated resentment and anger among neglected and exploited African American customers, feelings that exploded in the 1992 Los Angeles riots. He claimed that he was only surprised by how patient African Americans were and how long the riots were in coming. Yet, he also noted that Korean Americans had very little to do with the riots. His ostensibly contradictory insistence that the riots were caused by greedy Korean American shopkeepers and that Korean Americans in general had little to do with the riots can be clarified by noting that Korean Americans like him were above the fray.

Several second-generation Korean Americans were critical of their parents' generation, if not directly critical of their shopkeeper parents. They said that they have heard "racist" sentiments expressed by their parents or other Korean Americans during intimate conversations among family members and friends. This racism, which cannot be sustained in their multiethnic environment, nonetheless found expression among first-generation Korean Americans. In other words, from the perspective of some second-generation Korean Americans, the first generation predictably incurred the wrath of African Americans by their racist words and deeds. From this view, racism emerges as a major culprit.

The charge of Korean American racism is a serious one. No doubt Korean Americans, like all groups, have their share of bigots and xenophobes. However, there is a complex etiology to first-generation Korean Americans' attitudes toward African Americans, which second-generation accusers overlook. Further, we should not simply deny many first-generation Korean Americans' assertions that they harbor no racist feelings toward African Americans.

Consider a Korean American woman's reaction to the Soon Ja Du–Latasha Harlins incident. She complained that "over and over all they showed was the orange juice, again and again just the orange juice, nothing about how the girl grabbed her, and the hundreds of Koreans who have died." She continued that she could fully understand Du's rage, rage at young customers' cavalier attitude toward older shopkeepers. After three Korean shop owners had been murdered during a single day, one Korean American social service worker explained that riot victims were growing more and more angry at all the Latasha Harlins commotion: "Yes, her life was important, but what about the dozens of Korean merchants? What about their lives? Don't they matter?" Given the growing number of Korean American merchants murdered by African Americans in South Central Los Angeles, we might therefore conclude that there is an intense African American racism against Korean Americans adding fuel to the raging Black-Korean conflict. Yet, the anger and frustration of Korean Americans should not lead to a conclusion about Korean American racism or to a conclusion about the significance of an interethnic conflict.

A crucial ideological source of first-generation Korean immigrants' attitudes toward African Americans is the pervasive U.S. presence in South Korea. The U.S. military presence has contributed to the racializing of many South Koreans. They have observed the segregated restaurants, bars, and brothels and the black-white division of the U.S. military in Korea: the heavy concentration of African American troops at the demilitarized zone and the "whiter," easier assignments in Seoul. In addition, South Korea has been racialized by American popular culture. American movies and television shows, aired at theaters and on South Korean television stations and the American military station, bring the culture of the United States and its racism to South Korea. One Korean American explained, "I had the idea that blacks were dirty and aggressive from American films and from our experience with black soldiers. My very first day in America, I was afraid to go outside because of the dangerous blacks" (quoted in Rieder 1990: 17). As Jan Sunoo stated, Korean immigrants "are captives of their own prejudices because of their narrow exposure to African-American culture and lifestyles. They get it the same way the majority of Americans get it—from movies" (quoted in George 1992: 83). American racism thus rides on the coattails of American cultural dominance.

In the United States, the pervasive ideological devaluation of African Americans undoubtedly contributes to Korean Americans' attitudes toward African Americans. In addition, there is a troubling material foundation for Korean American entrepreneurs' prejudice. As a result of their daily troubles with shoplifting and violence, some shopkeepers come to negative overgeneralizations about African Americans. Many Korean immigrants, bred on fervent nationalism in Korea, are wont to see the social world in an ethnonationalistic frame. Thus, many Korean American shopkeepers operating in poor neighborhoods are prone to overgeneralize based on their encounters with poor African Americans.

The influence of existing Korean American prejudice, however, should not be exaggerated. Unlike white racism, which has long had a tremendous impact on African American lives, Korean American prejudices play a relatively minor role in African American lives. The point we wish to emphasize is that the existence of negative stereotypes—indeed, racism—among some Korean Americans (and African Americans) does not translate into a widespread and sustained interethnic conflict. What the Black-Korean conflict does, in effect, is to transmute instances of Korean American prejudice into a major cause of an interethnic conflict. There is a sleight of hand involved in this ideological move. Although Korean Americans—like all groups in the United States—hold negative stereotypes about many other groups, and, in fact, also experience conflicts with white customers and Latino employees, we are not awash with stories about the "Korean-White conflict" or the "Korean-Latino conflict."

In sum, while we cannot deny that Korean American prejudice against African Americans exists—although many Korean Americans deny that they themselves harbor racist feelings—we should not exaggerate its importance. Above all, such prejudice alone does not add up to a Black-Korean conflict.

KOREAN AMERICANS' AMERICAN DREAMS

In spite of the underemphasis, and even the denial, of racism, the issue of Korean American merchants' exploiting the African American community remains. Although some Korean American merchants invoke political and economic causes for the root of the African American crisis, particularly citing poverty as the cause of the riots, their responses remain pragmatic. Korean American merchants merely follow the rules of the capitalist game. Consider perhaps the most persistent criticisms leveled against Korean American merchants in South Central Los Angeles: they do not live there or put profit back into the community. Korean Americans, as mobility-oriented immigrants, seek to maximize their profit in order to achieve their personal Americans dreams. The shop owners who offered compelling political-economic explanations nonetheless do not propose structural solutions. Rather than community betterment, the object for them is to move away from poor areas and petty entrepreneurship. In other words, they came to make money in, not change, the United States. Some Korean Americans, in addition, blame African Americans for their plight. Although critical of America's media frame, Korean American merchants still, in part, espouse the American Dream.

Ultimately, however, African Americans are incidental to Korean Americans' visions of life in the United States. African Americans in South Central Los Angeles are seen as temporary customers by most Korean Americans, in pursuit of their private American dreams. So many have sought their fortune in predominantly poor African American neighborhoods, including South Central Los Angeles, mainly owing to structural constraints (Abelmann and Lie 1995: Chap. 5).

Korean American merchants and employees who come into contact with African Americans express complimentary opinions of African Americans' friendliness and strong communal ties, although these opinions are coupled with remarks on their lack of education and even laziness. Although Korean American shopkeepers seldom project the infernal image of a war zone, they nonetheless speak of a poor neighborhood. This complexity and ambivalence constitute the human essences of the media-constructed interethnic conflict.

CONCLUSION

The interethnic conflict, outside of its historical political-economic context, misses the central problems facing both ethnic groups and South Central Los Angeles at large. After all, the Black-Korean conflict is not the fundamental problem facing either group. It is misleading to stress the interethnic conflict or its importance in the Los Angeles riots. The ideological constitution and construction of the Black-Korean conflict should alert us not only to the importance of the broader political economy but also to the necessity of rethinking dominant American ideologies.

There are at least two negative repercussions of the persistence of this Black-Korean conflict frame. First, the dissemination of interethnic conflict discourse may heighten individual suspicion and hatred; in this way, it could become an instance of self-fulfilling prophesy. Some people have suggested that the media coverage of the Black-Korean conflict contributed to African American hate crimes against Korean Americans. Second, the focus on the Black-Korean conflict averts our gaze from more serious and pressing issues facing South Central Los Angeles in particular and the United States at large. As some Korean American merchants insisted, it is not them but the larger political economy that hinders African American mobility. To pin the blame on Korean Americans not only scapegoats them, but it may serve to perpetuate the intolerable status quo.

NOTES

1. There is a growing literature on the Black-Korean conflict. See, among others, Abelmann 1991; Chang 1993a, 1993b; Cho 1993; Kang et al. 1993; Kim 1991; Kô and Rî 1993, Min 1991; and Stewart 1993. See also Lew 1993; Min 1994; and Smith 1994.

2. Equally significant was the virtual silence of many Korean American organizations. Most Korean American organizations were concerned with South Korean, not Korean American, affairs. Hence, their views were largely irrelevant during and after the riots. The absence of effective first-generation Korean American media

representatives catapulted second-generation Korean Americans into the role of media spokespeople for Los Angeles Korean Americans.

REFERENCES

Abelmann, Nancy. 1991. Transgressing headlines: Reporting race in the African American/Korean American conflicts. Paper presented at the Association for Asian Studies meeting, New Orleans, La.

Abelmann, Nancy, and John Lie. 1995. *Blue dreams: Korean Americans and the 1992 L.A. riots.* Cambridge, Mass.: Harvard University Press.

Alan-Williams, Gregory. 1994. *A gathering of heroes.* Chicago: Academy Chicago.

Chang, Edward T. 1993a. Jewish and Korean merchants in African American neighborhoods: A comparative perspective. *Amerasia Journal* 19 (2): 5–21.

——. 1993b. America's first multiethnic "riots." In *The state of Asian America: Activism and resistance in the 1990s,* edited by Karin Aguilar-San Juan. Boston: South End Press.

Cho, Sumi K. 1993. Korean Americans vs. African Americans: Conflict and construction. Pp. 196–211 in *Reading Rodney King/Reading urban uprising,* edited by Robert Gooding-Williams. New York: Routledge.

Davis, Mike. 1992. *L.A. was just the beginning: Urban revolt in the United States: A thousand points of light.* Westfield, N.J.: Open Magazine Pamphlet Series.

——. 1993. Who killed LA? A political autopsy. *New Left Review* 197:3–28.

George, Lynelle. 1992. *No crystal stair: African-Americans in the City of Angels.* London: Verso.

Hicks, Joe, Antonio Villaraigosa, and Angela Oh. 1992. Los Angeles after the explosion: Rebellion and beyond. *Against the Current* 40:44–48.

Hong, Roy. 1992. Korean perspectives. *Against the Current* 40:11.

Kang, Miliann, Julianna J. Kim, Edward J. W. Park, and Hae Won Park. 1993. *Bridge toward unity.* Los Angeles: Korean Immigrant Workers Advocates of Southern California.

Kim, Shin. 1991. Conceptualization of inter-minority group conflict: Conflict between Korean entrepreneurs and black local residents. Pp. 29–48 in *The Korean American community: Present and future,* edited by Tae-Hwan Kwak and Seong Hyong Lee. Seoul: Kyungnam University Press.

Kō, Changū, and Sū Rī. 1993. *Amerika, Koriataun* [America, Koreatown]. Tokyo: Shakai Hyōronsha.

Lew, Walter. 1993. Black Korea. Pp. 230–35 in *Charlie Chan is dead,* edited by Jessica Hagedorn. New York: Penguin.

Madhubuti, Haki R., ed. 1993. *Why L.A. happened.* Chicago: Third World Publishers.

Min, Katherine. 1994. K-Boy and 2 Bad. *TriQuarterly* 89:38–51.

Min, Pyong Gap. 1991. Korean immigrants' small business activities and Korean-Black interracial conflicts. Pp. 13–28 in *The Korean American community: Present and future,* edited by Tae-Hwan Kwak and Seong Hyong Lee. Seoul: Kyungnam University Press.

Portes, Alejandro, and Alex Stepick. 1993. *City on the edge: The transformation of Miami.* Berkeley and Los Angeles: University of California Press.

Reed, Ishmael. 1993. *Airing dirty laundry.* Reading, Mass.: Addison-Wesley.

Rieder, Jonathan. 1990. Trouble in store. *New Republic* July 2: 16–20.

Rodriguez, Richard. 1992. Multiculturalism with no diversity. *Los Angeles Times* May 10: M1.

Smith, Anna Deavere. 1994. *Twilight: Los Angeles, 1992.* New York: Anchor.

Stewart, Ella. 1993. Communication between African Americans and Korean Americans: Before and after the Los Angeles riots. *Amerasia Journal* 19 (2): 23–53.

Part 2 NEW YORK CITY

The Dynamics of Black-Korean Conflict: A Korean American Perspective

HEON CHEOL LEE

DESPITE THE FACT THAT BLACK-KOREAN CONFLICTS HAVE OCCURRED frequently over the past decade (e.g., Ogburn and Butler 1983; Eng and Sargent 1981; Cleaver 1983a-f; I. Kim 1981; Yoo 1981; Venerose 1987; Song 1989; Mills and Davis 1990; Burson 1988; Ford and Lee 1991) and are of obvious social significance, there have been virtually *no systematic* studies of the black-Korean conflict, especially of its conflict processes. There have been many publications of a nonacademic nature on the conflict, but these accounts are grossly inadequate from a sociological perspective. Many of the accounts in the news media and the official reports are too narrowly focused and biased because they are based on selective observations or politically motivated interpretations of the conflict. Examples are "Clash of Cultures" (Karwarth 1990), "Cultural Conflict" (Njeri 1989), and "incident-based conflict" (Mayor's Committee 1990b). Other widely circulated accounts assume, without citing adequate supporting evidence, that such conflicts stem from "misunderstandings rooted in cultural differences" (Banks 1985), from black racism against Korean Americans as a form of scapegoating (*New York Post* 1990) or as a form of "racial extortion" (*Flatbush Inquirer* 1990), from a white conspiracy of "divide and conquer" (Oh and Kim 1991), or from disparate economic opportunities between blacks and Koreans (Mayor's Committee 1990b). As Michael Banton (1988: 15) points out, such "popular ideas about racial relations reflect individual experiences and the images generated by the mass media. They do not provide a reliable basis for the understanding of what gives those relations their character."

One fundamental problem in those explanations is the lack of clear identification of what the black-Korean conflict is. Since the conflict, as a complex social process, emerges, escalates, and de-escalates with many different dimensions at different stages (Blalock 1989; Kriesberg 1982), before we explain why the black-Korean conflicts have occurred as they have, we need to specify exactly what black-Korean conflict we are actually trying to explain. In other words, since black-Korean conflict may mean a variety of different phenomena to different people, we have to make clear to what social phenomenon a black-Korean conflict refers.

Black-Korean Conflict: From Dispute to Boycott

What we are specifically dealing with in this chapter is an emerging pattern of black-Korean conflict. It usually starts with a dispute between a Korean merchant and a black customer at a Korean-owned store, is followed by an organized black boycott, and escalates into a large-scale intergroup conflict. The key event that changes the nature of the conflict from an interpersonal dispute to a collective intergroup conflict is the black boycott of Korean stores in black neighborhoods. Without an organized boycott of Korean stores, there would be no black-Korean conflict in the form of direct, overt, collective actions. Because of organized collective actions for and against the boycotts, the black-Korean conflict has emerged as an intergroup conflict at the collective level. For my purposes, it is the black boycott of Korean stores that determines the inclusion of a social phenomenon as an appropriate object of this study.

Therefore, the black-Korean conflict is defined as direct, overt, collective actions taken by blacks and Koreans to achieve their conflicting goals. In the cases of all such conflicts reported here, the conflicting goals revolved around either forcing Korean stores to close or keeping them open. The conflict is tentatively designated as a black-Korean conflict only because it involves black boycotts of Korean stores.

To understand the black-Korean conflict, then, it is important to understand the nature of black boycotts against Korean stores. One has to find out who organized the boycotts, what resources were available and were deployed for or against the boycott, and how these resources were mobilized or demobilized. One also has to find out what the boycott leaders wanted to achieve through the boycotts.

POWER DIFFERENTIAL: A KEY DETERMINANT
OF CONFLICT PROCESSES

The fundamental assumption underlying the question of why blacks boycott Korean stores is that without resources and the mobilization of those resources, the conflict could never have emerged, nor could it have escalated into an intergroup conflict at the collective level. Social conditions that generate strain and resentment among individuals are important, but an actual conflict can occur only when people who are capable of challenging the conflictual situation actually take collective actions by organizing themselves and mobilizing resources, and when such organized collective actions promote the interests of either their whole collectivity or some of its members.[1]

In explaining specific collective actions, the resource mobilization approach has developed into an alternative paradigm to the collective behavior approach, and it offers greater explanatory power.[2] In the resource mobilization approach, the role of power (as mobilized resources) is central in explaining collective actions such as social conflicts, protests, and social movements. The difference in power between conflict parties determine not only the nature of the conflict but also the likelihood of conflict development.

Blalock (1989), in his "power model" of conflict, emphasizes the central role of power in conflict processes. The key factor, according to him, is the balance of power between conflict parties. The role of power has also been emphasized in the study of racial and ethnic conflicts. John Stone argues that "it is differences in *power*, and the dynamic change of power resources over time, that provide the key to an understanding of racial and ethnic conflict" (1985: 37). James Blackwell also believes that "*the most fundamental variables which undergird conflicts in the American society are those of differential power and race*" (1976: 197, emphasis in original).

From this perspective, among their various differences, power difference between blacks and Koreans is the single most important factor that determines the dynamics of the conflict between blacks and Koreans in New York City. For this study it is important to examine the dynamic power relations between blacks and Koreans both in American society in general and in New York City. The organizing capabilities of blacks and Koreans, the mobilizing and demobilizing ideologies, and the environments that facilitate or constrain the effective mobilization of resources are crucial elements that play significant roles in conflict processes.

From the perspective of the power model, it should be noted that the seemingly obvious and yet the most significant aspect of the boycott is that it is a *black* boycott of *Korean* stores in predominantly *black* neighborhoods in a *white* dominant society. The dynamics of a black-Korean conflict must be understood as the result of power relations between blacks and Koreans in a white dominant society. It should be stressed that, regarding the power relations between them, both blacks and Koreans are categorized as racial minorities in the United States. But the degree of their minority statuses is different, and they are inconsistent in different dimensions.

The central theoretical concern in my analysis of the power dimensions of the black-Korean conflict involves how the ethnic consciousness, identity, and group boundaries based on the physical differences of their group members were stressed, reinforced, and expanded in the process of ethnic mobilization, and how the same ethnic differentiation was challenged in the process of demobilizing ethnic resources. The uses of racism and the processes of racializing and ethnicizing people shall be looked at from this perspective of ethnic mobilization.

Data Collection

The data was collected primarily on the Church Avenue case during the period of the Church Avenue black boycott of Korean stores. This boycott broke out on January 18, 1990, and lasted until May 1991. It provided a rare opportunity to observe the conflict phenomena as they were unfolding in a real-world conflict situation.

Data was collected by observing picketings, rallies, marches, demonstrations, and community meetings, either for or against the boycott. I also attended news conferences, other conferences on the conflict, public hearings, and court hearings. At such events and collective actions, I was also able to get information about those who were directly involved in the conflict and the larger economic and political environment relevant to the conflict. While observing, I also conducted informal interviews with merchants, customers, picketers, boycott leaders, and other participants, such as the police and reporters. I was usually able to interview boycott leaders in the morning when not many people were inside the picket line. Across the police barricade, sometimes we could discuss a number of subjects. Such informal interviews, without prepared questions and prior appointments, proved to be good sources of information.

More formal interviews were then conducted with key players in the conflict. Most of them were identified during my observation of conflict phenomena. Using the purposive snowball sampling technique, the number of interviewees was expanded: I usually asked the interviewees to recommend any other persons whom they thought to be a good source of information. Overall, I tried to concentrate on the owners and managers of Korean stores that had been boycotted in New York City and black customers and boycott leaders who were directly involved in the conflict. More than fifty people were interviewed in a more formal, controlled setting: Korean store owners, managers, Korean and non-Korean employees of Korean stores, non-Korean store owners, black customers, local residents, local community leaders, Korean community leaders, Haitian community leaders, boycott leaders, lawyers, police officers, local politicians, and local historians.[3]

In addition to observations and interviews, I collected various documents related to the boycott. Flyers that were distributed to local residents in support of the boycott and sometimes, although rarely, against the boycott were especially informative. Transcripts of public hearings and court hearings, legal documents, police reports, news releases, public statements, and reports were collected and analyzed. Due to the high publicity of the conflict and sustained public interest, I was able to collect most of these documents from Korean merchants, boycott leaders, reporters, and lawyers.

Another source of information was the coverage in newspapers, magazines, and journals. To identify previous conflict cases and to obtain any missing information on the Church Avenue case, I monitored local Korean newspapers such as the *Korea Times New York* and black newspapers such as the *New York Amsterdam News*. Other New York newspapers, such as the *New York Times*, the *Post*, the *Daily News*, and *Newsday* were used. Despite the problems of omission, underrepresentation, incompleteness, and inaccuracies of some of this information, the survey of news reports by means of a computerized system gave me information on broad trends which supplemented the existing data.

THE BLACK BOYCOTT OF KOREAN STORES: AN ORGANIZED, PURPOSEFUL, COLLECTIVE ACTION

The sequence of the two events—an organized boycott of Korean stores following an incident at a Korean-owned store—gives one the impression that the black-Korean conflict at the collective level was *caused* by the incident. The boycotts appear to be simply the work of a group of angry black customers who wish to change Korean merchants' disrespect-ful behaviors. Based on this line of simple logic (or for political reasons), one may conclude that the black-Korean conflict is "incident-based."[4]

An incident is indeed important for the boycott and helps to generate support, but the way the conflict manifests at the collective level is quite independent of the nature and the causes of the original incident. A merchant-customer dispute and incident may have been a precondition for the black-Korean conflict, but it is not sufficient for the emergence of the black-Korean conflict at the collective level. Because the nature of the initial incident in fact does not explain much about the shape of the conflict, I believe that the black-Korean conflict is much more than an incident-based phenomenon. The black boycotts of Korean stores have been organized to achieve more than just the changing of Korean mer-chants' disrespectful behavior.

In light of the organized nature of the boycott, it may be more appro-priate to characterize the original incident as an "opportune" event for boycott organizers rather than as a precipitating event. The conflict may seem to have been precipitated by the incident, but the actual process of conflict development was not a precipitation but a series of deliberate, purposeful, organized collective actions. It should be pointed out that not all incidents that have occurred between Korean merchants and black customers have precipitated black-Korean conflicts. As happened in the Church Avenue case, the spontaneous protests usually die down within a few days after the incident, and the organized boycott starts as a new form of protest and movement.

A key question is, Who organized and led the boycott? To under-stand the dynamics of the conflict, it is important to identify the parties involved in conflict situations, particularly those who provide leadership (Blalock 1989; Kriesberg 1982). Although on the surface it seems obvious who the parties are in a black-Korean conflict, not all Koreans and blacks in New York City have been directly involved in the conflict and many blacks have been against the boycott. Therefore, it is essential to find out who among blacks organized either in support of the boycott or to protest against the boycott.

The boycott leadership changed hands throughout the various stages of the conflict. Only at the very beginning of the conflict were spontane-ous protests made by the local residents. Business at the two stores was halted for a couple of days by the angry demonstrations of local residents in front of the stores. Then, as the executive director of the Church Avenue Merchants Block Association observed, "It was free game for everybody to come in and do whatever they wished."

First, the local black activists tried to capitalize on the conflict situation. Under the leadership of George Dames, the Flatbush Coalition for Economic Empowerment was organized in order to raise the issue of disparate economic opportunities for blacks and to launch the black economic empowerment movement. The first organizing meeting was convened by Dames a few days after the incident, and several community organizations sent their representatives to voice their concern over disparate business ownership among blacks.

Less than a week afterward, a black nationalist group called the December 12th Movement, with the support of left-wing Haitian organizations, began to lead the boycott. Just a week after the boycott started, flyers were already being distributed to mobilize black residents to the first "Black Power Street Rally" on January 27, 1990. Flyers also requested that "the business community in an act of respect and solidarity with our struggle, and outrage at the police protection of the Koreans, and [police] occupation of our community" close all businesses on Church Avenue between Flatbush Avenue and East Seventeenth Street for an hour on Saturday. While urging residents to "boycott all Korean stores," the boycott leaders also announced through the flyers the coming of an "African People's Farmers Market." This rally was the beginning of a series of rallies, marches, meetings, and demonstrations organized by the same group of black nationalists using different names for their organizations, including the December 12th Movement, the Black Men's Movement, and the Flatbush Frontline Collective.

The Flatbush Frontline Collective was formed as the boycott frontline organization and comprised all these groups. As the boycott progressed, it became clear that the Flatbush Frontline Collective was replacing the Flatbush Coalition for Economic Empowerment. Local community leaders withdrew from the situation, and black nationalists such as Sonny Carson, Coltrane Chimurenga, Amowale Clay, and other members of the so-called New York 8+ began to control the course of events (Noel 1992). They are the same group of people who led the 1989 Fulton Street boycott and participated in the 1988 Harlem boycott (Lee 1988; English 1988). There were other groups involved, notably left-wing Haitian organizations such as Mokam, which had been organized primarily for political involvement in Haiti, not to serve the Haitian immigrants in New York City.

Although some local residents joined the picketing, marches, and demonstrations, those who organized and led the boycott were neither local residents and customers, nor local community leaders. A prominent local resident who occupied a political position believed that the boycott was "basically kept alive by people who don't reside there."

Another key question regarding the organized black boycott is, In what ways were black customers mobilized for the boycott? The first thing that the boycott leaders did was to racialize the issues (and people) in order to further differentiate blacks and Koreans into different racial-ethnic groups. There was a constant attempt to suggest that the Haitian customer involved in the original dispute, who was referred to as *sister Jhislaine*, was the victim of Korean racism and had not received equal justice because of white racism.

To effectively mobilize resources, the legitimacy of the boycott was stressed. Here, the issue of disrespect toward black customers by Korean merchants and its underlying notion of Korean racism was evoked and emphasized by boycott leaders. By organizing the black unity rallies and marches in an event entitled the "Day of Outrage against Racism," the boycott leaders attempted to put the boycott of Korean stores under the long tradition of black boycotts used effectively to fight against white racism. Regardless of the nature of the incident and sources of individual disputes, the boycott was defined as the result of Korean racism and portrayed as a continuation of blacks' "historical struggle for self-determination" (as stated on a flyer). Through such a racializing process, a dispute between a Korean merchant and a black customer was escalated into an interracial black-Korean conflict.

Black nationalism, especially the idea of "black control of the black community," was employed as a dominant ideology for the boycott by its leaders. Throughout the boycott, organizers denounced the economic conditions of urban America as "economic exploitation" and "a form of twentieth-century slavery." The only solution, according to the repeated assertions of boycott leaders, was for blacks to take control of all aspects of the black community, economic and political.

WHY DO BLACKS BOYCOTT KOREAN STORES?

Ostensibly, the black boycotts of Korean stores were launched to protest the "disrespectful" treatment of black customers by Korean merchants and to demand racial justice and the arrest of the alleged Korean attackers of a black customer. The chant "no respect, no money" was a constant refrain at picket lines in front of stores or at black unity rallies.

When one of the boycott leaders was asked why they were boycotting Korean stores, he answered: "People are outraged at the attack on sister Jhislaine, beaten by three Korean merchants. People are also fed up with the disrespect that they receive from Korean merchants."

Undoubtedly, the boycotts also served as a means to achieve the economic empowerment of blacks. According to the boycott leaders, the key question for blacks in the 1990s is, "Who is going to control the economic life of the Black community?" (as stated on flyers distributed during the Church Avenue boycott). Not surprisingly, the first organization formed after the start of the Church Avenue boycott was the Flatbush Coalition for Economic Empowerment. The formation of such an organization, its activities during the boycott, and, most of all, the overall economic conditions of urban America suggest that the visible presence of Korean business in black neighborhoods—or, to be more precise, the paucity of black business in these neighborhoods—has played a significant role in black-Korean conflicts.

Despite such ostensive purposes, it was found that the black boycotts of Korean stores were about much more than changing Korean merchants' alleged disrespectful behavior and achieving racial justice. The boycotts were also intended to promote economic empowerment of blacks in urban America, but this is still only a part of the whole story. What is at stake in this conflict is not just black control of the black economy. It is, much more importantly, the *political* control of black communities. The crucial underlying issue in the conflict is who controls black communities *politically*, in the broadest sense of the word. More specifically, the issue is *which* blacks control black communities in urban America.

The conflict situation related to Korean merchants and their business in black neighborhoods provided black activists and black political entrepreneurs with good political opportunities to promote their own interests and enhance their own political influence in urban America. Not only for the political empowerment of blacks as a whole but also for their own personal political empowerment, militant black nationalists deliberately escalated the interpersonal conflict to an interracial level and intensified it. In order to increase the race-based black power in urban America, blacks themselves were racialized and ethnicized during the conflict.

The political dimension of the black-Korean conflict will be better understood if we put the conflict within the contexts of black-white competition and black-black competition for scarce political resources in urban America. In other words, the conflict, although apparently between blacks and Koreans, should also be recognized as the result of black-white competition for political control of black communities and the black-black competition for black leadership and political influence in inner-city black neighborhoods.

In this regard, we must look at the black-Korean conflict in New York City in terms of "the politics of race" and the social movement of black empowerment for political gains. The shape of the conflict—its intensity, its duration, and the difficulty of achieving negotiated settlements—can be better explained if we consider the political dimension of the conflict and its "movement" aspect. In doing so, the role of black nationalism, which was seemingly employed to rally black customers for the boycott, can be better understood as an ideology of black empowerment.

BLACK-WHITE COMPETITION: WHITE OUTSIDERS AND THE POLITICS OF RACE

During the boycott, it was obvious that the overall black-white competition for political control of black communities and the "inflammatory racial politics" (Sleeper 1990) of militant blacks were significantly affecting the shape of the black-Korean conflict.[5] Speaker after speaker at the black unity rallies talked about the need to control "all aspects of black communities," and they devoted most of their time to criticizing the "white power structure" currently dominating black communities. One speaker at a black unity rally in front of the two boycotted stores expressed his view in this way: "We must take control of our own destiny. We must start this by building institutions economically for ourselves. We must control our community economically and politically."

The ideology of black nationalism, with the goal of "black control of black communities," provided black political entrepreneurs with an ideological weapon with which they could establish and maintain their political niche against the white politicians who have been representing black communities. Based on this ideology, they defined urban neighborhoods like Church Avenue as territorial bases from which to affirm their political power. They asserted that blacks should control these neighborhoods and categorized all non-blacks as "outsiders" to the black community who were exploiting blacks and did not represent black interests.

Mobilization efforts are not always for personal gain; often they are based on real underrepresentation. During the Church Avenue boycott, in 1990, it was found that Community Board 14, which has jurisdiction over the Church Avenue area, had a disproportionate underrepresentation of blacks. The members of the board are appointed by the Brooklyn Borough president based on the nominations of the district's City Council members. Blacks, who represented 40 percent of the district, held only 22 percent of the seats on the board. Furthermore, in 1990, white politicians actually occupied most of the important political positions representing the Church Avenue area. These white elected officials included U.S. Congressman Charles Schumer, New York State Senator Marty Markowitz, New York State Assemblyman Speaker Mel Miller, and New York City Councilwoman Susan Alter. In 1991, Alter ran for office in a different district and was elected. All of them were Jewish politicians, according to a boycott leader, who claimed: "They do not represent us, nor do they operate in our best interest!" (from a Black Power Rally flyer distributed during the Church Avenue boycott). The white politicians are still there, even though the racial-ethnic composition of the local population has changed. Now, black political entrepreneurs are knocking on the doors to succeed them. Una Clark, a black community leader, was elected from the district in which Church Avenue is located.

It was not clear how many boycott leaders actually ran, or intended to run, for the offices presently occupied by white politicians, but the political control of black communities was a dominant theme at the rallies and marches during the boycott. It was not a coincidence that one of the Church Avenue boycott leaders, Ernest Foster, also led the protests against the underrepresentation of blacks on Community Board 14 (Myers 1992).

BLACK-BLACK COMPETITION: THE STRUGGLE FOR BLACK LEADERSHIP AND BLACK OUTSIDERS

Against these "outsiders,"—white politicians and Korean merchants—the boycott leaders, using the ideology of black nationalism, advocated black control of black communities. However, the question of which blacks should control black communities in urban America remained. Blacks in urban America are a diverse group, and they are in competition against one another. I believe that the black-black competition for leadership within black communities and for political influence in New York City, more than anything else, has contributed to the development of black-Korean conflicts.

One example of such black-black competition was that between the longtime resident African American blacks and the recently immigrated ethnic blacks, particularly Haitian immigrants. This serious competition made a significant impact upon the dynamics of the black-Korean conflict. The leaders of the West Indian community asserted that the community was a West Indian neighborhood and the boycott leaders did not belong to the community itself. They were black but "outsiders," and as such they could not represent the interests of Haitian Americans—including the woman who was allegedly assaulted by the Korean merchants.

The conflict was also escalated because of the competition for control of the black community between the established moderate black integrationist groups and the yet-to-be established militant black separatist groups. The competition for black leadership among various black militant groups has played a significant part in molding the conflict. Among them, the most visible black-black competition was that between Al Sharpton's and Sonny Carson's groups. Their struggle for power among black communities seemed to repeatedly exacerbate the black-Korean conflict in New York City. Although Al Sharpton was actively involved in many of the controversial racial incidents in New York City, he was never directly involved in any black-Korean conflict cases. He publicly supported the boycotts (e.g., on a radio talk show at WLIB), but he never appeared on Church Avenue, nor did he participate in any rallies, marches, or demonstrations to support the boycott.

The most telling events indicating the competition between these two groups and its impact on intergroup conflict in New York City were their protest rallies in front of the Brooklyn Supreme Court. In May 1990, Sonny Carson came with his supporters to protest the *white* judge's ruling on the fifty-foot court injunction imposed on black boycotts of Korean stores. Two separate protest rallies, one led by Sharpton and one led by Carson, were held in the same courtyard, providing a vivid example of the power struggle for black leadership in New York City.

Such intense competition among black activist groups seems to be partially responsible for the increase in racial tension in New York City in general and for the intensity of the black-Korean conflict in particular. When an incident involving any black persons occurs in New York City, regardless of the racial and ethnic backgrounds of other parties, the two competing groups seem eager to put themselves in the middle of the controversy and use the occasion for their own purposes. It happened in Flatbush, Bensonhurst, Bedford-Stuyvesant, and Crown Heights.

Black "conflict" organizations such as the December 12th Movement in New York, the Brotherhood Crusade in Los Angeles (Stolberg 1991; Ford and Simon 1991), the African Nationalist Pioneer Movement (Jamison 1988), which led a boycott in Harlem, New York, and the Alliance for

Concerned People, which led a brief boycott of the R & N fruit and vegetable store in Brooklyn, New York, also played an essential role in the emergence and escalation of the conflict. The disputes were racialized and the conflict was sustained by these organizations to advance their own control of black communities. Boycotts became the first resort for any dispute, partly because such conflict situations provided an opportunity (or "a public forum," according to Sonny Carson) for the different conflict organizations and their leaders to establish themselves within black communities. One of the main reasons why the boycotts lasted so long is that they were organized by black "outsiders" to achieve their own goals of controlling black communities.

Black Empowerment and the "Africanization" of New Black Immigrants

A key underlying process in this black-black conflict is the ethnic empowerment of blacks for political purposes. This refers to the process through which blacks in urban America attempt to increase their power— be it economic or political—by racializing and ethnicizing new black immigrants as a group. It is the social process of ethnogenesis and group formation with the goal of gaining power on the basis of ethnicity (Pitts 1974; Taylor 1979; Mason 1982; Roosens 1989). In this process, blacks are constantly reminded by other blacks of the racially defined meanings of "being black in America." Black consciousness and identity are stressed, and group boundaries are redefined and reinforced because ethnicity brings people "strategic advantages" when it is "politicized" (Roosens 1989: 14). Ethnicity, as Joseph Rothschild observes in his book *Ethnopolitics*, "in certain historical and socioeconomic circumstances, is readily politicized" (1981: 1). Modern American society in general, and urban America in particular, have produced fertile circumstances under which the ethnicity among blacks can be readily politicized.

The problem is that black ethnicity cannot be taken for granted anymore in America. Black society in the 1990s is much more diverse and heterogeneous than it was in the 1960s. Black people are diverse in their culture, religion, language, national origin, class, and, most of all, in their approaches to the fundamental problems that blacks face in America. It is apparent, as James Blackwell points out, that blacks in America can no longer be treated "as a monolithic undifferentiated mass" (1985: 344). The real challenge for "Black Powerists" and black "political entrepreneurs" now is to generate and reinforce ethnic solidarity among diverse blacks in America and to construct and reconstruct blacks as a racial-ethnic group in order to politicize it as a power group.

Among the diverse subgroups of blacks, one significant division is that between native blacks and recent black immigrants. Ethnic diversity between them seems to be as important as the diversity between different racial groups. During the Church Avenue boycott, for example, the ethnic differences among blacks were often emphasized by Caribbean Americans, who were pursuing different interests. They were regularly heard saying "All blacks are not the same," and many even showed contempt toward the African American boycott leaders. English-speaking Caribbean immigrants also did not seem to feel strong ethnic attachments, as blacks, to Haitian immigrants; some openly expressed ethnic prejudice against Haitians. Black diversity, different interests among diverse black subgroups, and power relations among these subgroups are important structural elements we must consider in our discussion of the process of black empowerment.

The primary task of the Black Power Movement in the 1960s was to attach a sense of pride to being black among the native blacks. In the 1990s, the task is not only to enhance black consciousness among the native blacks but also to overcome black diversity by inculcating the social meaning of blackness in America to new black immigrants such as Haitians, Jamaicans, or Trinidadians—recent immigrants who are more likely to identify themselves by their homeland rather than simply as "blacks." As a speaker at a black power rally stated, "Black solidarity is essential for black power."

During the boycott there was a constant effort to "Africanize" new black immigrants as "African Americans," not only to conduct an effective boycott against the Korean stores but also to achieve unity among diverse blacks in order to enhance the political power of blacks in urban America. To reach these ends, the issues were formulated, and the conflict was intensified.

One important function of black unity rallies and marches for the boycott was to make these new black immigrants realize that, regardless of their personal heritage, in America they would be categorically treated as blacks. Speaker after speaker during the rallies stressed, "We are one people." One speaker asked the crowd, "Can you tell the difference between Haitian black and Jamaican black?" After hearing from the crowd the expected "no," he continued: "I don't care if she is a Haitian woman. She is black. She can be my mother."

By identifying with the alleged victim and characterizing the dent as a racial one, the boycott leaders were racializing new e blacks and redefining the group boundary in order to expand their r ce-based political power. By emphasizing the same racial distinctiveness rather than ethnic differences, the native blacks attempted to expand their group boundaries and thereby increase their social bases of power in American society.

THE BOYCOTT AS A STRATEGY FOR BLACK EMPOWERMENT: A BLACK DILEMMA

A Korean merchant who owned a store at Church Avenue and whose business was badly hurt because of the boycott sarcastically asked, "Black Power? Fine. But why against Korean merchants?" Is the black boycott of Korean stores an effective strategy for black empowerment? This is a relevant question because the likelihood of more black boycotts of Korean stores depends on whether the black-Korean conflict will provide favorable political opportunities for black activists or political entrepreneurs.

The effectiveness of such boycotts as a strategy for black empowerment, however, is questionable. First of all, attendance at the marches on the streets of Brooklyn, the rallies, and the picketing in front of stores clearly indicated that boycott leaders failed to mobilize black residents for a mass movement. Moreover, the black-Korean conflict gradually turned into a black-black conflict between the black boycotters and the black shoppers. In addition to the complications of black diversity, there was also a fundamental black dilemma in boycotting the stores owned by Korean merchants—who themselves were identified as a racial minority in America.

Blacks and Koreans are racial minorities in America in terms of their relative group positions against the dominant whites in the ethnic stratification system of America. But their "degrees of minority status" are different and inconsistent in various ways (Marger 1991: 66). Despite the higher rate of business ownership among Korean immigrants and their greater degree of integration into suburban white communities,[6] blacks are numerically, organizationally, and politically more powerful than Koreans in urban America. Blacks in the United States, in short, are a racial minority, but in urban America they are a dominant group among racial minorities.

The complex nature of the black-Korean conflict is due to the multidimensional, inconsistent minority statuses of blacks and Koreans in the

United States. Relations between these two minorities are not as consistent and clear-cut as black-white relations in America. Their inconsistently different minority statuses in America have affected their consciousness, their understandings of situations, and their strategies.

One striking phenomenon during the conflict has been the presence of a strong minority consciousness among both blacks and Koreans. Most Korean merchants strongly believed that they were targets of crimes and organized boycotts because they did not have power in comparison with blacks in America. Korean merchants tended to think that they were treated badly by blacks—in incidents such as boycotts, shoplifting, muggings, and other crimes—because they do not have power. One of the comments most regularly heard from Korean merchants is: "We have to be tough [to blacks]. Especially at the beginning of the new business we have to be tough to set the pattern. Otherwise, they will walk all over us." Such minority consciousness might have made some merchants react with unnecessarily rough actions to their customers. As for the boycott, Korean merchants also believe it was an instance of minority victimization, stating they were victimized because they do not have power.

The minority consciousness of both groups undoubtedly prolonged and intensified the conflict. "Winning the battle" has become an end in itself. Both blacks and Koreans seemed to believe that the outcome would have significant consequences upon their group status and emerging minority group relations. In addition, Koreans feared the likelihood of more boycotts in the future. An important strategy used both for and against the boycott was to define which group was the more victimized minority between blacks and Koreans. In order to mobilize ethnic resources, the groups' differences were stressed and their minority statuses were emphasized; both groups claimed that their group was the victim of racial discrimination.

The real dilemma of the black nationalists who organized the boycotts came from the fact that they were, or were perceived to be, more powerful than Koreans in urban America. As members of a dominant minority, they were employing a strategy of differentiating people according to their physical appearances in order to enhance or maintain their group interests—just as the dominant whites had been doing for such a long time against blacks. Group differentiation for the purpose of ethnic empowerment, as practiced by racial minorities, is essentially the same as the process of group differentiation for the purpose of racial discrimination, as practiced by dominant groups. Racial discrimination justified by the ideology of racism has been used by dominant groups as "a technique of dominance," while ethnic empowerment based on ethnicity has been used by minority groups as "a technique of empowerment" for the interests of the group. Both techniques are based on the same process of group differentiation, and both increase racial consciousness among racial minorities.

As the dominant American racial minority, with a history of racial victimization and urban riots, blacks in urban America have the "privilege" of challenging the structures of racial inequality through ethnic empowerment. Urban America has provided them with a favorable "structure of political opportunities" (Eisinger 1973) because of "the receptivity of vulnerability of the political system to organized protest by a given challenging group" (McAdam, McCarthy, and Zald 1988: 699). Absence of control by governmental agencies, who did not wish to take sides in this case, was clearly an indicator of favorable political conditions that black nationalists could exploit. From this perspective, the boycotts of Korean stores are only possible because they are done by blacks in America. Yet, there is a fundamental dilemma in employing the old technique of group differentiation and empowerment against the new racial minorities.

CONCLUSION

To understand the dynamic process of the black-Korean conflict, I focused my study on the organized collective actions related to the boycotts and counterboycott measures. Based on the resource mobilization perspective in social movement theories, my concentration was on how such "objective" social, economic, and political conditions were perceived, interpreted, defined, and used by the conflict parties to frame the issues, to mobilize resources, and to enhance the interests of each group.

The central role of power is a key in explaining the conflict processes. Blacks, as a dominant minority in urban America, are capable of challenging emerging ethnic order in urban America. Korean merchants, who are not yet ready to move up nor to pack up and move out of black neighborhoods, also have resources to defend their place in the ethnic order. The actual or perceived differences in power between blacks and Koreans in terms of resource mobilization have played the most significant role in shaping the dynamic process of conflict between these two groups.

As racial-ethnic groups with strong racial-ethnic consciousness and identification among their members, with their own organizations and institutions, and with clear group boundaries between them, blacks and Koreans in the United States have established and maintained highly separated intergroup relations. This high degree of separation and the absence of multiple ties and cross-relations among their members have become important factors contributing to the conflict. During the conflict, ethnic differentiation has been further prompted by both boycott leaders and Korean merchants in order to mobilize ethnic resources.

In this regard, it must be stressed that this is a conflict between two racial minorities in the United States: blacks and Koreans are racial minorities in terms of their relationship to whites in America. At both interpersonal and intergroup levels, their minority statuses and minority consciousness, as major frames of reference, have made a significant impact upon their relations. The main underlying process in black-Korean conflicts is that of ethnic empowerment of racial minorities based on utilizing ethnicity in a multiethnic society as a power base to be mobilized for the interests of the group rather than viewing it as a cultural subgroup.

To understand the process of ethnic empowerment, especially black empowerment, it is necessary to look at the black-Korean conflict in the political context of black-white relations in urban America. The former ideology of black nationalism and black power has been employed not just against Korean merchants but against dominant white institutions such as the police, the media, the courts, and, especially, the white politicians who have long represented black neighborhoods. The competition among blacks for the leadership within black communities has also significantly affected the emergence and development of the black-Korean conflict. The ideological and organizational competition among black integrationist groups, separatist groups, and diverse black militant groups has clearly escalated the conflict.

In rejecting more individualistic explanations based on either Korean racism and black racism or the cultural differences between the two groups, I have emphasized the economic and political contexts that contribute to the conflict. More specifically, I have treated the process of ethnic empowerment of blacks as the key element. In order to enhance the status of blacks in the United States and to promote their own political influence within black communities, many black leaders have attempted to boost the ethnic empowerment of blacks using the ideology of black nationalism and black power. It was not the frustrations or grievances of black merchants or customers that led directly to the boycott but rather the potential use of such a boycott as a strategy for black empowerment.

In this regard, it should be noted that the black-Korean conflict in New York City surrounding the boycotts of Korean stores and counter-boycott measures in the 1990s had an unmistakable similarity to the black-

Jewish conflict surrounding the 1968–69 New York City school strikes.[7] The common element in both cases is that the racial-ethnic differences were stressed to enhance group interests and the conflict situations were used by black nationalist groups to promote the black power movement.

The real paradox in both cases is that blacks, who have historically been been singled out as a racial category for differential treatment in the United States, are now using the same technique of group differentiation for the enhancement of their group interests. America has gradually come to recognize this as a voluntary group differentiation. Scarce resources have been allocated based more on the political power of each group than on individual merit. It seems that the black-Korean conflict is a particular case that reflects the general trend of ethnic empowerment among racial minorities in this multiethnic society, and it casts an ominous sign on the future of intergroup relations in the United States.

NOTES

1. This assumption is based on the so-called rational choice model of collective actions, as advocated by Olson (1965) and Blalock (1989), and the massive literature on the "resource mobilization approach" in social movement theories.

2. See Gamson 1990 (pp. 136–41 in 1975 edition) for a brief but well-summarized presentation of this point.

3. One notable figure who refused a formal interview is Sonny Carson, who was deeply involved in the conflict as an organizer and appeared at and addressed a number of rallies. Unlike his surrogates, who exhibited more cooperative attitudes, he refused to talk to any "Korean blood."

4. See the Mayor's Committee (1990b: 15–16), "The conflict on Church Avenue is incident-based. . . . The Committee has concluded therefore that the Family Red Apple Market and Church Fruits are targeted because of the January 18th incident."

5. For the political usage of race and the overall issue of racial politics in New York City, see also Green 1989 and Kasinitz 1992.

6. The level of Asian-white residential segregation is much lower than that of segregation between blacks and whites, see Langberg and Reynolds 1985.

7. For example, Sinden(1980) and Maynard (1970) have presented similar analyses. See also Bourgeois 1976 and Fantini, Gittell, and Magat 1970. For the analysis of black-Latino conflict in this category, see Oliver and Johnson 1984.

REFERENCES

Banks, Sandy. 1985. Korean merchants, black customers—tensions grow. *Los Angeles Times*. April 15: Sec. 2, p. 1.

Banton, Michael. 1988. *Racial consciousness*. New York: Longman.

Blackwell, James E. 1976. The power basis of ethnic conflict in American society. Pp. 179–96 in *The uses of controversy in sociology*, edited by Lewis Coser and Otto Larsen. New York: The Free Press.

——. 1985. *The black community: Diversity and unity*. 2d ed. New York: Harper and Row.

Blalock, Hubert M. 1989. *Power and conflict: Toward a general theory*. Newbury Park, Calif.: Sage Publications.

Bourgeois, Donald A. 1976. Community control and urban conflict. Pp. 94–97 in *School and community alternatives*, edited by Maurice M. Martinez, Jr., and Josepha M. Weston. Dubuque, Iowa: Kendall/Hunt.

Burson, Pat. 1988. Korean merchants meet with blacks to ease tensions and end picketing. *Atlanta Constitution*. October 19: C1.

Cleaver, James H. 1983a. Asian businesses in black community cause stir. *Los Angeles Sentinel*. August 11: A1.

——. 1983b. Asian attitudes toward blacks cause raised eyebrows. *Los Angeles Sentinel*. August 18: A1.

——. 1983c. Residents complain about alleged Asian problem. *Los Angeles Sentinel*. August 25: A1.

——. 1983d. Citizens air gripes about Asians. *Los Angeles Sentinel*. September 1: A1.

——. 1983e. Asians may face lawsuits. *Los Angeles Sentinel*. September 8: A2.

——. 1983f. Black agenda hosts Korean dialogue. *Los Angeles Sentinel*. September 15: A1.

Eisinger, Peter K. 1973. The conditions of protest behavior in American cities. *American Political Science Review* 67:11–28.

Eng, Peter, and Edward D. Sargent. 1981. A troubled American dream: Blacks and Asians at odds over money and territory. *Washington Post*. August 17: A1.

English, Merle. 1988. Black activists plan Korean store boycott. *Newsday*. September 22.

Fantini, Mario, Marilyn Gittell, and Richard Magat. 1970. *Community control and the urban school*. New York: Praeger.

Flatbush Inquirer. 1990. More racial extortion. Vol. 2 (May 15): 5.

Ford, Andrea, and John H. Lee. 1991. Racial tensions blamed in girl's death. *Los Angeles Times*. March 20.

Ford, Andrea, and Richard Simon. 1991. Group's role in boycott of L.A. store hit. *Los Angeles Times*. September 11: B1.

Gamson, William A. 1990. *The strategy of social protest*, 2d ed. Belmont, Calif.: Wadsworth.

Green, Charles. 1989. *The struggle for black empowerment in New York City: Beyond the politics of pigmentation*. New York: Praeger.

Jamison, Harold L. 1988. Groups says no to Korean peace effort. *New York Amsterdam News*. September 17.

Karwarth, Rob. 1990. Clash of cultures is more than just skin deep. *Chicago Tribune*. July 15: Sec. 2C, p. 1.

Kasinitz, Philip. 1992. *Caribbean New York: Black immigrants and the politics of race*. Ithaca, N.Y.: Cornell University Press.

Kim, Illsoo. 1981. *New urban immigrants: The Korean community in New York*. Princeton, N.J.: Princeton University Press.

Krajicek, David. 1987. N.Y. eight reject rep. *New York Daily News*. July 12: 33.

Kriesberg, Louis. 1982. *Social conflicts*, 2d ed. Englewood Cliffs, N.J.: Prentice-Hall.

Langberg, Mark, and Farley Reynolds. 1985. Residential segregation of Asian Americans in 1980. *Sociology and Social Research* 70:71–75.

Lee, Felicia R. 1988. Blacks and Koreans in Brooklyn forge an accord. *New York Times.* December 21: Sec. 2, p. 1.

Marger, Martin N. 1991. *Race and ethnic relations: American and global perspectives,* 2d ed. Belmont, Calif.: Wadsworth.

Mason, David. 1982. Race relations, group formation and power: A framework for analysis, *Ethnic and Racial Studies* 5 (4): 421–39.

Maynard, Robert C. 1970. Black nationalism and community schools. Pp. 100–110 in *Community control of schools,* edited by Henry M. Levin. Washington, D.C.: Brookings Institution.

Mayor's Committee. 1990a. *Transcript of the public hearing on the boycott on Church Avenue.* June 28.

———. 1990b. *Report of the Mayor's Committee investigating the protest against two Korean-owned groceries on Church Avenue in Brooklyn.* New York.

McAdam, Doug, J. D. McCarthy, and M. N. Zald. 1988. Social movements. Pp. 695–737 in *Handbook of sociology,* edited by Neil J. Smelser. Newbury Park, Calif.,: Sage Publications.

Mills, Marja, and Robert Davis. 1990. Roseland is no bed of roses for Korean merchants. *Chicago Tribune.* July 10: Sec. 2C, p. 1.

Myers, Steven Lee. 1992. A community board in conflict: In Flatbush, blacks are pressing for more seats on panel. *New York Times.* February 10: B1.

New York Post. 1990. Scapegoating New York's Koreans. Editorial, January 25.

Njeri, Itabari. 1989. Cultural conflict. *Los Angeles Times.* November 8: E1.

Noel, Peter. 1992. Death of a movement: How New York's black activists won and lost the struggle for a united front. *Village Voice.* August 18: 23–32

Ogburn, Robert, and Steve Butler. 1983. The tale of three cities unfolds. *Koreatown.* November 12.

Oh, Angela Eunjin, and Bong Hwan Kim. 1991. Don't fall for "divide and conquer." *Los Angeles Times.* September 4: B7.

Oliver, Melvin, and James M. Johnson, Jr. 1984. Inter-ethnic conflict in an urban ghetto: The case of Blacks and Latinos in Los Angeles. *Research in Social Movements, Conflict, and Change* 6:57–94.

Olson, Mancur. 1965. *The logic of collective action.* Cambridge, Mass.: Harvard University Press.

Pitts, James P. 1974. The study of race consciousness: Comments on new directions. *American Journal of Sociology* 80:665–87.

Roosens, Eugeen E. 1989. *Creating ethnicity: The process of ethnogenesis.* Newbury Park, Calif.: Sage Publications.

Rothschild, Joseph. 1981. *Ethnopolitics: A conceptual framework.* New York: Columbia University Press.

Sinden, Peter G. 1980. Anti-Semitism and the black power movement. *Ethnicity* 7:34–46.

Sleeper, Jim. 1990. *The closest of strangers: Liberalism and the politics of race in New York.* New York: Norton.

Song, Kyung Mi. 1989. Korean merchants in black neighborhoods: Facing perils in the inner city. Master's Project, Graduate School of Journalism, Columbia University, New York.

Stolberg, Sheryl. 1991. Issue of Brotherhood Crusade funding heats up over boycott. *Los Angeles Times*. September 26: B1.

Stone, John. 1985. *Racial conflict in contemporary society*. Cambridge, Mass.: Harvard University Press.

Taylor, Ronald L. 1979. Black ethnicity and the persistence of ethnogenesis. *American Journal of Sociology* 84:1401–23.

Venerose, Joseph R. 1987. Kimchi comes to Harlem: Blacklash to Korean immigration. Master's Project, Graduate School of Journalism, Columbia University.

Yoo, Woong Nyol. 1981. Business owners in New York's Harlem struggle against anti-Korean prejudice. *Koreatown*. October 19: 4.

7 Conflict between Korean Merchants and Black Customers: A Structural Analysis

Heon Cheol Lee

Since the early 1980s, a series of conflicts between Korean merchants and black customers have erupted at Korean stores in inner-city black neighborhoods. The conflict usually stems from a dispute between a Korean merchant and a black customer at a Korean-owned store, which is followed by a black boycott and escalates into a large-scale intergroup conflict.

Black-Korean conflicts of this nature have occurred in most cities in which significant numbers of Korean immigrants operate businesses in black neighborhoods. For example, on January 18, 1990, an incident occurred at a Korean-owned fruit and vegetable store on Church Avenue, in the Flatbush section of Brooklyn, New York. The merchant-customer dispute quickly escalated into a protest and boycott, which spread to another Korean store across the street and lasted more than a year. In 1991, the fatal shooting of a teenage black girl at a Korean store in South Central Los Angeles also developed into a long, bitter conflict (Ford and Lee 1991). Similar conflicts involving organized boycotts of Korean stores in black neighborhoods following an incident have been reported in Baltimore, Washington, Philadelphia, Chicago, Atlanta, and Los Angeles (e.g., Ogburn and Butler 1983; Eng and Sargent 1981; Cleaver 1983; Kim 1981; Yoo 1981; Venerose 1987; Song 1989; Mills and Davis 1990; Burson 1988). What accounts for these instances of black-Korean conflict in urban America?

Perhaps the most popular answer to this question, especially among black boycotters, is that something is wrong with Korean merchants.

Korean merchants are rude or disrespectful because they are prejudiced against blacks. Black boycotters have always asserted that the primary reason for the boycott was the "disrespectful" behavior of Korean merchants toward black customers.

Another popular explanation for the source of dispute and eventual conflict is "the differences in culture" between blacks and Koreans (Karwarth 1990; Njeri 1989) or "misunderstandings rooted in cultural differences" (Banks 1985). According to this view, Korean merchants might not intend to act disrespectfully. They are perceived to be disrespectful because some aspects of their cultural heritage, which prescribe them to behave in certain ways, are often misinterpreted by blacks. When Korean cashiers put change on a counter rather than in a customer's hand, it is because of their culture, not because of their racist attitudes. From this perspective, to prevent further conflicts between Koreans and blacks, what Korean merchants really need is "sensitivity training" to enhance their understanding of their customers' culture.

A third widely circulated explanation is that such conflicts stem from black racism as a form of scapegoating (*New York Post* 1990) or as a form of "racial extortion" (*Flatbush Inquirer* 1990). Blacks boycott Korean stores, according to this view, not so much because Korean merchants are disrespectful but because blacks are jealous of Korean success, frustrated and even embarrassed by it. Korean merchants are singled out as the scapegoats in such a scenario because, as new immigrants, they lack power. A community newsletter in Brooklyn, the *Flatbush Inquirer*, called it "a new breed of racism" and argued that blacks were in effect trying to extort money in the form of negotiated settlements, contributions to black organizations, or the use of local black institutions.

Previously published accounts of Korean racism or black racism fail to give satisfying explanations of why, contrary to their economic interests, Korean merchants are rude to their black customers, if they are rude at all. Nor do they explain in a satisfying manner and with supporting evidence why blacks are racially motivated to boycott Korean stores.

Conflict unfolds in time and can refer to a variety of phenomena. The factors that influence its development do not all operate simultaneously, and the factors that influence the merchant-customer dispute are different from the factors that influence the boycott. In this sequential model of conflict, a different conceptual framework is needed to explain the different stages of conflict development. Therefore, we have to specify the circumstances so that we know exactly what black-Korean conflict we are dealing with.

It is essential to make a clear distinction between a merchant-customer dispute at the individual level and a black-Korean conflict at the collective level. An individual dispute between a Korean merchant and a black customer and an incident resulting from it may be a precondition for the black-Korean conflict at the collective level, but it alone is not sufficient for the emergence of a black-Korean conflict at the collective level. The conflict at the collective level seems to have developed quite independently from any original incident.

Most misunderstandings of the black-Korean conflict and the erroneous solutions offered are the result of confusing these two different levels of conflict and mistakenly believing that the conflict is caused or precipitated by the incident. The conditions and processes that give rise to the collective conflict are distinct from and often unrelated to the sources of individual disputes. An attempt to identify the structural sources of the disputes should therefore enhance our understanding of the relationships between Korean merchants and black customers. In this chapter, I focus only on the merchant-customer disputes at the individual level.

Based on such a distinction, I attempt to answer several questions regarding the disputes between Korean merchants and black customers at Korean stores in black neighborhoods: How can Korean merchants do their business in black neighborhoods and yet, contrary to their economic interests, treat their black customers disrespectfully, if they actually do? Is it because of their racial prejudice against blacks? Or is it only because of their cultural differences that they are perceived to be rude? Are there more fundamental sources of tension that generate disputes between blacks and Koreans? If so, what are they?

Data Collection

The data was collected primarily during the period of the Church Avenue black boycott of Korean stores (January 1990–May 1991). With owners' approval and managers' cooperation, as a nonparticipant observer I was able to view the interactions between Korean merchants and black customers at various Korean stores in New York City and, more extensively, at two Korean fruit and vegetable stores on Church Avenue (in addition to one on Fulton Street in Bedford-Stuyvesant and one in Harlem). These two Korean fruit and vegetable stores, on the block next to the two boycotted stores, were ideal places for this purpose. During the long boycott period, their businesses flourished.

During the summer and fall of 1990, I conducted a survey among most of the Korean merchants who owned stores within five blocks of Church Avenue. That gave me an overall picture of how the ghetto economy functioned. A couple of group interviews with Korean merchants at the Brooklyn Market were also conducted at an office of the Korean Produce Association of New York. These interviews made it possible for me to do a comparative analysis among Korean businesses in different neighborhoods. Owners of other stores in New York City that had previously been boycotted were also interviewed during this period.

Expecting difficulties in getting reliable data from black interviewees due to my ethnic background, I started with Korean interviewees to fully sensitize myself to substantive issues. Then I interviewed black participants and, unless they objected, recorded the interviews. To ensure more reliable data, I told the interviewees clearly what the purpose of my study was and assured them of the confidentiality of my research. I had to interview some key informants more than once. In many instances, these second interviews turned out to be more productive as we got to know each other better.

THE KOREAN ANTIBLACK PREJUDICE EXPLANATION

From the interviews with Korean merchants and the observations of their interactions with black customers, it became clear that Korean antiblack prejudice does exist among Korean merchants in these neighborhoods and affects the nature of merchant-customer relations. One Korean merchant who owned a store on Church Avenue, while insisting that he was not a racist, argued: "Blacks cannot own and manage this kind of business. They are lazy. They are too ignorant. They don't have business skills and stamina." Another Korean merchant, in his analysis of black underrepresentation in small business, explained that "for the low-class blacks, especially, they are so much accustomed to enjoying their lives without working. No job is not a stigma to them any more." Then he went on to say, "I firmly believe that if all Korean merchants pack and leave this area, and blacks take over, this block will become a slum again."

Quite often, when these Korean merchants mentioned "Americans" in the middle of their casual conversations, they actually meant whites. It was also quite common for Korean merchants to use the derogatory term *Camdungi* instead of the more respectful *Heuk In* when they referred to a black person.

In a campaign to educate Korean merchants on how to prevent disputes with black customers, the *Korean Times New York*, based on its long coverage of black-Korean conflicts and selective interviews, issued a list titled "Ten Essentials for the Prevention of Black-Korean Conflict" (September 28, 1991). The first commandment for all Korean merchants is "Never use the word *Camdungi.*" The last is "Get rid of the equation 'black=ignorant.' "[1] The necessity for such guidelines clearly indicates that some form of racial prejudice is playing an important role in interactions between Korean merchants and black customers.

It is quite possible that Korean merchants have become prejudiced against blacks through their preimmigrant exposure to images of blacks, most of which were provided by various white media. A number of Korean store owners complained that the Korean employees who came to America rather recently tended to be rougher in their handling of black customers than were the more seasoned shopkeepers. Obviously, the language barrier could be a factor. The evidence of prejudice and rude behavior, however, is too overwhelming to blame only on poor English skills.

After immigration, shopkeepers' selective experiences with poor inner city blacks seem to reinforce their stereotypes about blacks. Crimes such as mugging, stealing, burglary, and arson, as well as other forms of "disrespectful" behaviors committed by some blacks seem to be confirming what Korean merchants had already "known" of blacks before they came to America. As their economic niche is further threatened because of boycotts, Korean merchants' racially prejudiced ideas seem to become even more ingrained, protecting their current position and solidifying their antiblack prejudice.

Overall, however, the existence of Korean antiblack prejudice does not fully explain their alleged disrespectful behaviors and the merchant-customer disputes. People simply do not always act in the ways their attitudes might prescribe. To Korean merchants whose customers are mainly black, their economic interests are too important to act disrespectfully, even if they are prejudiced against blacks. A Korean merchant's statement illustrates this point: "In this area, within four blocks on Church Avenue, there are six fruit and vegetable stores. Five of them are Koreans'. We are competing against each other. How could we be rude to our customers? If we are, we will lose our customers. We are not that stupid."

Most Korean merchants, in other words, are generally prejudiced against blacks but do not discriminate against their black customers because doing so would jeopardize their economic interests. For their businesses, they must suppress their antiblack prejudice. If we use Robert K. Merton's (1976) prejudice-discrimination typology, most Korean merchants may belong to the category of "prejudiced nondiscriminators."

An uneven process of modifying attitudes and behaviors seems to occur among Korean merchants. Because of their economic interests, Korean merchants' behavioral adjustment seems faster than their attitudinal one in this interracial contact situation. The longer Korean merchants deal with black customers, the more comfortable they become with them. One Korean merchant who sold her takeout fast food restaurant on Church Avenue and moved to Fulton Street in Brooklyn, another predominantly black neighborhood, said she felt more comfortable with black customers than with white customers.

It is also apparent that the antiblack prejudice among Korean merchants is exaggerated by black demonstrators, especially during a conflict. The view that Koreans harbor such prejudice is more forcefully presented by boycott leaders and black community leaders than black customers. Even during the boycotts, amid chants of "no respect, no money," other Korean stores continued to do business with their black customers. During the Church Avenue boycott, for example, a significant number of black customers came to both boycotted stores not just to shop but also to encourage the merchants. Since the middle of September 1990, after a court order to keep demonstrators at least fifty feet away from stores was enforced and Mayor Dinkins visited the stores, black customers started coming back to the boycotted stores in spite of continuing harassment from the picketers. This clearly indicates that ordinary black customers do not believe as strongly as do the boycott leaders that blacks are treated badly because of Korean merchants' racial prejudice.

Nevertheless, antiblack prejudice does exist among Korean merchants, and it has played a role in merchant-customer relations. Under certain circumstances this prejudice could be a source of the disrespectful behaviors of Korean merchants. Though if we consider the complex nature of merchant-customer relations and the dynamic process of conflict development, its role is rather minor and should not be exaggerated. We have to look at more fundamental sources of strains and disputes.

THE CULTURAL DIFFERENCES EXPLANATION

According to the cultural difference proponents, Korean merchants are perceived to be rude by blacks because of the differences in their cultures, not because of the Korean merchants' racist attitude.

This view of culture difference is well expressed by Connie Kang, who contributed an article to the *New York Times* entitled "Koreans Have a Reason Not to Smile." She believes that for Koreans, "a mechanical smile is hard to produce," and wonders if, "had she [the Haitian customer] known smiling at strangers just isn't part of the Korean culture, she would have reacted differently" (Kang 1990).

What are the behaviors attributed to Korean culture that are not suitable for dealing with black customers? This issue was addressed at a conference entitled "Human Relations: Racial and Cultural Diversity," held in August 1990 during the Church Avenue boycott. Twenty-five Koreans and the same number of blacks—of African, Haitian, and Caribbean heritage—participated in this three-day conference. One task was to identify those specific aspects of Korean culture that can lead to misunderstandings with black customers. According to Korean participants, Koreans are "culturally and traditionally" not supposed to show their feelings or emotions in public, which would preclude smiling at strangers. When they bump into other people on the street, Koreans do not say "Excuse me." Direct eye contact is not culturally acceptable, especially with older people or those of the opposite sex. Physical contact, not only kissing and hugging but any type of touching (especially between members of the opposite sex), is not permitted in public as a proscribed social norm. Men in Korea are expected to be more serious and less talkative. The patterns of behavior rooted in such Korean cultural expectations may be the source of misunderstandings and disputes between Korean merchants and black customers.

Korean merchants, then, would need to increase their sensitivity to American customers' needs and improve their understanding of customer expectations. To reduce racial tension and strain and to prevent further conflicts between Koreans and blacks, the Mayor's Committee, for example, suggests a need "to sensitize Blacks and Koreans to their cultural differences and similarities" (1990: 65). Yet the committee has never specified these differences in culture as the source of tension and conflict. It was proposed that Korean merchants would need a series of "cultural exchange" programs or "sensitivity training," or they might take a course in "multi-cultural literacy."

In my opinion, cultural differences also have been overemphasized. The role of cultural differences has been exaggerated in explaining not only individual merchant-customer relations but also the whole black-Korean conflict. Undoubtedly, the differences in their cultures have played some part in merchant-customer relations, but they do not fully account for the merchant-customer disputes in their daily interactions. In the rest of this chapter, I show how various structural elements of some Korean businesses are conducive to merchant-customer disputes and generate strain between Korean merchants and black customers.

STRUCTURAL CONTRADICTIONS OF KOREAN BUSINESSES IN BLACK NEIGHBORHOODS

More than simply a result of their antiblack prejudice and cultural differences, Korean merchants are perceived to be disrespectful of their black customers because of the structural conditions of some Korean businesses, which constrain merchants' behaviors in certain patterned ways. To examine these structural constraints, we first have to understand how the economy in poor urban neighborhoods works and how Korean merchants establish and operate their business in these neighborhoods.

Before we look at the ghetto economy and certain structural elements of Korean businesses, however, the fundamental nature of merchant-customer relations should be briefly discussed. In a commercial transaction between merchant and customer, the basic nature of their relation is a zero-sum equation. Other factors notwithstanding, if a merchant reduces the price, it is a gain for the customer and a loss for the merchant. Such contradictory interests are fundamental to merchant-customer relations.

One example I observed quite frequently at Korean fruit and vegetable stores illustrates this point. Whether to cut out one end or both ends of a yam, and how much of the ends should be cut, is one of the routine battles between Korean merchants and black customers. Since yams are sold by weight, no customer wants to pay for the inedible parts. However, since the whole package is weighed and bought as a unit when yams are purchased from wholesalers, merchants have to be concerned about how much of the yam is discarded at the customer's request. The more yam that is cut off, the less their profit will be. Korean merchants look quite mean when they are asked to cut the yam.

Merchants try to maximize their profits from each transaction while customers try to get the best deal at minimum expense. To remain a viable business enterprise, however, long-term relations should be more inter-dependent rather than exploitative, that is, maximizing only one party's interest. The key task for merchants is how to make a profit in the long run while also satisfying customers' needs. To be rude to customers is clearly contrary to merchants' long-term economic interests. What are those structural conditions, then, that constrain merchants' behavior and generate tensions and disputes between Korean merchants and black customers?

One significant structural factor is the size of the store. The limited number of cases makes generalizing difficult, but one notable pattern among the boycotted stores is their similar size—relatively big compared to most Korean fruit and vegetable stores but not as big as grocery supermarkets such as Pathmark or A & P. They are mid-sized fruit and vegetable stores, between 1,800 to 2,000 square feet, with seven to ten employees.

One consequence of such a medium size is its ambiguous nature with regard to merchant-customer relations. These are neither traditional corner stores nor modern supermarkets. They are not mom-and-pop stores: more than husband and wife have to work there. A set of proper rules have not been established and accepted by both merchants and customers at such markets. They do not have the same frame of reference and often seem to have contradictory expectations. The customer who may ask for a one dollar discount at a Korean store cannot ask for it at a neighborhood supermarket. Unlike the owner at a mom-and-pop store, an employed cashier at a Korean store cannot be as flexible to such non-routine requests as being asked for a discount.

Because of the size of Korean stores, furthermore, owners do not have effective ways of controlling and monitoring customers. The stores are neither big enough to accommodate impersonal, systematic control nor small enough to allow personal control. Modern surveillance technology to prevent shoplifting would be too costly for these stores, and merchants also cannot afford the added cost and time of checking the shopping bags of all customers when they come in. Korean merchants have not yet developed an effective control mechanism for such stores except the most primitive and cheapest one: watching while working.

Another problem related to store size is the limited space in which customers can shop. A single doorway serves as entry and exit. Through this passageway, boxes of merchandise are also brought into and out of the store; none of the five fruit and vegetable stores on Church Avenue had back doors for deliveries or trash removal. Through the small spaces between packed merchandise, shoppers and workers perilously move around either to shop or to bring merchandise back and forth.

A separate worry is the more vulnerable "store" at the outside of the building. Well-stocked displays of fresh apples, oranges, and other fruit and vegetables outside are common features of Korean stores in many streets of New York City. The outside display is there not just because of limited space inside but to generate the desire to buy. If a customer sees a sign advertising plantains "10 for $1.00," it's not so easy to pass them by. Such displays are intended to attract customers, but they also make shoplifting or "tasting" much easier. Merchants therefore watch customers outside carefully, and many will chase shoplifters who have stolen from these easily targeted displays.

Competition among Korean merchants is another important factor affecting merchant-customer relations. Before the Church Avenue boycott, for example, the two boycotted stores were in severe competition with each other. Such competition among Korean merchants is not limited to the stores on Church Avenue. According to the executive director of the Korean Produce Association of New York, the association was originally formed to coordinate the locations of Korean stores in order to reduce the competition among Korean merchants. Because of this competition, the profit margin per sale is low and the volume of overall sales must be high to cover costs and make some profit. As a result, the merchants have to process many more customers, at a much quicker rate, to compensate for the lower profit margins. A Korean merchant was highly critical of the competition between the two neighboring Korean stores:

> Since the price is so good, more customers come to the stores. Since many people come, the workers cannot be kind to the customers. They are too busy replenishing stock. I heard the volume of the sales of those two stores sometimes exceeded $40,000 per week. To sell fruits and vegetables for that amount of money, they have to work really hard without a split second of break. They even don't have time to go to the bathroom. Under the circumstances it's impossible to be nice to their customers. We have to be more concerned about the profit margin. With better price and profit margin, we may have fewer customers who we can serve better.

The competition among Korean merchants not only lowers profits but also destroys the basic pricing system. If the merchants lower prices to compete, then the customers feel they can challenge the prices as a form of discount. Furthermore, since the volume of sales requires more customers to wait in lines, it gives the impression that these stores are "raking in all the black money" from black neighborhoods.

The customers' buying habits in these neighborhoods further aggravate this problem. Customers do not buy a large amount of merchandise at one time. The average sale per customer at Korean fruit and vegetable stores in black neighborhoods is low, somewhere between $3.00 and $5.00

per sale. They buy little, according to a Korean merchant, not just because they have little money or do not plan to shop in bulk, but because they are "smart shoppers." By purchasing a little without spending much money, they can enjoy fresh fruit and vegetables every day without worrying about keeping produce fresh at home.

No customer likes to wait in long lines. For most customers, it is not worthwhile to wait long in order to buy just a few dollars' worth of goods. Furthermore, when people are in a hurry to buy only one item, they often do not bother going inside to pay the cashier but instead pay the clerk who is watching the produce outside. Because of such practices, it is sometimes very difficult to know if a customer is leaving after having made a payment or without having paid. One control mechanism is to give a shopping bag to those who have paid, but here also a contradiction exists: the need to maintain a monitoring system and the need to minimize expense. To reduce their expenses, cashiers are inclined not to use bags for just a few items.

Furthermore, because of minimal staff and the constant need to replenish merchandise, items usually are not completely organized and priced. Price tags may not be attached, and signs for prices may be unclear or confusing, especially to recent immigrants unfamiliar with the stores themselves and signs written in English. Crowds of customers are also clustered in the stores around rush hours and on weekends, which further hinders service. Under these circumstances, customers still expect to be processed as quickly as possible while at the same time being treated respectfully.

How Korean merchants raise initial capital and their overall financing system also affect their relations with customers and must be considered as a structural element. My study confirms the findings of other researchers (Light and Bonacich 1988; Min and Jaret 1984; Kim 1981), which report that Korean merchants do not use commercial banks to obtain their initial capital. Among more than twenty stores on Church Avenue and a few stores in Harlem and Fulton Street in Brooklyn that were investigated, none of the Korean merchants had borrowed money from a bank to start their business. Instead, they had borrowed from their family, friends, or other Korean businessmen, and used the borrowing system known as *Kye* to raise large sums of money or to pay back personal loans.[2]

One merchant described in detail how he amassed money to buy his first store.[3] His case is not unique among Korean merchants. Even though he was ready, in terms of business skills, to buy a fruit and vegetable store for himself, he had only about $5,000. He borrowed quite a large amount of money from his brother, sisters, and parents and borrowed another $60,000 from a Korean store owner. He then had to promise the owner selling the store an additional $120,00 over the next year, in amounts of $60,000 every six months. He then used the *Kye* to raise large sums of money and pay back the personal loans. Such personal loans, especially those from other businessmen, are basically short-term loans with high interest. They place enormous financial pressure on the borrower to pay them back as quickly as possible. Merchants in such stressful arrangements feel they have to make a lot of money quickly.

It was found that the owners of the stores boycotted in New York City had both owned their businesses for similar amounts of time, only about one or two years. This means that the merchants' finances were very tight, as they worked to pay back the money they had borrowed from their friends or relatives or to cover their slot or slots of *Kye*.[4] They might have had to hire fewer people and work longer and harder themselves, and they likely were less able to accommodate losses from shoplifting. The social obligation to pay loans back is enormous in this tightly controlled community of personal networks connected by kinship and friendship.

Korean stores are usually open long hours until late at night; some are open twenty-four hours a day. Often that is the only way they can afford to pay expensive rent or make money quickly to pay back their personal loans. Furthermore, by operating twenty-four hours, merchants do not have to move display stands every morning and evening. However, these long hours during the night create a greater chance of being robbed or mugged.

When a dispute arises, there is no institutionalized way of resolving it at the store. These shops have no customer service department. They are too small for that, and the space is too confined to isolate the nonroutine from the routine. There is no specialist who handles customer complaints; the store manager is usually brought in to handle such situations, but he or she is not trained, too busy, and has English skills that are inadequate for the task. Often, neither merchants nor shoppers know English very well. With limited English, they tend to speak shortly and bluntly.

Under these conditions it appears that even the most sensitized Korean merchants would not be able to behave in a sensitive way. They are too busy and too tired. They have to be very efficient and "work like a machine," as a black employee at a Korean store put it.

One incident I witnessed at a Korean fruit and vegetable store in Harlem demonstrates this situation. The store in question had been boycotted by blacks in 1984. At the time of my visit, the store's owner was working at the cash register. He was highly efficient, ringing up sales and making change very quickly. When he was complimented on his efficiency, the owner boastfully replied: "This is not the only thing I'm doing now. While working the cash register, I'm also watching customers, answering their questions, supervising employees and telling them which shelves to restock, and allowing you to interview me." This left me with the impression that for such businesses to remain viable, their owners must work with extraordinary efficiency, almost to the limit of their human capacity. While simultaneously handling multiple tasks, it is very difficult for merchants to be courteous to all customers. In my opinion, any disrespect they show toward blacks may not necessarily be a reflection of their underlying racial prejudice or cultural differences but could rather be an outcome of the structural contradictions of some Korean businesses.

In many respects, the poverty and related problems such as unemployment and crime in these neighborhoods has provided business opportunities for Korean immigrants. At the same time, these conditions have created an environment that has strained the relationships between Korean merchants and black customers. As far as merchant-customer disputes are concerned, I have come to reject any individualistic explanations solely based on Korean racism or black racism or on the cultural differences between the two groups.

Instead of the conflict being generated by the cultural differences, the conflict itself seems to generate ethnic myths about both Koreans and blacks in America. The various accounts of incidents and boycotts, and their causes as reported by the news media, appear to have taken root in this society as popular ideas. Generalizations such as "Koreans are rude" or "blacks are jealous of Korean success," which were largely constructed during the conflict, seem to have become a significant independent factor contributing to the subsequent black-Korean conflict.

RACIAL, ETHNIC, AND MINORITY CONSCIOUSNESS

I have identified multiple sources of the disputes between Korean merchants and black customers, and I have stressed the significant role of structural contradictions in some Korean-owned businesses. In addition to such objective conditions that constrain behavior, however, we must also take into account the frames of reference with which both blacks and Koreans perceive and interpret their daily experiences. A discussion of the subjective components of their behaviors will enhance our understanding of why such minor disputes between Korean merchants and black customers have developed into "racial" incidents and collective conflict between them.

The critical factor here is that both blacks and Koreans are racial minorities in the United States. Self-consciousness of their minority status and a constant fear of being treated differently because of their group status are strong currents among both Korean merchants and black customers. This consciousness clearly influences their perceptions and interpretations, but what differentiates the two groups is the different self-consciousness attached to their particular group statuses: their racial, ethnic, and minority consciousness. These three different types of consciousness among blacks and Koreans make a significant difference not only in their interpretations of disputes but also in the process of conflict escalation.

With the long history of racial discrimination in America, many black customers are likely to interpret certain behaviors in racial terms and believe that they are being discriminated against because they are black. As long as they believe that they are being treated differently because of their physical appearance, their understanding of the situation will be based on their racial consciousness.

In addition to a strong racial consciousness, recent black immigrants such as Haitians have a strong ethnic consciousness of their own. The customer involved in the dispute at the Family Red Apple store happened to be a Haitian American woman. Therefore the strong resentment among Haitian immigrants of racial-ethnic prejudice towards Haitians in America, even from other blacks, made a significant impact on the dynamics of the Church Avenue conflict. Haitians in America believe that they suffer great prejudice, but more for being Haitian than for being black. A Haitian American woman at the public hearing said, "Being a Haitian student growing up in America, I suffered a lot of racism because I was a *Haitian*." One young Haitian leader who actively participated in the boycott and made a speech at a black unity rally said, "If you are a Haitian, not just Koreans disrespect you, everybody disrespects you. Americans disrespect you, Dominicans disrespect you."

During the Church Avenue boycott, the strong ethnic resentment among Haitian Americans exploded when the Haitian "connection" to AIDS was reported by the news media. On April 20, 1990, a large number of Haitian Americans participated in a rally against prejudice then came to Church Avenue and held the biggest Haitian rally for the boycott. Such labeling as "the people who brought AIDS" and other types of racial and ethnic discrimination "even by Koreans" is seen as unbearable to Haitian Americans, who have enormous "Haitian pride" as the people who won independence and established the first black independent country in the Western Hemisphere.

In addition to racial and ethnic consciousness, minority consciousness, which is prevalent among Korean merchants in these neighborhoods, also has played a critical role in merchant-customer disputes. Korean merchants tend to think that they are treated badly by blacks because they do not have as much power. Such minority consciousness among Korean merchants might have encouraged some merchants to be unnecessarily rough to their customers. This issue of different consciousness becomes much more important when blacks and Koreans get collectively involved in a boycott.

CONCLUSION

Even if antiblack prejudice among Korean merchants and misunderstandings rooted in cultural differences between Korean merchants and black customers play some role in merchant-customer disputes, from my observations it has been the structural contradictions of some Korean stores that largely account for the strains, tensions, and disputes between Korean merchants and black customers. Furthermore, racial, ethnic, or minority consciousness has affected perceptions and interpretations on both sides and exacerbated relations.

However, I want to note that, considering the number of Korean stores in black neighborhoods and the volume of daily contacts between Korean merchants and black customers, the overall relations between Korean merchants and black customers were not as bad as they were presented by the boycott leaders and news media.[5] Business was still conducted at other Korean stores on Church Avenue during the boycott, quite a number of black customers attempted to enter the boycotted stores even under the intimidation of protesters, and most black customers came back to the stores after the boycotts ended. As the research progressed, I became increasingly puzzled at the fact that Korean merchants could conduct their business under such adverse conditions and maintain relatively stable economic relations with black customers.

One thing that was clear was that the black-Korean conflict was not the result of explosive dissatisfaction among ordinary black customers with Korean merchants' so-called disrespectful behaviors.[6] Since the black boycotts of Korean stores appear to grow out of individual merchant-customer disputes, we are led to believe that the black boycotts have been employed as a means to change a pattern of racial discrimination against black customers by Korean merchants. Various evidence strongly suggests that the role of merchant-customer disputes was disproportionately exaggerated and strategically racialized for the boycott. Such hostilities between black customers and Korean merchants (e.g. *New York Times*, May 18, 1992) seems more or less a condition created as a consequence of the conflict rather than the conflict's cause.

A dispute between a Korean merchant and a black customer may be one of the necessary preconditions for the black-Korean conflict at the collective level, but it alone is not a sufficient one. Such a dispute in fact creates an opportunity for black activists to raise more fundamental issues such as the disparate economic opportunities between blacks and Korean immigrants. It also provides black nationalists with a good political opportunity for the social movement of black empowerment. In an attempt to understand the dynamics of the black-Korean conflict, therefore, it is very important to consider, in addition to the merchant-customer disputes, the fundamental economic conditions and the process of ethnic empowerment among blacks in America.

NOTES

1. "The ten essentials" (my translation) are as follows: (1) Never use the word *Camdungi*, (2) Don't speak Korean loudly or finger point at the store, (3) Don't show off you have made lots of money, (4) Participate in local community activities, (5) Don't chase shoplifters outside of the store, (6) Try not to use arms, (7) Please learn English or Spanish, (8) Try not to use the word *no* to the customers, (9) Keep in your mind all the time that "black is beautiful." (10) Get rid of the equation of "black = ignorant."

2. A *Kye* is an old institution commonly used in Asian countries to raise money. There are many different types of *Kyes*, but essentially it is a rotating credit association in which each participant gives a certain amount of money to the designated receiver each month. By rotating, each member of the *Kye* receives the *Kye Don* (money) at his or her turn.

3. How one has raised money to buy a store is a very sensitive subject among Korean merchants. Only after building up personal trust with merchants and assuring them they would not be identified was it possible for me to get reliable information.

4. It is not unusual for members to have more than one slot. By having multiple slots of *Kye*, they can amass money more quickly, but they obviously have to put in much more money each pay term.

5. There were twenty-four Korean stores (including the two boycotted stores) within five blocks of Church Avenue in 1990. This number is more than one-third of the total small businesses in the area. The Korean Produce Association of New York estimated in 1990 that about 1500 Korean fruit and vegetable stores were located in predominantly black neighborhoods of New York City.

6. This statement is based on my observations and interviews with Korean merchants and black customers. As of now, no survey data on the satisfaction or dissatisfaction of ordinary black customers is available.

REFERENCES

Banks, Sandy. 1985. Korean merchants, black customers—tensions grow. *Los Angeles Times*. April 15: Sec. 2, p. 1.

Blalock, Hubert M. 1989. *Power and conflict: Toward a general theory.* Newbury Park, Calif.: Sage Publications.

Burson, Pat. 1988. Korean merchants meet with blacks to ease tensions and end picketing. *Atlanta Constitution*. October 19: C1.

Cleaver, James H. 1983. Asian businesses in black community cause stir. *Los Angeles Sentinel*. August 11: A1.

Eng, Peter, and Edward D. Sargent. 1981. A troubled American Dream: Blacks and Asians at odds over money and territory. *Washington Post*. August 17: 1.

Flatbush Inquirer. 1990. More racial extortion. Vol. 2 (May 15): 5.

Ford, Andrea, and John H. Lee. 1991. Racial tensions blamed in girl's death." *Los Angeles Times*. March 20.

Kang, Connie K. 1990. Koreans have a reason not to smile. *New York Times*. September 8: Sec. 1, p. 23.

Karwath, Rob. 1990. Clash of cultures is more than just skin deep. *Chicago Tribune*. July 15: Sec. 2C, p. 1.

Kim, Illsoo. 1981. *New urban immigrants: The Korean community in New York.* Princeton, N.J.: Princeton University Press.

Kriesberg, Louis. 1982. *Social conflicts*, 2d ed. Englewood Cliffs, N.J.: Prentice-Hall.

Light, Ivan H., and Edna Bonacich. 1988. *Immigrant entrepreneurs: Koreans in Los Angeles, 1965–1982.* Berkeley and Los Angeles: University of California Press.

Mayor's Committee. 1990. *Report of the Mayor's Committee investigating the protest against two Korean-owned groceries on Church Avenue in Brooklyn.* New York.

Merton, Robert K. 1976. Discrimination and the American creed. Pp. 189–216 in Merton, *Sociological ambivalence and other essays.* New York: The Free Press.

Mills, Marja, and Robert Davis. 1990. Roseland is no bed of roses for Korean Merchants. *Chicago Tribune*. July 10: Sec. 2C, p. 1.

Min, Pyong Gap, and Charles Jaret. 1984. Ethnic business success: The case of Korean small business in Atlanta. *Sociology and Social Research* 69 (3): 412–35.

New York Post. 1990 Scapegoating New York's Koreans. Editorial. January 25.

Njeri, Itabari. 1989. Cultural conflict. *Los Angeles Times*. November 8: E1.

Ogburn, Robert, and Steve Butler. 1983. The tale of three cities unfolds. *Koreatown*. November 12.

Oh, Angela Eunjin, and Bong Hwan Kim. 1991. Don't fall for "divide and conquer." *Los Angeles Times*. September 4: B7.

Song, Kyung Mi. 1989. Korean merchants in black neighborhoods: Facing perils in the inner city. Master's Project, Graduate School of Journalism, Columbia University.

Venerose, Joseph R. 1987. Kimchi comes to Harlem: Blacklash to Korean immigration. Master's Project, Graduate School of Journalism. Columbia University.

Yoo, Woong Nyol. 1981. Business owners in New York's Harlem struggle against anti-Korean prejudice. *Koreatown*. October 19: 4.

8 The Middleman Minority Characteristics of Korean Immigrants in the United States

PYONG GAP MIN AND ANDREW KOLODNY

IN MANY COUNTRIES AROUND THE WORLD, PARTICULAR ETHNIC MI-
norities have played the role of tradesmen and small businessmen. These
groups include the Jews in Europe, the Chinese in Southeast Asia, the
Indians in Africa, and the Parsees in India (Eitzen 1971; Palmer 1957;
Porter 1981). These middlemen occupy a unique position of intermediate
status as they operate between the elite and the masses, between the
producers and the consumers (Bonacich 1973). The similarities in the
social, political, and economic situations of these various groups are reflected in what has been referred to as "the Jews of" metaphor (Zenner
1991: 52–54). For example, the Chinese have been described as "the Jews
of Siam" and "the Jews of the East," and Indians as "the Jews of East
Africa." Indeed, this metaphor has been applied to many different ethnic
groups by both Western and non-Western observers.

Middleman minorities are often hated by both sides of the host society's distinct status gap. They are perceived as being clannish, disloyal,
and unscrupulous outsiders. These stereotypes, along with the often different physical characteristics of the middlemen, serve to identify and
isolate them as scapegoats. During periods of economic or political dis-
tress, reactions to middlemen have included boycotts, riots, expulsions,
and genocide. For example, Indians in Africa have been the victims of
violent riots and expulsions (Palmer 1957); the Chinese have confronted
hostile host societies in both Thailand and the Philippines (Eitzen 1971);
and Jewish communities in Europe have suffered pogroms, expulsions,
and genocide (Zenner 1991).

Middleman minorities are usually found in societies marked by distinct strata boundaries, very often between two racial-ethnic groups (Rinder 1959). In the United States, stratification is diverse and strata boundaries are flexible. However, an economic gap, if not a status gap, does exist between whites and the minority residents of low-income inner-city neighborhoods. Many Jews in the United States played a vulnerable role as merchants, filling the gap between the residents of black and Hispanic neighborhoods and the dominant classes controlling banks, economic institutions, and political power structures (Porter 1981). Black anti-Semitism has been due, in part, to the economic role that Jews have played in black neighborhoods. Although Jewish Americans have been more sympathetic than other white ethnic groups to the civil rights movement and the economic struggles of blacks (Feagin 1989: 150), Jewish merchants were the victims of boycotts and violent riots in black neighborhoods across the country, including Harlem, Detroit, and Watts (Weisbord and Stein 1970: 45; Capeci 1985; Cohen 1970).

A large proportion of Korean immigrants in the United States currently occupy the same position in minority areas that many Jews once held. Korean immigrants have been highly entrepreneurial, and a significant proportion of Korean businesses are located in low-income black neighborhoods. Because of Korean entrepreneurs' minority-oriented commercial activities, many researchers (Bonacich 1980; Bonacich and Jung 1982; Kim 1981; Min 1991; Portes and Manning 1986; Waldinger 1989) have concluded that they play a middleman minority role in the United States.

Social scientists, focusing on different aspects of the middleman minority phenomenon, may disagree over the way middleman minorities are defined. However, based on the work of several scholars who have contributed to the development of middleman minority theory (Blalock 1967; Bonacich 1973; Bonacich and Modell 1980: Chap. 1; Porter 1981; Rinder 1959; Turner and Bonacich 1980; Zenner 1991), we have deduced that a middleman minority group in the United States would be likely to display the following characteristics: (1) a concentration in small business, (2) a focus on providing services to minority customers, (3) a dependence on U.S. corporations for supply of merchandise, (4) a strong ethnic cohesion, (5) a subjection to stereotyping, and (6) experiences of hostility from the host society. Our aim is to determine the extent to which Korean immigrants in the United States exhibit these characteristics.

The above summary provides a clear idea about our definition of middleman minorities. However, since Edna Bonacich's widely read arti-

cle (1973) has provided another definition, we may need a further clar-
ification of middleman minorities as applied in this chapter to the Korean
group. In her version of middleman minority theory, Bonacich argued
that middleman groups originate as sojourners or temporary residents in
host societies who plan to eventually return to their home countries. The
economic effects of sojourning include a tendency toward thrift to hasten
a return home and concentration in certain occupations easily liquidated
and transportable, such as commerce and trade. The noneconomic effects
of sojourning include a high degree of internal solidarity and the preser-
vation of distinctive cultural traits.

Several researchers have criticized Bonacich's middleman minority
theory for different reasons. Robert Cherry (1989) and Walter Zenner
(1980) have indicated that Jews in the United States, which Bonacich
considered a typical middleman minority, were not sojourners. Eugene
Wong (1985) criticized Bonacich's sojourning theory for stereotyping Chinese and Japanese in the United States as "sojourners," "inassimilable,"
and "aliens." Both Cherry and Wong do not agree with Bonacich's sojourning theory partly because it gives the impression that Jews or Chinese in the United States entered small business *by choice* and thus ob-
scures the reality that discrimination and disadvantage forced them to do
so. Still other researchers (Aldrich et al. 1983; Ward 1984) showed that,
based on empirical studies, sojourners are more likely to prefer other
employment over self-employment. Finally, Cherry (1989), Wong (1985),
and others disagree with the characterization of Jewish, Japanese, Chinese, and Korean Americans as middleman minorities because, in their
view, the middleman minority thesis, like the model minority thesis,
depicts Jewish and Asian groups as economically successful, therefore
excluding them from the opportunity to welfare programs.

We consider Korean immigrants in the United States a middleman
minority, but not in the way Bonacich (1973) defined it, that is, not in the
sense that Korean immigrants are sojourners. Survey studies (Min 1988a;
Park et al. 1990: 102) have shown that most Korean immigrants are permanent residents who plan to live in the United States for good. As we
discuss later, Korean immigrants' language barrier and other disadvantages for employment in the general labor market, not a sojourning orien-
tation, have been the main contributors to Koreans' concentration in
small business.[1] We consider playing the intermediary (commercial) role,
connecting producers and consumers, in the delivery of goods and services to be the central characteristic of middleman minorities. By considering Korean immigrants a middleman minority, we never intend to give

the impression that Koreans are economically successful and free from problems. We rather wish to emphasize that Korean immigrants' disadvantages for employment in the general labor market have forced them into small business and that their middleman role has increased intergroup conflicts and host hostility.

DATA SOURCES

Los Angeles County has the largest Korean population in the United States, approximately 200,000. The New York–New Jersey metropolitan area, home to about 130,000 Koreans, is the second largest Korean center. This chapter analyzes the middleman minority characteristics of Korean immigrants largely in the contexts of the Los Angeles and New York Korean communities. Although we have utilized findings from several previous studies on Korean immigrants, we rely mainly on the following sources.

First, our research included a survey of Korean merchants and their customers in black neighborhoods in New York City conducted in spring 1992. For the survey, 155 Korean merchants were randomly selected from directories of Korean merchants' associations in three predominantly black areas in which a large number of Korean businesses are located. Ninety-five of them were successfully interviewed over the phone by four Korean students. Five hundred households in the three areas, located close to the addresses of the selected Korean stores, were also randomly selected from the New York City public telephone directories. From these households, 151 telephone interviews were successfully completed by two white and two black students. Ninety-seven of the respondents were black and fifty-one were white.

Second, personal interviews with representatives of Korean trade associations in New York and Los Angeles provided another source of data. Interviews with leaders of business associations in Los Angeles were conducted in August 1990, and interviews in New York were conducted in the fall of 1991. These interviews focused primarily on Korean merchants' business-related intergroup conflicts and their reactive solidarity. They also provided information on the number of businesses in each category, the approximate racial distribution of customers, and the extent of hostility from customers.

Finally, stories relating to Korean-black conflicts have been well covered in Korean ethnic dailies. All articles on Korean-black conflicts that appeared in the *Korea Times New York* between 1970 and 1992 have been used, as have articles on Korean-black conflicts that appeared in the *Sae Gae Times* and the *Korea Central Daily New York* between 1988 and 1992. For an analysis of Korean-black conflicts in Los Angeles, articles published in the *Korea Times Los Angeles* have been used as the major data source.

CONCENTRATION IN SMALL BUSINESS

The current Korean community in the United States is largely a by-product of the 1965 Hart-Celler Act. Korean immigration steadily increased in the late 1960s and early 1970s. The annual number of Korean immigrants reached 30,000 in 1976 and continued to exceed that number until 1990 (Kim and Min 1992). Nearly a half million Koreans came to the United States as legal immigrants between 1970 and 1990. As a result, the Korean population in the United States increased from 70,000 in 1970 to 800,000 in 1990. Korean American scholars estimate that in 1993 there were approximately one million Koreans living in the United States.

The post-1965 Korean immigrants, particularly those who came in the 1970s, were highly educated and generally had held white-collar and professional occupations in Korea. However, because of language barriers and unfamiliarity with American society, most Korean immigrants could not retain their white-collar and professional occupations.[2] As an alternative to blue-collar occupations with which they were not familiar, Korean immigrants began opening small businesses (Min 1984). Owing to their lack of business experience and training, Korean immigrants in the 1970s were at a disadvantage when establishing their own businesses. Moreover, few of these Korean immigrants arrived with enough capital to start their own businesses. Therefore, most worked for many years as employees before they were able to establish their own businesses.

The Korean immigrants who have come to the United States since the early 1980s, in contrast to the Korean immigrants who arrived in the 1970s, have had enormous advantages in opening their own business. Working as employees for Korean-owned stores, newly arriving immigrants have been able to acquire business information and training more easily.[3] Also, due to the improvement in economic conditions in South Korea and recent changes in emigration policy there, Korean immigrants have been able to arrive to the United States with more money than they had previously been allowed to bring. For example, according to a pre-departure survey conducted in Seoul, a prospective Korean immigrant in 1986 planned to take an average of $14,500 to the United States and later send an additional average amount of $25,200 (Park et al. 1990: 66). Re-

TABLE 8.1 New York City Married Koreans' Self-employment Rates, by Sex

Job Type	Husbands		Wives		Total	
	N	%	N	%	N	%
Self-employed	172	61.4	102	48.8	274	56.0
Employed in Korean firms	69	24.6	76	36.4	145	29.7
Employed in non-Korean firms	39	13.9	31	14.8	70	14.3
Total	280	99.9	209	100.0	489	100.0

Source: Min 1992.

cently arriving Korean immigrants can also borrow money from friends and relatives who are already settled.

According to available data, the Korean community has witnessed a phenomenal increase in the self-employment rate since the early 1970s. For example, a survey conducted in 1973 (Bonacich, Light, and Wong 1976) indicated that 25 percent of Korean household heads in Los Angeles were self-employed. The self-employment rate of household heads in the Los Angeles Korean community increased to 40 percent by 1977 (Yu 1982). A 1986 survey showed that 45 percent of Korean workers in Los Angeles and Orange Counties were self-employed, with another 30 percent employed in Korean-owned stores (Min 1989). A 1988 survey of married Korean women in New York City revealed an even higher self-employment rate: 49 percent of Korean wives and 61 percent of Korean husbands in New York City were self-employed in 1988, with only about 14 percent of Korean husbands or wives employed in non-Korean firms (See Table 8.1). Case studies conducted in Chicago and Atlanta also indicate that approximately one-third of Korean adult immigrants in each of these cities are self-employed (Hurh and Kim 1988; Min 1988a). These studies demonstrate that Korean immigrants in the United States are heavily concentrated in small business, one of the common characteristics of middleman minorities.

A middleman minority bridges two groups in a racially or ethnically stratified society, often distributing products made by the dominant group to the consuming masses. Korean immigrants in the United States can be shown to play a role similar to the one played by traditional middleman minorities by presenting two aspects of Korean immigrant business: (1) a large proportion of Korean businesses are located in black and Hispanic neighborhoods, and (2) Korean merchants largely depend on U.S. corporations for the supply of their merchandise.

CONCENTRATION IN MINORITY NEIGHBORHOODS

Korean businesses serve whites, minority members, and co-ethnic customers. However, they serve a much larger proportion of black and Hispanic customers than would be dictated by national averages. Korean merchants in New York depend heavily on black and Hispanic customers.[4] Residentially, Koreans in New York City are heavily concentrated in Queens, with less than 9 percent residing in Brooklyn and the Bronx. However, a significant proportion of Korean-owned stores are located in Brooklyn and the Bronx. According to Korean business leaders, about 3,000 Korean-owned stores are located in Brooklyn, and 1,500 are located in the Bronx. They respectively make up 25 percent and 13 percent of the Korean-owned businesses in New York City. The vast majority of Korean-owned stores in Brooklyn are located in black neighborhoods in which black immigrants from Haiti, Jamaica, and other parts of the Caribbean islands constitute the majority of the population. The Bronx is heavily populated by Hispanics, and Korean businesses there are concentrated in these Hispanic neighborhoods. Korean merchants also own many businesses in Harlem (on Manhattan) and Jamaica (in Queens), two primarily black areas. In addition, more than 600 Korean peddlers and flea market vendors also serve mainly black and Hispanic customers.

We conducted a survey of Koreans in Los Angeles and Orange Counties in 1986, which included data on the racial composition of customers of Korean-owned businesses in these two counties. The percentage of Korean businesses serving primarily black and Hispanic customers was nearly equal to the percentage of those mainly serving non-Hispanic white customers, approximately 35 percent (the other 30% served Koreans). An examination of the ethnic composition of the population in Los Angeles and Orange Counties in 1980 and 1990 reveals that Korean merchants were serving a disproportionately high percentage of minority customers. Furthermore, Korean merchants' dependence on black and Hispanic customers has drastically increased since we conducted the 1986 survey. In 1985, Korean immigrants in Los Angeles began developing indoor swap meet businesses, "a new form of retailing in which individual sellers lease booths in a large building and sell their wares independently" (Chang 1990). According to the president of the California Swap Meet Sellers' Association, approximately 100 out of 130 indoor swap meets in Southern California were owned by Koreans in 1994, and 80 percent of the Korean-owned swap meets were located in black or Hispanic areas.

Types of Korean-Owned Businesses in Minority Neighborhoods

There is a significant correlation between the type of Korean-owned business and the ethnic composition of its customers. Generally speaking, Korean retail stores are heavily concentrated in minority neighborhoods. In Los Angeles, the most common type of Korean-owned business located primarily in black and Hispanic neighborhoods are grocery and liquor retail stores. According to an informal survey by the *Korea Times Los Angeles*, as of December 1991, 80 percent of the grocery and liquor stores and gas stations located in South Central Los Angeles were owned by Koreans (*Korea Times Los Angeles* 1992a). In other cities, the percentage of Korean-owned grocery and liquor businesses is even greater. For example, in 1982, Korean grocery, vegetable, and liquor stores constituted 31 percent of all Korean businesses in Atlanta (Min 1988a: 43), and 36 percent of Korean shop owners in Toronto engaged in the grocery business (Yu 1986). Korean immigrants clearly dominate the grocery and liquor retail trade, a prototype middleman occupation in many inner-city black neighborhoods throughout the country.

As noted above, Korean-owned outdoor and indoor swap meet retail stores have mushroomed in Los Angeles since 1985, an overwhelming majority of which are located in black and Hispanic neighborhoods. In New York, grocery and produce retail stores are the most common Korean business, and a large percentage of these are located in black and Hispanic neighborhoods. Retail stores dealing in wigs, handbags, jewelry, and other manufactured goods located in New York City's black and Hispanic neighborhoods are also owned primarily by Korean immigrants.

In contrast, Korean nonprofessional service businesses such as dry-cleaning shops and nail salons are heavily concentrated in white middle-class neighborhoods. According to the 1986 Los Angeles survey, 75 percent of Korean professionals such as medical doctors, lawyers, and accountants primarily served other Korean Americans (Min 1989).

Reasons for Concentration in Minority Neighborhoods

The two most common Korean-owned businesses in minority neighborhoods are (1) grocery, liquor, and produce retail stores and (2) stores dealing in fashion items such as wigs, clothing, handbags, jewelry, hats, and shoes. A close examination of the nature of each of these two types of small business will help us understand why they are overrepresented in minority areas.

In white neighborhoods, Korean-owned small grocery stores are unable to compete with large chain supermarkets. In low-income minority neighborhoods, due to the low spending capacity of the residents, high crime rates, and vandalism, large grocery chains are unwilling to invest in opening stores (Light and Bonacich 1988; Min 1988a: 73). For the same reasons, independent white business owners are also reluctant to open grocery stores in these areas (Min 1988a: 73). As a result, Korean immigrants can open up small grocery stores in these areas without fear of competition from large chain supermarkets or white store owners. Moreover, the capital needed to operate a store, including commercial rents, is significantly lower in a low-income minority area than in a middle-income white area, allowing disadvantaged Korean immigrants to start grocery businesses with a smaller amount of capital.

The other major type of Korean-owned stores in minority areas consists of those dealing in fashion items (wigs, handbags, hats, clothing, jewelry, shoes) imported from South Korea and other Asian countries. The easy access that Korean store owners have to Korean wholesalers and importers has led to these stores' rapid development.[5] These merchants have also not had to compete with department stores, which (like supermarket chains) are often unwilling to invest in low-income areas. Furthermore, structural changes in the U.S. economy have provided Korean-owned fashion stores with an additional advantage: Because fashion cycles have become shorter in the contemporary post-industrial economy, large department stores, which must operate through several channels before new merchandise can be ordered, have faced difficulties in quickly obtaining "hot" items that independent Korean merchants acquire directly from Korean suppliers (Chang 1990).

Comparison with Other Entrepreneurial Immigrant Groups

Korean businesses serve all three groups of customers: non-Hispanic whites, minority members, and Koreans. However, compared to other immigrant business owners, Korean merchants depend more heavily on low-income minority customers. Although Cubans in Miami have developed a high level of immigrant entrepreneurship, most Cuban businesses are located in Cuban enclaves and serve co-ethnic members (Portes 1987;

Portes and Bach 1985). Thus, Cuban immigrants in Miami follow an enclave economy pattern rather than a middleman minority pattern (Wilson and Portes 1980).

Chinese immigrants are also active in small businesses, but only a small percentage of Chinese businesses depend primarily on blacks and Hispanics. Chinese restaurants, garment manufacturing establishments, and gift shops selling manufactured goods imported from Asia are the three most common types of Chinese business (Kwong 1987; Zhou 1992). Whereas Chinese restaurants serve both Chinese customers and the general American population, Chinese gift shops, most of which are located in Chinatowns, serve visitors there, particularly white tourists. Chinese garment factories, as well as Korean garment factories, subcontract work from large manufacturers.

Small groceries owned by Iraqi Chaldean Christians in Detroit are heavily concentrated in black neighborhoods (Sengstock 1974). However, unlike Korean immigrants, who have concentrated their small business in minority neighborhoods in cities throughout the United States, Iraqi Christians appear to play this role only in Detroit.

Dependence on U.S. Corporations

The classic middleman merchant acts as a go-between, distributing products to the masses on behalf of the ruling class. In contemporary U.S. society, there is no fixed "ruling class" and strata boundaries are more flexible. However, it is true that large corporations dominate the American economy. Korean immigrants in the United States can be considered to play a middleman minority role not only because they cater to a disproportionately large number of minority customers but also because many of them depend on large American corporations for their merchandise. Korean grocery and liquor retailers distribute corporate products to minority customers, whereas Korean garment subcontractors, although not engaged in retail trade, also benefit large U.S. manufacturers by providing them with sources of low-cost labor (Bonacich 1980; Bonacich, Light, and Wong 1976; Light and Bonacich 1988).

Table 8.2 lists the major Korean-owned businesses in New York. Korean grocery and liquor stores constitute more than 12 percent of the total number of Korean businesses in the New York metropolitan area. Korean grocery and liquor retailers are prototype middleman merchants because they depend entirely on U.S. corporations for their supplies while operating stores primarily in minority neighborhoods. Two other types of

TABLE 8.2 Major Korean Businesses in New York (December 1991)

Business Type	Number		Percent	
Produce Retail	1,800		12.0	
Grocery and Liquor Retail	1,850	(2,950)*	12.3	(19.7)*
Dry Cleaning Service	1,500		10.0	
Wholesale of Asian- and Korean-Imported Items	500		3.3	
Retail of Asian- and Korean-Imported Items	2,220		14.8	
Nail Salons	1,400		9.3	
Fish Retail	720		4.8	
Garment Manufacturing	350		2.3	
Other	5,360		35.7	
Estimated Total	15,000		100.0	

Source: interviews with leaders of Korean business associations in New York
*Those 700 Korean-owned stores selling both green groceries and general groceries are included in both produce retail and grocery retail categories. Therefore, the total number of Korean-owned stores engaged in produce or grocery retail should be 2,950 rather than 3,650, the sum of the two subtotals.

Korean-owned businesses in New York that depend completely on U.S. corporate suppliers are produce shops and fish stores.

There are about 350 Korean-owned garment manufacturing businesses in New York. According to our interviews with staff members of the Korean Garment Subcontractors Association of New York, 95 percent of these establishments subcontract work from large garment manufacturers. Garment subcontracting is more common among Koreans in Los Angeles; there are approximately 700 Korean garment subcontractors there. Strictly speaking, Korean garment subcontractors are not middlemen because they do not serve disadvantaged minority customers. However, they can be considered middlemen in the sense that they connect U.S. manufacturers with non-Korean workers, particularly Hispanic employees. Chinese garment subcontractors usually hire co-ethnic workers—new immigrants from mainland China and Hong Kong (Kwong 1987)—and thus they do not play a middleman role. In contrast, Korean garment subcontractors in both Los Angeles and New York largely depend on Hispanic employees (Light and Bonacich 1988; My interview with the president of Korean Garment Subcontractors Association of New York). Hispanic garment employees are exploited, earning low wages and working under poor conditions, but the ultimate beneficiaries of their exploitation are the manufacturers, not the Korean garment sub-contractors (Bonacich 1993).

There are approximately five hundred Korean-owned wholesale businesses in the New York metropolitan area. Korean retail stores dealing in fashion items and related manufactured goods depend on these co-ethnic wholesalers to supply them with imported items from South Korea and other Asian countries. Because Korean retailers selling imported fashion items primarily serve disadvantaged minority members and have encountered hostility from their customers, they may be seen as middlemen, although in a limited sense.[6] Clearly, some types of Korean businesses exhibit more middleman minority characteristics than others.

Ethnic Cohesion

Many social scientists emphasize an unwillingness to assimilate and strong group ties as major middleman minority characteristics. While the middleman groups' internal cohesion often facilitates their commercial activities, it may also increase hostility toward them. Some researchers view such strong internal cohesion as a trait rooted in the middleman groups' culture (Light 1972), whereas others note that economic activities and ethnic cohesion mutually reinforce each other (Bonacich and Modell 1980; Reitz 1980).

Like middleman minority groups in other societies, Korean immigrants in the United States maintain strong ethnic cohesion. For example, Won Moo Hurh and Kwang Chung Kim (1988) report that 90 percent of Korean immigrants in Chicago spoke Korean at home and 82 percent were affiliated with one or more Korean organizations. A comparative study of three Asian ethnic groups revealed that a much larger proportion of Korean Americans (75%) than Filipino (50%) or Chinese Americans (19%) belonged to at least one ethnic association (Mangiafico 1988: 174). In June 1992, one month after the Los Angeles riot, KSCI-TV (Channel 18) asked Gallup to take a survey of Korean, Filipino, and Chinese Americans on ethnic attachment and assimilation. The results of this survey demonstrated that Korean respondents were more likely to retain their native language and form friendships with co-ethnic members than were the Filipino and Chinese respondents (*Korea Times Los Angeles* 1992d).

Is there a cultural basis for the strong ethnic cohesion found among Korean immigrants? Korea's cultural homogeneity may provide a cultural basis for the strong group ties formed by Korean immigrants in the United States (Min 1991). South Korea, from which almost all post-1965

Korean immigrants originated, is a small country where there is a single race with one language. Having only one language gives Korean immigrants an enormous advantage over other Asian immigrant groups in maintaining their ethnicity in the United States. Nearly all Korean immigrants can read Korean-language ethnic newspapers and understand ethnic television programs. Because regional differences are nearly insignificant in South Korea, Korean immigrants, regardless of their province of origin, identify themselves as Korean or Korean American. Indian and Filipino immigrants, on the other hand, need to use English in their ethnic media because they come from countries where many languages and dialects are spoken. Unlike Korean immigrants, they are more likely to identify themselves as belonging to a particular region (Pido 1986; Saran 1985). Chinese immigrants originated from several different countries: mainland China, Hong Kong, Singapore, and Vietnam. Immigrants from Taiwan and mainland China differ significantly in political ideologies, socioeconomic backgrounds, and other characteristics. Even immigrants from mainland China consist of several regional subgroups who use different native languages.

While the middle-class background of Korean immigrants plays an important role in their ability to establish a business, their ethnic resources may be equally as important (Light and Bonacich 1988: chap. 6; Min 1988a; Yoon 1996). Like middleman minorities in traditional societies, the commercial activities of Korean immigrants maximize their use of ethnic resources. Whereas help from their children is not as important for Korean business owners as it was for Chinese businesses during the prewar period (Light 1972), husband-wife coordination has been found to be central to Korean immigrants' success in small business (Min 1988a: 113–17). Although Korean merchants do hire non-Korean workers, only rarely do the latter handle cash or work as cashiers (Min 1988a). Ivan Light and Edna Bonacich (1988: 233) demonstrated that in 80 percent of the cases, Korean liquor store owners in Hollywood sold their businesses to other Koreans. Although Korean immigrants' class resources—individual earnings and money brought from Korea—are the most important source of their business capital, Korean immigrants are more likely to rely on private co-ethnic loans for business capital than are native-born Americans (Min 1988a: 80–81).

Korean immigrants' cultural homogeneity contributes to their internal cohesion, which in turn facilitates their ethnic business development. However, Korean immigrants' concentration in small business has also further enhanced their ethnic cohesion (Min 1988b, 1991). Concentration in small business has partly strengthened ethnic ties by segregating Koreans into an ethnic subeconomy. Most Korean immigrants are self-employed, and many other Koreans are employed in co-ethnic business. This economic segregation increases Koreans' social segregation. Koreans in such an ethnic subeconomy (which includes the vast majority of the Korean work force) interact with fellow Koreans, speak the Korean language, and practice Korean customs more frequently than do those Korean Americans in the general economy (Min 1989). Moreover, to deal efficiently with business-related intergroup conflicts, Korean businessmen have had to unite, further strengthening their ethnic cohesion.

STEREOTYPING AND HOSTILITY

Middleman minorities are commonly charged with being clannish, cheap, and disloyal. Irwin Rinder (1959) believed that these negative stereotypes, as well as the middleman minority's visibility and vulnerable position in the economy, has led to scapegoating. Here, we examine the degree to which black and white respondents accept negative stereotypes of Korean immigrants and discuss the various forms of hostility that Korean merchants have encountered.

In our 1992 New York City survey, black and white respondents were asked to indicate their level of agreement with four statements. Three of these four statements reflect the image of Korean merchants as overly money-oriented, inassimilable, and clannish. Table 8.3 shows the percentages of black and white respondents who either *strongly agreed* or *moderately agreed* with each statement. As expected, a large proportion of the respondents accepted each negative stereotype. However, a significantly larger percentage of black respondents than white respondents endorsed each statement. The greater number of negative responses of blacks is not surprising, considering that Korean merchants in black neighborhoods have encountered more hostility than those in white neighborhoods.

In their study of anti-Semitism in the United States, Gertrude Selznick and Stephen Steinberg (1969) included in one of their surveys the statement "Jews only care about their own kind." Forty-three percent of blacks agreed with this statement. We substituted *Koreans* for *Jews* in the statement for our 1992 survey and obtained a nearly identical result. Selznick and Steinberg conducted their study in the late 1960s, when many Jews occupied the same position in the ghetto economy that Koreans presently occupy. While the middleman group itself has changed, the stereotype remains the same.

TABLE 8.3 Percentages of Black and White Respondents who Accepted
Stereotypes of Koreans

Stereotypes	Black Rs (N=97)	White Rs (N=50)	Significance
(1) Koreans are overly concerned with making money.	45.4	26.0	$p < .05$
(2) Koreans do not try to learn English and American customs.	34.4	24.4	$p > .1$
(3) Koreans only care about other Koreans.	44.3	30.0	$p < .1$
(4) Koreans are in general rude and nasty people.	22.7	8.0	$p < .05$

Source: Min 1996: 124.

The economic position, visibility, ethnic cohesion, and outsider status, of middleman minorities are believed to provoke hostility toward them. The middleman minority is often disliked by both sides of the traditional society's distinct status gap. Although our 1992 New York City survey indicated that a significant percentage of whites accepted negative stereotypes of Koreans, Korean immigrants have not had to confront white anti-Korean hostility or active anti-Korean governmental policies. Whereas Korean merchants in Hispanic neighborhoods have not encountered overt hostility (Cheng and Espiritu 1989), Korean merchants in black neighborhoods have suffered racially motivated verbal and physical attacks, boycotts, looting, arson, and murder.

The recent riots in South Central Los Angeles, in which about 2,300 Korean businesses were looted or burned, have attracted attention to Korean-black conflicts there. However, in the 1980s Korean-black conflicts were more severe in New York than in Los Angeles. In that decade, the New York Korean community encountered four long-term black boycotts of Korean stores and several cases of arson. These boycotts, which were usually organized by black nationalist groups against a particular store, often spread to other neighborhood Korean-owned stores.

The longest and most intense anti-Korean boycott occurred in 1990 in the Church Avenue–Fulton Street area of Brooklyn. This boycott, like the others, began after a scuffle occurred between a black customer accused of shoplifting and a Korean employee accused of assaulting the customer. When the residents heard that a black customer had been beaten in the store, they quickly gathered and began picketing in front of the store. A few days later, black boycotters began picketing a Korean store across the street.[7] During the first week of the boycott, over 150 black people rallied in front of the two stores. Although the boycott had originally been organized by a Haitian community organization, Sonny Carson's black nationalist group, the December 12th Movement, intervened and turned the demonstration into a long-term boycott that lasted for nearly eighteen months. The boycott continued until the owner of the grocery store originally targeted sold his business to another Korean.

During the boycott, several Korean merchants in Brooklyn were verbally and physically assaulted. An owner of one of the boycotted stores was spat upon and beaten by twenty young black men on the way home from his store, and the other store owner's wife was beaten by a picketer inside her own shop (*Sae Gae Times* 1990a). Another Korean merchant in the area was robbed and beaten after arguing with a customer who had eaten fruit without paying; two days later, a gunshot was fired into his store and a Mexican employee was attacked and beaten. The store was later boycotted and picketed for three days (*Korea Central Daily New York* 1990).

Although there were Korean-black tensions in Los Angeles during the 1980s, the Los Angeles Korean community maintained better relations with the black community than did their New York counterparts before 1990. By the summer of 1990, Korean-black tensions in Los Angeles nevertheless became severe: Anti-Korean pamphlets calling for the elimination of Korean merchants from black communities were widely distributed by black nationalists, and several Korean merchants in South Central Los Angeles were attacked in their stores (*Sae Gae Times* 1990b). In March 1991, a fourteen-year-old black girl in South Central Los Angeles was shot to death by a female Korean store owner in a confrontation over an unpaid bottle of orange juice. The girl had punched the owner three times before she was shot. A few months later, a black man was shot to death by a Korean liquor store owner in South Central Los Angeles while attempting to rob the merchant. These two incidents escalated black anti-Korean violence in the latter half of 1991; several Koreans were physically attacked and the two stores in which the shootings had occurred were boycotted and firebombed.

Black hostility toward Korean merchants climaxed during the 1992 Los Angeles riots. During these riots, approximately 2,300 Korean businesses were looted or burned, one Korean was killed, and forty-six Koreans were injured (*Korea Times Los Angeles* 1992b). The property damages Korean merchants suffered were estimated to be more than 350 million

TABLE 8.4 Damage Statistics of Korean-Owned Businesses (Looted or Burned) in Los Angeles, May 6, 1991–May 11, 1992, Compiled by *Radio Korea*

Categories of Businesses	Number Estimated	Costs Damage ($)
Car Repair Shops	61	9,707,000
Beauty Salons	39	5,607,300
Dry Cleaners	82	21,269,000
Electronic Stores	60	16,085,000
Furniture Stores	21	4,215,000
Gas Stations	39	4,792,000
Jewelry Shops	49	6,316,000
Liquor Stores	187	41,812,000
Grocery Markets	273	66,873,850
Swap Meets	336	54,941,300
Restaurants	93	10,797,900
Clothing Stores	222	34,458,734
Video Shops	29	4,192,500
Other	376	65,894,810
Total	1,867	346,962,394

Source: Korea Times Los Angeles, English Edition, May 11, 1992

dollars, accounting for about 45 percent of the total property damages from the riots (see Table 8.4). Although a disproportionate number of small businesses in South Central Los Angeles were owned by Koreans at that time, there is evidence that Korean merchants were specifically targeted. An inquiry by the Federal Bureau of Investigation indicated that in planning the riots, black gangs had selected specific Korean-owned stores to be destroyed and looted (*Korea Times Los Angeles* 1992c). Although the violence did not begin there, businesses in the neighboring community of Koreatown, over three miles away, were looted and burned as the rioting progressed.

During periods of stress and unrest, middleman minorities have often served as a scapegoat, acting as a shield for the superordinate by bearing the brunt of the subordinate's hostility. The Los Angeles riots began after a nearly all-white jury's acquittal of the policemen that had beaten Rodney King. Yet most white Americans remained insulated from black anger while Korean immigrants and their stores were attacked. Acting as scapegoats during the riots, Korean immigrants replayed the classic middleman minority role. Historically, governments have often failed to protect the rights of the middleman minority during periods of civil unrest, often taking a passive position (Blalock 1967: 84). This passive position was exemplified by the Los Angeles police department's failure to protect Korean merchants during the riots (*Korea Times Los Angeles* 1992e). The police's failure to enforce a court order to keep picketers fifty feet away from the entrance of the Family Red Apple Market during the 1990 Brooklyn boycott may be seen as another example of the government's failing to protect the rights of a middleman minority (*Korea Times New York* 1990).

As noted, Korean merchants have encountered overt hostility only in black neighborhoods. We must examine the role of antimiddleman ideologies in provoking host hostility to help explain why Korean merchants in white and Hispanic neighborhoods have not encountered such overt hostility. In response to Bonacich's article on middleman minorities (1973), Sheldon Stryker points out that in some societies, middleman minorities have not faced host hostility and hatred (1974). According to Stryker, such antagonism develops in the context of a particular political configuration. He noted that middleman minorities have been persecuted in societies where an ideology associated with "emergent nationalism" has developed. In his recent book on middleman minorities, Walter Zenner argues that antimiddleman ideologies play a critical role in spawning hatred toward middleman minorities. In his view, "Anti-Semitism fits the nationalist conception that the nation must control its own economy and sees dangers in letting important sections fall under the control of strangers, such as Jews" (1991: 49). Like Stryker, Zenner suggests that host hostility toward middleman minorities develops in societies that are influenced by nationalist ideologies.

Black nationalists have consistently emphasized the importance of economic autonomy in black communities (Carmichael and Hamilton 1967; Turner 1973). In their analysis of Korean-black conflicts in Los Angeles, Ivan Light and his colleagues (1994) argue that black nationalism has played a significant role in shaping the anti-Korean views of blacks. In the past, black nationalists have focused on the economic role played by Jews, Italians, and other white ethnic groups in black communities. Presently, they are targeting Korean merchants, who own a large number of businesses in black neighborhoods.

Boycotts of Korean stores are commonly organized by black nationalist organizations. Sonny Carson, chairperson of the December 12th Movement, has played an influential role in organizing and intervening in all five major boycotts of Korean stores in New York. In many interviews during the boycotts, Carson expressed the black nationalist concern about outsiders' economic invasion of the black community. During a 1990 interview, for example, he stated: "The Koreans become intruders, upstarts, exploiters. . . . You get a certain ethnic dynamic that can easily become uncontrollable. . . . Right now, all these folks come in, make the money, and take it out before the sun goes down" (English and Yuh 1990). Black nationalists have referred to Korean merchants as "vampires" and "bloodsuckers" who prey upon the black community. This perception is widely accepted in the black community. In our 1992 New York City survey, 54 percent of black respondents agreed with the statement "Korean merchants drain black economic resources."

Conclusion

The middleman minority phenomenon is largely the product of pre-industrial and colonial societies, and its development is closely related to the economic, social, and political structures of such societies. Theoretically, contemporary American society in the advanced capitalist stage is unlikely to be conducive to the development of a middleman minority. However, Korean immigrants in the United States clearly exhibit their characteristics.

In traditional societies, middleman minorities bridged the status gap between the ruling class and the masses. Highly entrepreneurial Korean immigrants in the United States operating small businesses in inner-city minority areas may be seen as filling the gap that exists between the margins of the low-income black underclass and the dominant white society. By distributing corporate products to these disadvantaged inner-city minority customers, Korean grocers and liquor retailers play a role similar to that of a middleman minority. Although Korean-owned businesses are diverse and some exhibit more middleman minority characteristics than others, Korean immigrants are more likely to engage in minority-oriented businesses than any other immigrant-ethnic group.

Korean immigrants, like middleman minorities in other societies, maintain strong ethnic cohesion. They utilize their ethnic resources, along with their class resources, to facilitate the development of their business. Korean immigrants' ethnic cohesion might be due, in part, to Korea's cultural homogeneity. However, there is little doubt that Korean immigrants' concentration in small business has enhanced their ethnic cohesion by socially and economically segregating Koreans from mainstream U.S. society. Furthermore, Koreans' business-related intergroup conflicts have solidified not only Korean merchant relations but the Korean community as a whole.

Middleman minorities often confront hostility from the host society. Yet Korean merchants operating businesses in white and Hispanic neighborhoods have not received the overt hostility that those operating in black neighborhoods have suffered. Black hostility toward Korean merchants climaxed during the 1992 Los Angeles riots, during which 2,300 Korean-owned stores were destroyed. Many black nationalists have emphasized the importance of economic autonomy in their communities and opposed nonblack businesses in their neighborhoods. The lack of such an antimiddleman, nationalist ideology in white and Hispanic neighborhoods may explain the dissimilar reactions to Korean merchants in different neighborhoods.

As we can see from the Jews in Medieval Europe, the Chinese in the Philippines during the Spanish colonial period, and the Asian Indians in South Africa, traditional middleman minorities passed down their middleman occupations over generations. However, second-generation Korean Americans are not inheriting middleman businesses from their parents. The 1990 census shows that only 11 percent of native-born Koreans in the Los Angeles metropolitan area were self-employed, a rate lower than even that of the native-born white population (13%) (Light and Roach 1996). Traditional middleman minorities, located in rigidly stratified societies, maintained their middleman businesses over generations because they were not allowed to move into more desirable occupations. In contrast, voluntary immigrant groups in contemporary America have far more opportunities for social mobility than traditional middleman minorities. Therefore, native-born Korean Americans, who are fluent in English and familiar with American customs, are not attracted to running businesses in minority neighborhoods which involve long hours and physical danger. Contemporary Korean immigrants have, for now, filled the small business vacuums in minority neighborhoods created by Jewish and other white ethnic groups' intergenerational mobility. Newer immigrant groups are likely to undertake Korean immigrants' middleman businesses in the future, as Korean immigrants' children move into the mainstream economy.

NOTES

1. This interpretation is close to the view held by Robert Cherry (1989) and Eugene Wong (1985), that discrimination forced Jews and Chinese in the United States to make the occupational adjustment into small business.

2. Korean immigrants, although highly educated, have more language barriers than other Asian immigrant groups with white-collar and professional backgrounds.

For example, Filipino and Indian immigrants spoke English in their native countries and thus usually arrive to the United States more fluent in spoken English than Korean immigrants.

3. Since Korean immigrants are concentrated in several business specialties, it is now easier for new Korean immigrants to acquire business information from their relatives and friends already involved in such specialties.

4. Some Hispanic Americans, like African Americans and some Caribbean Americans, are black. For this reason, many social scientists prefer to use the term *African Americans* rather than *blacks* to differentiate blacks of African origin from black Hispanic Americans. However, in this chapter we use the term *blacks* and *Korean-black conflicts* instead of *African Americans* and *Korean-African American conflicts* because Korean merchants serve Caribbean immigrant blacks as well as native-born African Americans, and Koreans have been subject to hostility by both groups of the black population.

5. Non-Korean white Americans also import fashion items from South Korea and other Asian countries, but they distribute these imported items mainly to department stores in white areas.

6. Edna Bonacich considered Japanese farmers in California in the early twentieth century a middleman minority (1973; Bonacich and Modell 1980). However, as indicated by David O'Brien and Stephen Fugita (1982), Japanese farmers did not depend on non-Japanese suppliers, nor did they hire non-Japanese employees. Thus, they never acted as economic intermediaries in the movement of goods or services. Korean retail store owners who depend on Korean suppliers but largely serve minority customers possess more middleman characteristics than did Japanese farmers in California.

7. Blacks picketed this store because its owner had allowed a Korean employee from the originally boycotted store to hide in his store from angry black residents.

REFERENCES

Aldrich, Howard, John Carter, Trevor Jones, and David McEvoy. 1983. From periphery to peripheral: The South Asian petit bourgeoisie in England. Chap. 1 in *Research in the sociology of work*, vol. 2, edited by I. H. Simpson and R. Simpson. Greenwich, Conn.: JAI Press.

Blalock, Herbert. 1967. *Toward a theory of minority group relations.* New York: Wiley.

Bonacich, Edna. 1973. A theory of middleman minorities. *American Sociological Review* 37 (5): 583–94.

———. 1980. Middleman minorities and advanced capitalism. *Ethnic Group* 2:211–19.

———. 1993. Asian and Latino immigrants in the Los Angeles garment industry. Chap. 3 in *Immigration and entrepreneurship: Culture, capital, and ethnic networks*, edited by Ivan Light and Parminder Bhachu. New Brunswick, N.J.: Transaction Publishers.

Bonacich, Edna, and Tae Hawn Jung. 1982. A portrait of Korean small business in Los Angeles. Chap. 4 in *Koreans in Los Angeles: Prospects and promises*, edited by Eui-Young Yu, Earl H. Phillips, and Eun-Sik Yang. Los Angeles: Koryo Research Institute and Center for Korean-American and Korean Studies, California State University.

Bonacich, Edna, Ivan Light, and Charles Choy Wong. 1976. Small business among

Koreans in Los Angeles. Pp. 437–49 in *Counterpoint: Perspective on Asian America*, edited by Emma Gee. Los Angeles: Asian American Studies Center.

Bonacich, Edna, and John Modell. 1980. *The economic basis of ethnic solidarity: Small business in the Japanese American community*. Berkeley and Los Angeles: University of California Press.

Capeci, Dominic, Jr. 1985. Black-Jewish relations in wartime Detroit: The Marsch, Loving, and Wolf surveys and race riots of 1943. *Jewish Social Studies* 5:221–42.

Carmichael, Stokeley, and Charles Hamilton. 1967. *Black power: The politics of liberation in America*. New York: Vintage Books.

Chang, Edward. 1990. New urban crisis: Korean-black conflicts in Los Angeles. Unpublished dissertation, Ethnic Studies Department, University of California at Berkeley.

Cheng, Lucie, and Yen Espiritu. 1989. Korean business in black and Hispanic neighborhoods: A study of intergroup relations. *Sociological Perspectives* 32 (4): 521–34.

Cherry, Robert. 1989. Middleman minority theories: Their implications for black-Jewish relations. *Journal of Ethnic Studies* 17 (4): 117–38.

Cohen, Nathan. 1970. *The Los Angeles Riots: A sociological study*. New York: Praeger.

Eitzen, D. Stanley. 1971. Two minorities: The Jews of Poland and the Chinese of the Philippines. Pp. 117–38 in *Majority and minority: The dynamics of racial and ethnic relations*, edited by Norman R. Yetman and C. Hoy Steele. Boston: Allyn and Bacon.

English, Merle, and Ji-Yeon Yuh. 1990. Black-Korean conflict simmers. *Newsday*, February 13: 4.

Feagin, Joe R. 1989. *Racial and ethnic relations*. Englewood Cliffs, N.J.: Prentice-Hall.

Hurh, Won Moo, and Kwang Chung Kim. 1988. Uprooting and adjustment: A sociological study of Korean immigrants' mental health. Final Report Submitted to the National Institute of Mental Health.

Kim, Hyun Sook, and Pyong Gap Min. 1992. The post–1965 Korean immigrants: Their characteristics and settlement patterns. *Korea Journal of Population and Development* 21 (2): 121–43.

Kim Illsoo. 1981. *New urban immigrants: The Korean community in New York*. Princeton, N.J.: Princeton University Press.

Korea Central Daily New York. 1990. Black boycott spreads to Belmont Ave. August 28.

Korea Times Los Angeles. 1992a. Korean businesses in South Central Los Angeles. January 1.

——. 1992b. Special issue on the April 29 race riots. May 23.

——. 1992c. Korean stores were selectively targeted for arson. June 11.

——. 1992d. Korean Americans are the most insulated group. July 2.

——. 1992e. The Los Angeles City government should apologize to the Korean community. July 7.

Korea Times New York. 1990. "I will enforce the temporary restraining order." September 19.

Kwong, Peter. 1987. *The new Chinatown*. New York: Noonday Press.

Light, Ivan. 1972. *Ethnic enterprise in America: Business and welfare among Chinese, Japanese and blacks*. Berkeley and Los Angeles: University of California Press.

Light, Ivan, and Edna Bonacich. 1988. *Immigrant entrepreneurs: Koreans in Los Angeles, 1965–1982*. Berkeley and Los Angeles: University of California Press.

Light, Ivan, Hadas Har-Chvi, and Kenneth Kan. 1994. Black/Korean conflict in Los

Angeles. Chap. 4 in *Managing divided cities*, edited by Seamus Dunn. Keele: University of Keele.

Light, Ivan, and Elizabeth Roach. 1996. Self-employment: Mobility ladder or economic lifeboat? Chap. 7 in *Ethnic Los Angeles*, edited by Roger Waldinger and Mehdi Bozorgmehr. New York: Russell Sage Foundation.

Mangiafico, Luciano. 1988. *Contemporary Asian immigrants: Patterns of Filipino, Korean, and Chinese settlement in the United States*. New York: Praeger.

Min, Pyong Gap. 1984. From white-collar occupations to small business: Korean immigrants' occupational adjustment. *Sociological Quarterly* 25 (3): 333–52.

——. 1988a. *Ethnic business enterprise: Korean small business in Atlanta*. Staten Island, N.Y.: Center for Migration Studies.

——. 1988b. Korean immigrant entrepreneurship: A multivariate analysis. *Journal of Urban Affairs* 10 (2): 197–212.

——. 1989. Some positive functions of ethnic business for an immigrant community: Koreans in Los Angeles. Final Report Submitted to the National Science Foundation.

——. 1991. Cultural and economic boundaries of Korean ethnicity: A comparative analysis. *Ethnic and Racial Studies* 14 (2): 225–41.

——. 1992. Korean immigrant wives' overwork. *Korea Journal of Population and Development* 21 (1): 23–36.

——. 1996. *Caught in the middle: Korean merchants in America's multiethnic cities*. Berkeley and Los Angeles: University of California Press.

Noel, Peter. 1981. Koreans vie for Harlem dollars. *New York Amsterdam News*, July 4.

O'Brien, David, and Stephen Fugita. 1982. Middleman minority concept: Its explanatory value in the case of the Japanese in California agriculture. *Pacific Sociological Review* 25 (2): 185–204.

Palmer, Mabel. 1957. *The history of Indians in Natal: Natal regional survey*, vol. 10. Oxford: Oxford University Press.

Park, Insook Han, James Fawcett, Fred Arnold, and Robert Gardner. 1990. *Korean immigrants to the United States: A pre-departure analysis*. Paper No. 114. Honolulu: Population Institute, East-West Center.

Pido, Antonio J. A. 1986. *The Filipinos in America: Macro/micro dimension of immigration and integration*. Staten Island, N.Y.: Center for Migration Studies.

Porter, Jack N. 1981. The urban middleman: A comparative analysis. *Comparative Social Research* 4:199–215.

Portes, Alejandro. 1987. The social origin of the Cuban enclave economy of Miami. *Sociological Perspectives* 30 (4): 340–72.

Portes, Alejandro, and Robert Bach. 1985. *Latin journey*. Berkeley and Los Angeles: University of California Press.

Portes, Alejandro, and Robert Manning. 1986. The immigrant enclave: Theory and empirical examples. Chap. 2 in *Competitive ethnic relations*, edited by Susan Olzak and Joane Nagel. New York: American Press.

Reitz, Jeffrey. 1980. *The survival of ethnic groups*. Toronto: McGraw-Hill.

Rinder, Irwin. 1959. Strangers in the land: Social relations in the status gap. *Social Problems* 6 (3): 253–60.

Sae Gae Times. 1990a. [Man Ho Park] responded to boycotters with a six million lawsuit. May 24.

——. 1990b. LA Korean stores become targets of attack by black youngsters. August 16.

Saran, Parmatam. 1985. *Asian Indian experiences in the United States*. Cambridge, Mass.: Schenkman Books.

Selznick, Gertrude, and Stephen Steinberg. 1969. *The tenacity of prejudice*. Berkeley and Los Angeles: University of California Press.

Sengstock, Mary. 1974. Iraqi Christians in Detroit: An analysis of an ethnic occupation. Chap. 2 in *Arabic speaking communities in American cities*, edited by B. Aswad. Staten Island, N.Y.: Center for Migration Studies.

Stryker, Sheldon. 1958. Social structure and prejudice. *Social Problems* 6 (4): 340–54.

——. 1974. A theory of middleman minorities: A comment. *American Sociological Review* 38:281–82.

Turner, James. 1973. The sociology of black nationalism. Pp. 232–52 in *The death of white sociology*, edited by Joyce Ladner. New York: Random House.

Turner, Jonathan, and Edna Bonacich. 1980. Toward a composite theory of middleman minorities. *Ethnicity* 7 (2): 144–58.

Waldinger, Roger. 1989. Structural opportunity or ethnic advantage? Immigrant business development in New York. *International Migration Review* 23 (1): 48–72.

Ward, Robin. 1984. Minority settlement and the local economy. In *Approaches to economic life: Economic restructuring, employment, and the social division of labor*, edited by Bryan Robert, Ruth Finnegan, and Duncan Gallie. Manchester: Manchester University Press.

Weisbord, Robert, and Arthur Stein. 1970. *Bittersweet encounter*. Westport, Conn.: Negro University Press.

Wilson, Kenneth, and Alejandro Portes. 1980. Immigrant enclaves: An analysis of the labor market experiences of Cubans in Miami. *American Journal of Sociology* 86 (2): 295–316.

Wilson, William. 1987. *The truly disadvantaged: The inner city, the underclass, and public policy*. Chicago: University of Chicago Press.

Wong, Eugene. 1985. Asian American middleman minority theory: The framework of an ethnic myth. *Journal of Ethnic Studies* 3 (1): 51–86.

Yoon, In-Jin. 1991. The changing significance of ethnic and class resources in immigrant businesses: The case of Korean businesses in Chicago. *International Migration Review* 25 (2): 303–32.

Yu, Eui-Young. 1982. Occupation and work patterns of Korean immigrants. Chap. 3 in *Koreans in Los Angeles: Prospects and promises*, edited by Eui-Young Yu, Earl H. Phillips, and Eun Sik Yang. Los Angeles: Koryo Research Institute and Center for Korean-American and Korean Studies, California State University.

Yu, Jong Soo. 1986. Koreans in Canada. Chap. 5 in *The current status and future prospects of overseas Koreans*, edited by Dae Kil Lee. New York: Research Institute on World Affairs.

Zenner, Walter. 1980. Middleman minority theories: A critical review. Pp. 419–25 in *Sourcebook on the new immigration*, edited by Bryce Laporte. New Brunswick, N.J.: Transaction Books.

——. 1991. *Minorities in the middle: A cross-cultural analysis*. Albany: State University of New York Press.

Zhou, Min. 1992. *Chinatown*. Philadelphia: Temple University Press.

Part 3 CHICAGO

9 Contemplating Black-Korean Conflict in Chicago

InChul Choi

"No respect, no dollars" and "no exchange, no refund" are slogans frequently shouted by African American boycotters in front of Korean American stores. Why are African Americans boycotting Korean American stores? How much of what the marchers complain about the merchants is authentic? What needs to be done to mitigate the so-called black-Korean conflict? What is the significance of this relatively new urban phenomenon for the Korean American community in the United States? These are the questions I will try to answer in this chapter.

Like all major U.S. cities, Chicago has experienced its share of black-Korean conflict during the years 1990–94. Although the conflict has been neither as enduring as the Red Apple boycott in New York nor as dramatic as the 1992 riots in Los Angeles, Korean American merchants in Chicago have been threatened with boycotts and their stores have been damaged in celebrations of the Chicago Bulls' NBA championships. Though there were agonizing and tormenting moments on several occasions, it seems that the conflict has been relatively well contained in Chicago, partly due to the concerted mediation efforts of the Korean American community and partly due to sheer luck, namely, the lack of incitant events such as the death of Latasha Harlins in Los Angeles.

Incidents of Conflict and Their Containment in Chicago

From 1990 to 1994, there have been three boycotts staged in Korean American shopping strips in Chicago. The first one began in Roseland on the far South Side of the city on June 30, 1990, and continued until July 11 (Lee 1994). The second boycott was staged on August 3, 1991, and was fueled by demonstrations on several subsequent Saturdays, and the third occurred on December 18, 1993. Both of these later boycotts happened in Englewood, and the boycott demonstrations lasted just two to three hours. In all three boycotts, the demands of the marchers included the standard repertoire: respectful treatment of customers, employment opportunities, a fair refund and return policy, community contributions, and banking in African American banks.

The 1990 Roseland boycott, organized by a local alderman, ended in a peaceful manner when all forty-two Korean American store owners involved paid membership dues totaling $6,300 ($150 per store) to the Roseland Business Development Council (RBDC), a local economic development organization with which the alderman had close ties. It was later found out that collecting these fees for the RBDC had in fact been the ulterior motive of the boycott leaders. The 1991 and 1993 Englewood boycotts were organized, respectively, by the Chicago chapter of the Majestic Eagles, a national organization that supports small minority business and minority business, and the 21st Century Voices of Total Empowerment (VOTE), a political group alleged to have links with a local gang organization called the Gangster Disciples.

In the Majestic Eagles boycott, only about twenty people marched, including some high school students. In retrospect, the boycott organizers had a twofold aim: to promote an African American–operated mini-mall, which had just opened in the middle of a Korean American shopping strip, and to support an ousted alderman, who had fallen into the status of a paper tiger but was trying desperately to regain his fading base in the community. The 21st Century VOTE leaders, despite their apparent protest against Korean American business practices, also had two ulterior motives behind their boycott efforts. They wanted to test their mobilizing capacity in preparation for their support of two local candidates running for seats in the U.S. House of Representatives and Illinois State House of Representatives in the upcoming primary election on March 15, 1994, and to market their own merchandise in Korean American stores. Their alleged link to a gang organization, however, raised questions of legitimacy in the eyes of Korean American merchants, the mainstream media, city officials, and other African American community leaders.

Why were these boycotts relatively contained in Chicago? Their containment does not at all mean that the degree of African American discontent is negligible, the merchants are particularly "nicer," or socio-economic indicators in urban ghettos are more promising. There are, however, several factors that led to the boycott containment, some specific to Chicago and some general to the overall national situation.

First, leadership with vision and selfless commitment to the common good is a rare quality that can make the followers have something akin to a "conversion" experience, as illustrated in the charismatic leadership of Malcolm X and Martin Luther King, Jr. (West 1993). The boycott organizers in Chicago, however, showed petty leadership in their desire to capitalize on African Americans' discontent with Korean American merchants in order to advance their own ends—namely, to attain their own private economic gains or to promote their political ambition by using the merchants as scapegoats. They did not seem to care to change the situation, that is, improve relations between the two groups, as long as their own self-interests were fulfilled. Leadership with contaminated motives, dictated by an overt or covert selfish agenda, cannot create a volcanic power for any organized activity.

Second, the dichotomy of "good guys/bad guys" is hard to identify in black-Korean conflicts. A target group must be portrayed as the "bad guys" in order to intensify the magnitude of mobilization. It is not difficult to rebuke white supremacists, the Ku Klux Klan, or Jim Crow legislation as immoral. Initially, Korean Americans may naturally be sympathetic with the merchants, and African Americans antipathetic with the merchants, but a thorough observation leads concerned citizens of both communities to the conclusion that the merchants' and consumers' complaints are equally understandable. Furthermore, these problems are magnified by the media, at the cost of losing the bigger picture. Blocking our eyes with our hands will not erase the scenery of inner cities in America, which is indeed bleak, blighted, and broken.

Third, there was no concrete sparking incident in Chicago that could have ignited lengthy and potent boycotts, such as the Church Avenue incident in New York or the Soon Ja Du–Latasha Harlins incident in Los Angeles. Had there been an injured Haitian woman or a teenage girl shot and killed, a concrete, singled-out "victim" of the black-Korean conflict, the situation might have been different.

Fourth, a well-funded and skillfully orchestrated program with the merchants, community leaders, and organizers, on the one side, and African American city officials and community leaders, on the other, has helped ease the tension and contain the boycott. The Korean American Community Services (KACS) in Chicago received a three-year grant in the amount of $230,000 from the United Way of Chicago in July 1991 to launch the Community Mediation Project (CMP) to improve African American–Korean American relations. In addition to this grant, the KACS received program funds from the Polk Brothers, Kraft General Foods, the Quaker Oats Foundations, and the Wood Fund of Chicago. These grants allowed the KACS to hire two full-time community mediators, one Korean American and one African American, who assisted the merchants in establishing links with community organizations in the area where they do business. The mediators also endeavored to expose the residents to Korean culture and to publicize the merchants' contribution to the community. Hand in hand with the Korean American Merchants Association of Chicago (KAMAC), an affiliate of the KACS which has its office at KACS headquarters, a rigorous program has been carried out since 1990 to alleviate the tension. It is much more efficient and effective to establish a durable and systematic apparatus in the Korean American organizational setting than the African American counterpart, because the conflict is much more urgent and threatening to Korean Americans than to African Americans, for whom it may be merely one of many issues, perhaps toward the very bottom of their agenda. The apparatus, however, cannot succeed, if it does not extensively and intensively coordinate with the African American community.

The Chicago Bulls' NBA Championship Disturbance

Despite the containment of boycotts and a concerted mediation program, Korean American merchants in Chicago experienced their share of looting and destruction in June 1991 and again in June 1992 when the Chicago Bulls won the NBA championship. After the Bulls won the first championship, seven Korean American stores were looted, resulting in total financial damages of about half a million dollars. This unexpected incident led the Korean American community to extensively lobby for police protection when it began to seem likely that the Bulls would repeat their championship victory in spring 1992. The Los Angeles riots on April 29, 1992, further alarmed the Korean American community in Chicago, which then escalated its efforts to lobby the Chicago Police Department, the City Commission on Human Relations, the office of Governor Jim Edgar, the Cook County State's Attorney's office, and the Illinois State Police.

Although an additional 1,300 policemen were deployed during the final game of the Bulls' championship game on June 14, 1992, forty-five

TABLE 9.1 1992 Bulls' Championship Damage, Tabulated by KACS

	African Americans	Arab Americans	Korean Americans	Total
Number of stores damaged	61	116	45	222
Estimated amount of damages ($)	2,950,440	6,578,900	4,929,210*	14,458,550

Source: KACS 1992b

* A five-story department store was totally destroyed by arson. The estimated damage of that store was three million dollars.

Korean stores were set on fire and looted, resulting in financial damages of roughly five million dollars. Of the additional officers dispatched throughout the city on the night of the disturbance, seven hundred were sent to the North Side area to protect white neighborhoods and businesses, three hundred were positioned around the Bulls' stadium, and three hundred were scattered on the South and West Sides, predominantly African American neighborhoods where many Korean and Arab American businesses are located.[1] After midnight, more police officers were transferred from the North to South Side, but by then most of the damage had been done. This situation appears to be analogous to the Los Angeles riots, in which preferential police protection was given to the white Beverly Hills area while South Central and Koreatown were largely ignored.

The 1992 Bulls' championship riots, however, were not a Korean American–targeted incident, as illustrated by the damage data collected by the Korean American Community Services and Chicago Police Department (Tables 9.1 and 9.2). Whereas 61 African American stores and 116 Arab American stores were affected, only 45 Korean American stores were damaged (Table 9.1). The police department's preliminary report (Table 9.2) differs from the KACS figures (Table 9.1), but both indicate that the riots were not racially motivated. Only 16 percent of the total damaged stores were Asian American–owned, while Arab American–owned and African American–owned stores together comprised 43 percent.

Most of the affected merchants later managed to reopen their shops or relocate their business to "safer," middle-class African American neighborhoods. Some contemplated moving out of the African American area permanently but never acted on such a desire. One merchant said, "I have invested so much to do a trade in black neighborhoods, I can't start from scratch in white neighborhoods." In 1992, the KACS arranged for two merchants who had suffered damages to obtain state loans and another two shopkeepers to receive city emergency loans. One merchant whose business was destroyed twice, first in 1991 and again in 1992, had also obtained a city loan in 1991. Going to the African American suburban area to resume his business, he said, "I hope this twice-repeated calamity eventually changes into a blessing." Despite low interest rates, applying for government loans was quite troublesome for most of the merchants because collateral could hardly be secured and the required paperwork, such as tax returns, could not meet the guidelines set by the city and state.

When the Bulls won their third NBA championship on June 20, 1993, the Chicago Police Department put 2,500 additional officers on the streets, spending an extra 1.5 million dollars per game.[2] Intensive community lobbying paid off and resulted in much less damage; there were five minor incidents of breaking windows, with total damages of Korean stores at less than a thousand dollars. According to the police report, while roughly two hundred stores were damaged citywide, including thirty-three Arab American stores and thirty-seven African American stores, there was only one reported incident of damage at a Korean American business. The five Korean American merchants affected by minor incidents who reported the damage to the KAMAC hotline perhaps did not even bother to file a report with police or were categorized as Asians in the police department's summary report.

Immediately following the final championship game, there was a sense of relief and a widespread jubilant mood in Chicago's entire Korean American community (the minor incidents of damage to other stores became known to the KACS three weeks later). The 1993 Bulls' NBA

TABLE 9.2 1992 Bulls' Championship Damage, Tabulated by the Chicago Police Department

Ethnicity	Number of Stores Damaged	Percentage
Arab	89	26.33
Asian	55	16.27
Black	56	16.57
White	33	9.76
Hispanic	4	1.18
Unknown	97	28.70
Other	4	1.18
Total	338	99.99

Source: Chicago Police Department 1992

TABLE 9.3 1993 Bulls' Championship Damage, Tabulated by the Chicago Police Department

Ethnicity	Number of Stores Damaged	Percentage
Asian	7	3.55
Korean	1	0.51
Arab	33	16.75
Black	37	18.78
Hispanic	7	3.55
White	7	3.55
Indian	1	0.51
Jewish	2	1.02
Unknown	102	51.78
Total	197	100

Source: Chicago Police Department 1993

championship experience illustrates how much a concerted grass-roots effort can influence policymakers in their decision-making process and benefit the community.

KEY CONCEPTUAL POINTS OF PROGRAMMING

In order for programming aimed at reducing black-Korean tension to be viable, if not successful, it is necessary to have a core group, or an "inner circle," consisting of committed merchant leaders and full-time staffers, which must include African Americans and respected community activists who can strategize and theorize. It is also essential to secure program funds and to generate moral and financial support from the community. The merchants, for example, have continued to raise increasing amounts of money each year from their fellow members and the Korean American community at large. In 1990 the KAMAC raised $24,000, in 1991, $31,000, and in 1992, $52,000. Foundations and individual donors are also providing fuel to help the CMP excel.

The merchants have a direct interest in easing the tension, namely, to make their commercial activities more profitable and safer. The merchants are not, however, genuinely interested in building durable links with African Americans for the sake of, say, enhancing societal equity in pluralistic America. Despite this self-interest of the merchants, their efforts constitute the pivotal part of the CMP's ability to mobilize the human and monetary resources within the Korean American community at large.

It is, however, dangerous for the merchants alone to mediate the conflict, for conflict resolution involves political, social, cultural, religious, and other extramercantile dimensions. Developing and managing a public grant requires a seasoned nonprofit agency administrator. To implement numerous programs such as religious, musical, cultural, youth, journalistic, and athletic exchanges, it is necessary for community organizers to orchestrate the input of community leaders, clergymen, artists, athletes, and concerned journalists. Moreover, most of the Korean American merchants, who have not mastered the English tongue, have no choice but to take recourse in articulate community strategists who can link them to elected and appointed city and state officials and African American leadership.

In order to accomplish any mission, be it commercial, governmental, or religious, it is essential to win the support of a core group of indigenous people who can better communicate with their peers on behalf of those who are initiating the mission. To reach out to a racial or ethnic minority community, the government is likely to employ a person from that community to be its liaison. Likewise, African American staff in a Korean American agency can offer immense contributions to its mission of easing the conflict. African American staff members can balance or objectify the situation, help establish and smooth relations with African American officials, community leaders, and journalists, and organize particular components of exchange programs. Such liaisons may initially be perceived as "sellouts" by their peers, regardless of noble intentions. However, as programs bring in more peer interaction and merchants increase their participation in African American community affairs, the balanced position of such key members is soon appreciated by both sides. As Korean American colleagues develop an extensive network and personal friendships with African Americans, they will come to be be truly familiar with, and respectful to, African Americans as a people. Finally, sponsored events such as food basket donations, scholarships, and choral concerts cannot be implemented unless financial and moral support is rendered by the Korean American community at large. The efforts to mobilize these resources cannot be successful unless there is a systematic, durable, and centralized apparatus in place.

Numerous exchange programs can create effervescence in an interracial audience, and thus generate or renew commitment to interracial harmony. For example, when several hundred African Americans and Korean Americans sang *Hallelujah* together, a feeling of brotherhood resonated throughout the auditorium. It is questionable how long this feeling was sustained by the merchants themselves, but periodic, ritualistic exposure and cooperation may help shopkeepers look into themselves for possible flaws in their own attitudes. By exposing the community to a different culture, such events also help people of both racial groups not only to conceptualize diversity but also to experience and appreciate it.

THE INNER-CITY CONTEXT OF KOREAN AMERICAN STORES

There are roughly seven hundred Korean American stores on the South and West Sides of Chicago, where African Americans and some Latino Americans are highly concentrated. A majority of these are men's, women's, and children's clothing stores; the remaining shops deal in shoes, sportswear, jewelry, cosmetics, and general merchandise. There are no Korean-owned grocery or liquor stores.

Citywide rates of poverty and unemployment among African Americans in 1989 were 33.2 percent and 19.4 percent, respectively (City of Chicago 1992a, 1994). More depressing, the unemployment rate among sixteen- to nineteen-year-old African Americans was 45.8 percent in Chicago (Chicago Urban League 1992). According to the 1990 U.S. Census, some Chicago communities had extremely high poverty rates, such as Grand Boulevard, in which there are currently twenty Korean American stores and 64.7 percent of the residents are below the poverty line. Near West Side, with thirty-two stores, had a poverty rate of 54.5 percent, and East Garfield Park, with forty stores, 48.1 percent (*Chicago Reporter* July 1992: A9).

Aggravated by the high incidence of male incarceration, female-headed households, drugs, gang violence, high school dropouts, and teen pregnancies, the entire community is disarticulated and losing social control, that is, the ability to regulate themselves (Janowitz 1978). As middle-class African Americans, equipped with educational credentials and benefiting from affirmative action, climb the social ladder and move away from the inner city, they leave the urban ghettos to the underclass, the "truly disadvantaged" (Wilson 1987). Korean American merchants in these areas are not dealing with African Americans in a generic sense but, specifically, the urban poor of African American descent. The eclipse of hope, the overwhelming sense of powerlessness, and the perpetuating culture of poverty, frustration, and aggression, in which those suffering must find an outlet for their rage in order to remain sane, are some of the grim realities faced by merchants doing business in these areas.

Neither the white nor the black middle class will venture into the ghetto area to start a business. Most of the major department stores fled the inner city in the 1970s, and Korean American businessmen reinvested in the blighted area, filling the gap. Meanwhile, many of the African American underclass are not yet quite ready to start a small business. As society moves into the postindustrial era, losing a significant number of manufacturing jobs, the vacuum created has had a detrimental effect on more and more people in the inner city areas.

Black-Korean conflict is then a pathological manifestation of an American dilemma. Interminority relations between the two communities no doubt need to be improved, but a greater focus must be given to the bleak macrosocietal picture. Any social phenomenon must be seen in as comprehensive a context as possible. To decontexualize the problem and assert the current dysfunctional relation as merely the "black-Korean conflict" is partial, incomplete, and half-true. In many cases, half-truths can have more malignant ramifications than outright lies.

BUSINESS SAFETY

Business safety is perhaps the most acute concern of Korean American merchants in African American neighborhoods. The merchants often joke among themselves that their lives are at stake for their livelihood. Homicides, life-threatening armed robberies, and burglaries happen from time to time, and countless incidents of shoplifting are experienced by the merchants on a daily basis. During the years 1990–94, the KACS filed with the Illinois Attorney General's office four cases of homicide and five cases of personal injury of merchants in African American neighborhoods, enabling the victims or their families to receive monetary compensation of up to $25,000 each (Table 9.4). The four homicide cases represent the total for the Korean American community in Chicago, but the list of injury cases may be partial since only some injured merchants might have sought assistance with KACS. Mrs. Kim, wife of a homicide victim, said upon the death of her husband, "I feel so guilty because my husband has been saying 'let's move out of this area.' The business was not so good and the competition was fierce. My husband really wanted to get out. But I said to him, 'let's stay little more and the business will get better.' I am regretting that now. I should have listened to my husband."

TABLE 9.4 List of Crime Victims

Date	Nature of Crime	Type of Business	Community
01-31-90	Death	Beauty supply	Austin
02-07-90	Death	General merchandise	Garfield Park
06-29-90	Serious injury	General merchandise	Garfield Park
12-18-90	Serious injury	Apparel	Garfield Park
03-28-91	Death	Laundry	Chicago Lawn
11-03-92	Minor injury	General merchandise	Humboldt Park
03-27-93	Death	Wig	Beverly
04-03-93	Serious injury	Shoes	Rogers Park
04-03-93	Serious injury	Shoes	Rogers Park

Source: KACS Crime Victims Case Files.

In recent years, congenial working relations with the police department have dramatically contributed to business safety. The CMP staff gathered business safety data from Korean merchants to present at workshops in 1991 and 1992 with the Chicago Police Department. Because the workshops aimed to bring about strengthened police protection, the merchants, either consciously or unconsciously, might have exaggerated their experiences of crime. Regardless, assuming that any propensity for exaggeration remained the same over those two years, the data show an improved situation. Robbery and attempted robbery dropped from 102 cases in 1991 (0.57 per store) to 24 cases in 1992 (0.15 per store). Burglary and attempted burglary dropped from 321 cases in 1991 (1.78 per store) to 174 cases in 1992 (1.07 per store). The sensitivity to business safety promoted by the KAMAC and the KACS might have encouraged more merchants to report crimes to police, leading to an increase of reported crimes from 61 percent to 85 percent, and yet only 65 percent (in 1991) and 53 percent (in 1992) of those who filed police reports went to court to testify. The merchants explain that their testimony may contribute to the determent of crime, but they find it very inconvenient and costly to close the store for several hours in order to testify at court.

In 1992, 162 merchants reported 799 cases of shoplifting, roughly five incidents per store over one year. Whatever the numbers may indicate, the issues related to shoplifting lead to a deterioration of relations between merchants and customers. Rude treatment by the merchants, including suspicious looks and following after customers, indeed upsets innocent shoppers. Their resentment is quite authentic and understandable. However, merchants encounter daily incidents of lost merchandise

TABLE 9.5 Business Safety

	October 1991*	October 1992**
Number of stores responding	180	162
Type of Crime		
Robbery	20	11
Attempted robbery	82	13
Burglary	170	59
Attempted burglary	151	115
Group robbery	9	22
Shoplifting	N/A	799
Hold-up	12	13
Merchants reporting crime to police	109 (61%)	137 (85%)
Merchants testifying in court (of those who file reports)	71 (65%)	73 (53%)
Financial Losses	$141,310***	$461,940

Source: KACS 1991b, 1992c

*The 1991 figures cover up to late October. A questionnaire was prepared by the CMP and given to presidents of area merchants' associations, who then distributed and gathered the forms from individual merchants. The findings were presented on November 7, 1991.

**The 1992 figures cover up to early October. The method of collecting the data was the same as the previous year. These data were presented on October 14, 1992.

***This figure does not include loss from shoplifting.

and occasionally face life-threatening situations. In this routinized "at-risk" setting, the merchants, being human, become programmed to *suspect* their customers rather than to *trust* them. Humans tend to generalize after just one or two examples. When this generalization is done in a negative way, it is called *stereotyping*. However inaccurate and unfortunate, stealing has been deeply embedded as a stereotypical behavior of African Americans in the collective conscious of Korean American merchants. Deprogramming this automatic suspicion would require not only painstaking self-cultivation (and possibly a recourse to religion) on the part of the merchants but also drastic behavioral change on the part of African American customers. As three merchants in a 1992 survey confess:

> In my opinion, two out of ten blacks are very innocent and affectionate. The other eight are obsessed with inferiority both economically and socially or with groundless superiority. It seems they feel that they are entitled to certain compensation, despite their behavior's inflicting harmful effects on others.

Those with jobs and family, and who live a normal life, even if they are asked to steal, they would never do it. For troublemakers, however, even if jobs are given to them, it is just for short time and they would repeat troubles. . . . In my experience, they seem to feel that 'why should I work? I can feed myself without working.'

Their lifestyle is problematic. But I think our attitude also has to change. It must be a top priority on the part of the merchants that with genuine human concerns, we have to yield and make compromises. (KACS 1992c)

The vicious cycle of stealing and suspicion, which reinforces innocent shoppers' feelings of disgust, in short, this *aracial* merchant-customer dispute, is one of the major elements in the black-Korean conflict. Merchants or customers, Korean Americans or African Americans, people get angry over little things. A mom-and-pop store is not an ideological arena in which participants can discuss the civil rights movement or multiracial coalition; it is a place where many of these *little things* happen every day and simply make people angry.

African American Employment at Korean American Stores

Boycott leaders have complained that Korean Americans do not hire African Americans. Are Korean American merchants indeed obligated to create job opportunities for African Americans since they make money in their neighborhoods? Is providing jobs one of the meaningful ways Korean American merchants should contribute to the community where they trade? This demand implies that jobs are scarce in inner-city African American neighborhoods. Were there plenty of jobs in such neighborhoods, say, at industrial plants, people would never make such a demand on small-business merchants, who can provide only a handful of jobs.

In the early 1970s, when Korean Americans began to open stores in African American neighborhoods, they all started their businesses as mom-and-pop operations. Shopkeepers could establish themselves only by working seventy to eighty hours a week and by dividing all the labor between husband and wife and, in some cases, a few other relatives. As business operations became large enough to accommodate hiring workers not in the owner's family and as merchants increasingly saw the necessity of hiring local people for better customer relations, some employment opportunities began to open up for African Americans.

To assess the boycotters' demand of African American employment, we have surveyed merchants on several occasions. Our findings consistently indicate that over 75 percent of the Korean American stores in the Chicago area hire African Americans and that Korean American merchants have many more African American employees than they do Korean American employees; in the May 1992 survey, for example, 80 percent of all employees in Korean American stores were African Americans. The average number of African American employees, however, is only about two per store, indicating the small-scale operation of these establishments.

In October 1992, we also asked the merchants if they hired African Americans as managers. Out of 162 respondents, 27 (17%) answered affirmatively, while 107 merchants responded negatively and 28 did not reply. Further research could be done on what caused some merchants to hire African Americans as managers and whether or not the hiring of a man-

TABLE 9.6 African American Employment at Korean American Stores

	July 1990*	May 1992**	October 1992
Total stores	238	176	162
Total employees	—	483	—
African American employees	459	364 (80%)	227
Average African American employees per store	1.93	2.07	1.40
Korean American employees	—	119 (20%)	—
Stores hiring African Americans			
Yes	189 (79%)	—	121 (85%)
No	46 (19%)	—	28 (17%)
Unknown	3 (1%)	—	13 (8%)
Stores hiring African Americans as managers			
Yes	—	—	27 (17%)
No	—	—	107 (66%)
Unknown	—	—	28 (17%)

Source: Chicago Commission on Human Relations 1990; KACS 1992a, 1992c
*Inhe Choi, then community resource specialist with the Chicago Commission on Human Relations, conducted this survey in the midst of the Roseland picketing in July 1990. The KACS processed these data in June 1992 with volunteer help of Professor Michael Chwe, Department of Economics, the University of Chicago, and his associates.
**CMP staff at KACS collected these data in the aftermath of the L.A. riots to present at a meeting with Operation People United to Serve Humanity (PUSH).

TABLE 9.7 Englewood

	May 1992	December 1993
Total stores	52	41
Stores hiring African Americans	N/A	41
Total employees	217	167
African American employees	157 (72%)	129 (77%)
Korean American employees	60 (28%)	38 (23%)
Average employees per store	4.17	4.07
Average African American employees per store	3.02	3.15

Source: KACS 1992a, 1993

ager is correlated with the amount of the merchant's business experience in African American neighborhoods.

Although the information above is insufficient to draw conclusions, Table 9.6 seems to imply that the number of Korean American stores in the inner city areas of Chicago is decreasing. Many merchants have closed their shops and left the area. In 1990, leaders of merchant organizations estimated there were 1,200 Korean American stores in the inner city, but they have recently decreased the figure to 700 stores.[3]

The Englewood shopping strip currently has fifty-five Korean American stores, the highest concentration among all commercial districts on the South and West Sides of Chicago. Merchants also consider this area to be the most profitable. In order to respond to the employment opportunity demand of the 21st Century VOTE, the KACS gathered data in December 1993 (Table 9.7), which again approximates the earlier figures in Table 9.6. About three out of four Englewood employees are African Americans, 72 percent in May 1992 and 77 percent in December 1993, and the average number of workers per store was over four, attesting to the relatively larger business operations here compared to other areas.

REFUND AND EXCHANGE POLICY

Incidents involving refund and exchange policy also emerge as one of the major issues in black-Korean conflicts. Do Korean American merchants refuse to give refunds and exchanges because they were enculturated with the common mercantile practice in Korea that every sale is final? Are they then failing to adapt to the American way of doing business? This consumer argument may contain a grain of truth. Typical

TABLE 9.8 Refund and Exchange Policy

	July 1990	October 1992
Total stores	238	162
Return policy posted at visible place?		
Yes	134 (56%)	142 (88%)
No	30 (13%)	6 (4%)
Unknown	74 (31%)	14 (9%)
No cash refunds	—	53 (33%)
No exchanges	—	3 (2%)
Refunds with receipts	—	66 (39%)
Exchanges with receipts	—	136 (84%)
Unknown	—	23 (14%)

Source: Chicago Commission on Human Relations 1990; KACS 1992c

merchant arguments against a refund policy for inner-city residents are: they just buy and wear an evening dress for a party, then the next day bring it in for a refund, or they buy a shirt, are broke a couple of days later, tear off the shirt, then ask for a refund for the damaged good. These complaints may also contain a grain of truth. The complaints of both consumers and merchants have some merit, but all are partial. In future research, statistics might be collected to see whether or not there are more claims for refunds in the inner city area than in wealthier neighborhoods. Researchers should also investigate the hypothesis that the longer a merchant has been operating in the inner city, the fewer disputes over refunds he encounters.

To address this issue of refunds, the City of Chicago passed a city ordinance on November 16, 1992, requiring every store to post a refund policy at the cash register or some other conspicuous location and to give out a receipt with the store name and address on it (City of Chicago 1992b). Even prior to this ordinance, however, a majority of merchants— 88 percent in October 1992 and 56 percent in July 1990—had already been complying with this policy. As of October 1992, 84 percent of Korean American merchants allowed exchanges with receipts, and 39 percent granted refunds with receipts. Since the ordinance's implementation and the following rigorous campaign efforts and policy poster distributions by the CMP and the KAMAC, as well as the issuance of violation citations by the Department of Consumer Services, the compliance rate has increased to almost 100 percent. However, just as a reasonable policy should be implemented by the merchants, responsible shopping should be equally encouraged among African American residents.

SIGNIFICANCE OF THE BLACK-KOREAN CONFLICT

What is the significance of black-Korean conflict? Is no one at fault or is everyone to blame? What lessons should be learned from this ongoing conflict? Has it been portrayed exclusively as a microscopic malfunctioning? Why are people, especially policymakers and mainstream media spokespeople, refusing to survey the macroscopic urban terrain in present America? Should not societal ills be encountered directly, with courage?

The conflict has enlightened the Korean American community, which now strives to see life beyond the confines of ethnic boundaries. Socializing within one's ethnic boundaries is perhaps natural and comforting. However, to participate in building a multiracial coalition and to invite non–Korean Americans to appreciate and accommodate Korean values, as well as to acculturate Korean Americans into the American way of living, ethnic confinement must be cheerfully destroyed—at least in the realm of gesellschaft; it may be impossible in that of gemeinschaft. Korean Americans are now building an interracial bridge, however fragile, with African Americans. Korean American merchants have generously supported the candidacies of many African American office seekers. Although such political participation is motivated by merchants' own interests, this support nevertheless helps build a coalition with non–Korean Americans.

White and Latino communities also need to partake in future exchange programs between the African American and Korean American communities, both as participants and as observers. This is especially important given that the white community is extremely segregated from the underclass, not only residentially but also culturally. Multiracial programming and exchanges represent an effort to correct the misperception that the black-Korean conflict is a biracial phenomenon (Chap. 2) and to narrow the widening sociocultural distance between African Americans and white people.

The Los Angeles riots and the Bulls' championship riots in Chicago, as well as merchants' constant desire, conscious or subconscious, to retreat from the ghetto area, have made the community as a whole explore the possibility of diversifying business. Merchants increasingly talk about starting a franchise or developing a shopping strip in white neighborhoods. Planned projects like a business development center can help this community agenda of business diversification.

For African Americans, the memories of the civil rights movement are fading. Malcolm X is mythologized at the cost of losing perspective on a painful reality. Passion, responsibility, and a sense of proportion, all qualities required of political leaders, are hard to find in present African American leadership (Weber 1946). The boycott leaders, driven only by their self-interests, are far from this leadership ideal. To encourage Korean Americans to share in the glorious movements of the 1960s and to enlighten them that they are direct beneficiaries of the civil rights era, African Americans must be twice-born themselves.

The data presented here have been gathered in hopes of defending inner-city merchants from African American demands. As is possible in any such study, merchants may have inflated figures or lied on surveys for their advantage. Neither the CMP staff nor I verified survey data through personal interviews. Although the validity of such methodology may be questioned, responses nevertheless seem to reflect reality fairly well and serve to refute African Americans' misperceptions about merchants.

Hiring African Americans, implementing a refund and return policy, and suffering daily encounters with violence do not, however, make the merchants innocent parties in this conflict. Even though the economic structure in the United States may have dictated that Korean American immigrants were better able to set up business in the inner city, doing so was, after all, their own decision. Because individuals are not completely shaped by their environment, each person must focus on changing their own attitude, in spite of all obstacles. As one merchant testifies:

> Honestly speaking, we have looked down upon blacks, and this has not changed at all. Of course, a bigger problem lies with blacks than with the merchants, but in the long run our attitude must change. Making little money makes some merchants restless and arrogant in front of blacks, and they break morals and ethics among the merchants. We must also think over how we treat each one of our customers and how we treat each one of our employees, too. (KACS 1992c)

Structural evils must be criticized and changed in collaboration with all Americans, including Korean Americans; however, much like it requires two wheels to rotate an axle, unless behavioral changes on the part of African Americans accompany the societal consensus to change this overall structure, the energy for such change cannot be generated. The easiest change, individual behavioral modification, can be the first step in undertaking a grand task.

To portray black-Korean conflict as the black-Korean conflict does not make it a black-Korean conflict. In the past few years, however, the mainstream media have, consciously or unconsciously, excessively depicted the interracial dimension of the conflict. As words like *poverty* and *violence* have degenerated into cliché, sounding more like dull statistics than a hot topic, the media, which by their intrinsic nature must pursue new items, found their new story in the conflict. It was wholly a novelty to journalists, so they covered the conflict ardently—but too textually. If the conflict is contexualized, it becomes evident that members of the white majority, especially government decision makers, are participants, however invisible, of this urban phenomenon. They can be effective in revitalizing urban America and creating job opportunities. Korean merchants are targeted by African Americans for the several hundred jobs, at most, that they can offer in the entire city. Meanwhile, white industrialists can evade this issue and remain blameless after relocating their plants and headquarters, and therefore thousands of jobs, to suburbs, other states, or foreign countries.

FORECASTING THE FUTURE

In social conflict, it seems issues come and go without changing anything. Especially when it is virtually impossible to designate the "bad guys," anger alone has a limited ability to sustain and propel a conflict. It is unlikely that the merchants will be targeted again and again. Societal attention will shift from housing to health care, from Bosnia to South Africa. The black-Korean conflict as an issue will fade in the years to come. If the verdict in April 1992 was the climax of the conflict, the aftermath of the second Rodney King verdict in March 1993 was its anticlimax. The same repertoire, over and over, will someday prove tiresome to inner-city African Americans as well. In the next twenty to thirty years, many more Korean Americans will leave the ghettos. A harbinger of ethnic succession is already seen in the numbers of Arab and Pakistani Americans who now penetrate inner-city neighborhoods and compete with Korean American merchants still there. Rude treatment of customers, however, will take hold as a stereotypical trait of all Korean Americans, a label that will then pass on to the next generation, just as Jewish Americans, as the predecessors of Korean Americans in ghettos, are still haunted by the spectres of bloodsuckers. Every quarter century, a Watts riot can always return in a new form, over a new racial incident. Should Americans work to prevent this reincarnation or allow ourselves to repeat it?

NOTES

1. Telephone conversation with deputy chief of patrol on the night of June 14, 1992. A twenty-four-hour hotline was operating at KACS headquarters from June 14 to June 17.

2. Private conversation with Deputy Superintendent Edwin Bishop of the Chicago Police Department.

3. Private conversation with Chang Kun Kim and Sung Bae Kim, past presidents of the KAMAC.

REFERENCES

Chicago Commission on Human Relations. 1990. *Korean American merchants survey*.
Chicago Police Department. 1992. *Preliminary report: Bulls damage 1992*. June 26.
———. 1993. *Summary report of the Superintendent of Police*. Prepared by Commander Anthony Chiesa. July 12.
Chicago Reporter. July 1992. Table A-9, The deepening of poverty.
Chicago Urban League. 1992. *The changing economic standing of minorities in the Chicago metropolitan area, interim report*. Chicago: Latino Institute, Northern Illinois University.
City of Chicago. 1992a. *Social and economic characteristics of Chicago's population: Community area profiles*. Department of Planning and Development.
———. 1992b. *Rules and regulations applicable to merchandise retailers other than establishments with certified alternative price systems effective November 16, 1992*. Department of Consumer Services.
———. 1994. *Demographic characteristics of Chicago's population: Community area profiles*. Department of Planning and Development.
Janowitz, Morris. 1978. *The last half century: Societal change and politics in America*. Chicago: University of Chicago Press.
Kim, Kwang Chung, and Shin Kim. 1999. The multiracial nature of Los Angeles unrest in 1992. In this volume.
Korean American Community Services (KACS). 1991a. *The Korean American store damage during the 1991 Bulls' NBA victory*. Unpublished report. Chicago.
———. 1991b. *The 1991 Korean American merchants business safety survey*. Unpublished report. Chicago.
———. 1992a. *African American employment at Korean American stores*. Unpublished report. Chicago.
———. 1992b. *Damage report of the 1992 Bulls' NBA victory*. Unpublished report. Chicago.
———. 1992c. *The 1992 Korean American merchants survey*. Unpublished report. Chicago.
———. 1993. *African American employment at Korean American stores in Englewood*. Unpublished report. Chicago.
Lee, Yoon Mo. 1994. Perception and reality of the relationship between Korean mer-

chants and African-American customers. Chap. 14 in *Korean Americans: Conflict and harmony*, edited by Ho-Youn Kwon. Chicago: North Park College and Theological Seminary.

Weber, Max. 1946. Politics as vocation. Chap. 4 in *From Max Weber*, edited by H. H. Gerth and C. Wright Mills. Oxford: Oxford University Press.

West, Cornel. 1993. The crisis of black leadership. Chap. 3 in *Race Matters*. Boston: Beacon Press.

Wilson, William Julius. 1987. *The truly disadvantaged: The inner city, the underclass, and public policy*. Chicago: University of Chicago Press.

[10] Portrait of a Community Program: The African American and Korean American Community Mediation Project

InChul Choi and Shin Kim

THE SUMMER OF 1994 WAS QUIET IN CHICAGO. IT SEEMED THAT THE friction between African Americans and Korean American merchants had subsided. Whenever equality in urban America is threatened or lacking, collective black anger will always come back to challenge or provide "feedback" to our political and societal system. It is implausible, though, that such collective anger will recur in a form that encourages damaging or boycotting Korean American stores. Although individual merchants will continue to encounter individual consumer complaints and grievances, collective protests against a whole group of merchants are unlikely to be repeated. The same tune played over and over, however justifiable, has lost its freshness and newsworthiness in both Korean American and African American communities. African American citizens will even agree that Korean American merchants have contributed to revitalizing once-blighted areas and that intraethnic competition among Korean American merchants brings prices down to a very affordable level. Harrowed by the 1992 riots in Los Angeles and the Bulls' NBA championship riots in Chicago, Korean American merchants are now well aware that better customer relations are critically important to their business in the inner city. Merchants are, and must continue to be, prudent to avoid the recurrence of a *Latasha Harlins* flash point, which could overturn all that the mediation efforts have achieved.

The Chicago Bulls were eliminated early in the play-off series of 1994, allowing a more leisurely summer for Korean American merchants and concerned members of Chicago's Korean American community. The

Bulls' championship games had evoked disorderly conduct among inner city residents in June 1991, 1992, and 1993. In 1991's play-off disturbance, the City of Chicago and the Korean American community were caught off guard, and seven Korean American stores were damaged. In 1992, despite a two-month-long intensive lobby, forty-five Korean American stores were partially or wholly destroyed. Most of the damage, however, occurred outside the major shopping strips controlled by Korean American merchants. Determined to avoid another incident in 1993, the Chicago Police Department and Korean American merchants worked very closely to prevent another episode of disorder. No major damage was inflicted upon Korean American stores that year.

The Bulls' championship play-offs came to be a major annual event, requiring four months of involvement from merchants and community staff. This involvement consisted of preseries police and government lobbying and merchant meetings, a hotline during the series, and postseries damage control and assessment. Chicago's inner-city merchants talked ambivalently about Michael Jordan and the Bulls during these times: they were delighted to see Jordan's awe-inspiring talent, yet they would pray for the Bulls' early elimination. Lately, however, the merchants' conversation varies here and there: "It is so good for us that Michael Jordan retired," "Economy is still not picking up," "I am fed up with the South Side trade, will there be an alternative?" "How about starting a franchise store in white suburban areas?" and so on. The Bulls' championship violence has, for the time being, faded into antiquity.

In retrospect, the other crisis that Korean American merchants have faced in Chicago, boycotts, have been both threats and opportunities. The boycotts have motivated merchants to create and strengthen their own organization in order to mobilize monetary and moral support for their programs throughout the community, to improve their business rapport and build better public relations with consumers, and to network with African American community leaders, clergy, police, and elected and appointed public officials. Since the first Chicago boycott in July 1990, the Korean American community in general and Korean American merchants in particular have diligently and consciously orchestrated efforts to publicize how they were contributing to the well-being of the community where they were doing business. Thus, when any subsequent conflict occurred or seemed likely to occur, the merchant leadership could point to their track record and statistics to counter the claims of boycott organizers.

This chapter describes the process of black/Korean community mediation efforts in Chicago. As a portrait of a community program, our approach is descriptive rather than analytic. Since we view the urban controversy from the Korean American perspective, it may be countered that our description, though comprehensive, is biased toward the merchants' defense. It is of little relevance to discuss whether our portrait is objective or subjective, as long as the example of the Chicago community mediation efforts demonstrates how much a community program can contribute to educating and empowering the merchants and community and to protecting merchants' means of livelihood during times of crisis.

The Beginning of the Black/Korean Mediation Efforts

Approximately seven hundred Korean American stores are located in African American and Latino neighborhoods around Chicago's South and West Sides. The Community Mediation Project (CMP) of the Korean American Community Services (KACS) brings together 331 stores in seventeen shopping strips (Table 10.1). The merchant leaders estimate that two hundred stores are spread throughout the near North Side and far West Side and another two hundred stores are scattered sporadically throughout the entire South Side.

Headquartered at and supported by KACS, the Korean American Merchants Association of Chicago (KAMAC) represents and protects the interests of these 331 Korean American member merchants and promotes harmonious relations between its member merchants and African American consumers. Officers are selected from major shopping areas that have a high concentration of Korean American stores. Although the KAMAC also draws support from minor shopping strips, participation of these merchants is considered modest at best.

Anxious over a possible contagious effect from the Red Apple incident in New York, Chicago's inner-city merchants banded together in haste and founded the KAMAC on April 26, 1990. Immediately afterward, its organizational strength was rigorously tested when a two-week boycott erupted on June 30, 1990, in Roseland (Lee 1994). The entire Korean American community was well orchestrated under the leadership of the founding president of the KAMAC, Chang Kun Kim. The merchants learned from the Roseland boycott that it would be necessary to befriend local aldermen, high-ranking bureaucrats, police authorities, church ministers, and community leaders, all of whom could buffer the merchants from direct and excessive community demands.

TABLE 10.1 Location and Number of Korean American Stores

Name of Community	Street Location	Korean American Stores
Major shopping strips		
Englewood	63rd / Halsted	55
Garfield Park	Madison / Pulaski	40
Near West Side	12th / Halsted	32
Roseland	111th / Michigan	33
South Chicago	91st / Commercial	24
Grand Boulevard	47th / King	20
	subtotal	204
Minor shopping strips		
Woodlawn	63rd / Cottage Grove	6
South Shore	71st / Jeffery	11
Avalon Park	79th / Jeffery	8
Avalon Park	87th / Stony Island	9
Auburn Gresham	79th / Halsted	7
Chatham	79th / Cottage Grove	7
Chatham	87th / Cottage Grove	5
Chatham	87th / Dan Ryan	11
New City	47th / Ashland	20
	subtotal	84
Latino / African American mixed areas with minor shopping areas		
South Lawndale	26th / Kedzie	23
New City	47th / Halsted	20
	subtotal	43
Total		331

Source: Community Mediation Project, February 1994

After witnessing the intensity and magnitude of African American boycotting efforts firsthand, the KAMAC and KACS leadership realized the urgency of developing a durable and structured program to improve race relations between the two communities. In late July 1990, following the Roseland resolution, the KACS pursued a funding opportunity with the Chicago Community Trust and the United Way of Chicago to embark on its planned Community Mediation Project. Although the Trust decided to grant $2,000 for a plan to conduct a comprehensive needs-assessment study, the United Way rejected the grant proposal to launch the project. This required the KACS to return the approved grant to the

Trust. Since the KAMAC was an emerging organization without a budget of its own, the KACS was acting (as it still does act) as an umbrella organization for the KAMAC, providing technical assistance, program support, and fiscal management.

In the fall of 1990, leaders of the KAMAC and the KACS discussed the need to present a visible public event that would show Korean American merchants' contribution to the African American community. They concluded that a Christmas food basket presentation to needy families in the area would be a suitable gesture of goodwill. In less than two months, they raised over $24,000 in annual membership dues and contributions toward the food basket project; with this funding they prepared 1,000 baskets, each containing goods worth about twelve dollars in wholesale price.

In February 1991, the KACS again applied to the United Way, this time for a three-year priority grant on studying ways to reduce discrimination. After the preliminary phase of United Way's grant review, the KACS was invited to submit a full application by April 1991. This was accomplished, and a grant in the amount of $230,000 was approved in July 1991. This funding enabled the KACS to hire two full-time community mediators, one African American and one Korean American, in September 1991. In collaboration with the merchants, the KACS board, and the community at large, the CMP has since then worked to improve race relations and to overcome several crises. Although the United Way funding ceased in June 1994, the City of Chicago's Community Development Block Grant and grants from three foundations currently support the project, and the KAMAC has grown and is now able to raise a significant portion of its operating expenses.

PROGRAMMING OF THE COMMUNITY MEDIATION PROJECT

The CMP aims to encourage Korean American merchants to play a more visible and active role in community affairs where their stores are located, while also educating them on African American culture, customs, and history. Similarly, the project has sought to expose African Americans to Korean customs and culture. To encourage merchants' economic empowerment, the CMP also provides seminars and workshops on such topics as American business law and practice, sales promotion, commercial opportunities, insurance, and business safety. For both communities, numerous citywide cross-cultural events such as holiday concerts, athletic and journalistic programs, and youth exchanges have helped promote the values of cultural pluralism. The CMP has developed nine major programs, outlined in the following pages.

Geographic Area Committees

Geographic area committees have provided a common ground for Korean American merchants and African American residents to engage in face-to-face discussions and solve problems. Apprehensive about sensitizing the issues, Korean American merchants have passively participated in area committee meetings. Their involvement has also been inhibited by English language problems, difficulties in leaving stores during business hours, and frustration over the slow, if democratic, process of lengthy discussions over a series of meetings. In spite of these discouraging factors, geographic area committees have achieved two outstanding goals.

First, the Garfield Park Area Committee, which covers the Madison Street and Pulaski Road area, has evolved into a multiracial chamber of commerce, one in which Korean, Arab, and African American merchants, community residents, and city officials have cooperated to lay the groundwork. Efforts to organize a chamber were initiated before the Bulls' NBA championship riots in June 1992. Most heavily hit by these riots, the Garfield Park merchants regretted that their area did not have a viable chamber of its own and accelerated their efforts to organize one.

Second, the Englewood Area Committee initiated teamwork in order to draft a solid exchange and refund policy in the summer of 1992. By October 1992, this policy was adopted citywide by Korean American merchants and was printed on posters; a month afterward it became a city ordinance.

When local chambers of commerce became active, however, the CMP staff encouraged merchants to be an integral part of chambers rather than maintain an area committee. Once Korean American merchants had been mobilized to participate in community affairs through a chamber of commerce, as happened in Garfield Park, area committees often then became superfluous. Furthermore, despite the proactive function of area committees, the CMP staff found it very difficult to induce merchants to come to the committee meetings. Although the CMP leadership tried (and modestly succeeded) to maintain overall neutrality, African American staff tended to argue on the side of African Americans, and, likewise, Korean American staff tended to argue for the Korean American side.

Food Basket Presentations

Since 1990, the KAMAC has raised funds for annual food basket presentations. The KACS then helps distribute about a thousand baskets to the needy families in Chicago's African American neighborhoods. Usually fifty to one hundred baskets are allocated to each alderman's office or local church, from which they can then be presented to individual families. The CMP staff always invites state, city, and local dignitaries to the ceremony and solicits ample coverage from the mainstream press. In December 1993, United States Senator Carol Moseley-Braun of Illinois, the first African American woman to be elected to the U.S. Senate, served as the chairperson of this event.

Critics may note that this annual event lacks the genuine spirit of Christmas, which is to give unconditionally. Being a public relations event, the KAMAC food basket program is unquestionably a politicization of Christmas, not an unfamiliar occurrence in the modern tradition of commercializing the holiday season. The merchants themselves would not refute this ethical charge, but neither would they claim that the food baskets are more a forced gesture than a cheerful gift. The food basket program fulfills Korean American merchants' desperate need to demonstrate a tangible contribution to the community, while at the same time fulfilling a community's desperate need to help impoverished families. Local aldermen have been quite supportive of this event, and the extensive media coverage has been favorable.

Scholarships

In June 1991, as a way of returning a share of their profits to the community, Chicago Korean American merchants initiated a scholarship program for African American high school seniors. From 1991 to 1995, they awarded a total of fifty-five scholarships, adding up to an amount of $12,950. Five high schools were chosen in the areas with the highest concentration of Korean American stores. Each year, the CMP staff asks the principal to nominate three students, one in each of three areas: academic achievement, community service, and "most improved." Merchant leaders and the CMP staff always attend the award ceremony and present scholarship checks with engraved plaques.

From 1991–93, the KACS also helped select the African American recipients for a scholarship program established by the Canaan Korean Presbyterian Church in Glenview. Of ten $1,000 scholarships, the Canaan Church designated two scholarships for African Americans: one to fund a college student and one to fund a seminarian. The CMP staff reviewed roughly forty applicants and submitted a list of four finalists to the church scholarship committee for its final selection. An award presentation and worship service took place on the Sunday after Thanksgiving.

The Canaan scholarship illustrates that once a consistent program is established and recognized, community resources can be centralized and channeled through that program. Before the CMP gained momentum and visibility, there were several organizations and churches that sponsored or participated in community events, with the aim of healing the deteriorating relations. Establishing these events, however, became a problem because maintaining organizations' efforts were not routinized. With no central apparatus in the community to coordinate mediation efforts, such events could degenerate into clashes of egos among the self-proclaimed leaders of the community, sporadic goodwill events with negligible publicity, or mere localized dialogues and debates with African Americans. Although a centralized apparatus cannot and should not monopolize certain issues in the community, the handling of black/Korean conflict issues was gradually delegated to and virtually monopolized by the KAMAC and KACS in Chicago. As the CMP established a track record and subsequently received extensive media attention, Korean American resources were almost exclusively directed into the CMP, and the project's staff were sought after by numerous African American groups for panel discussions, public lectures, and keynote speeches.

Cross-cultural Concerts

Two cross-cultural concerts took place in Chicago, in December 1991 and December 1992. The first concert was staged at Kennedy-King College, a predominantly African American city college, and featured a 250-member choir consisting of six Korean American congregations and five African American congregations. More than six hundred Korean American and African American people were present to appreciate diverse forms of Christian expression. When the audience and choir all sang hymns together, unity resonated throughout the auditorium. The rhythmic dances and drumming of African Americans, which most Korean Americans had only seen on television, added to a cultural experience that became deeply embedded in the collective memory of the Korean American community.

The second concert was presented at Apostolic Faith Church. Despite the concert's title, *One in Christ*, the cooperation of churches was much more difficult to mobilize this time than the previous year. There was a smaller audience and choir, and overall the participants seemed to demonstrate less enthusiasm, less enjoyment, and less empathy. Although the December concerts were originally planned as an annual event, the KAMAC and KACS leadership and the CMP staff, despite some initial efforts, failed to stage a third concert the following year.

The brotherhood felt during a concert is simply not translatable into feelings of brotherhood at a store. It is doubtful that any individuals experienced a heartfelt conversion at the concerts. A few sensitive merchants and community members were bothered by religious concerns, though they still helped put the event together, but most merchants qua merchants overlooked the religious dimension of the event. Calculation and goal-orientedness have always been two of the cardinal aspects of a merchant's nature. A cross-cultural concert provided a rare opportunity for Korean merchants to improve their tainted image. It was a success theatrically but perhaps a failure theologically, for the ultimate reality was manipulated, as it is in business dealings. Is such profanation of the sacred in community programming justifiable, if not redeemable, as long as it contributes to the improvement of the community? The students of social sciences are likely to agree, though perhaps reluctantly.

Athletic Programs, Cultural Programs, and Youth Exchanges

The CMP staff has coordinated numerous interracial youth, cultural, and athletic events. Children of each community have presented their songs, dances, and skits in the other community. Young African American dancers have frequently been invited to perform at Korean American functions. In front of an audience of two thousand people at *DanceAfrica 1992*, African American and Korean American youths jointly performed a dance entitled *Respect the Elder*, choreographed by Chuck Davis, a renowned African American dancer. Children from both communities had sweated together for two months in practice to prepare for this performance.

Korean American youth have also been taken on tours of African American neighborhoods and to the DuSable Museum, an African American history and culture museum. Meanwhile, African American children have likewise been amazed by the prowess displayed at Tae Kwon Do demonstrations. Children from both communities have enjoyed hot dogs together and played games at joint picnics. The CMP staff has encouraged Chicago's youngsters to express pride in their own culture and to appreciate the culture of others from an early age. Korean American merchants have always underwritten expenses for such events with a smile and donated ample clothes, shoes, and toys as gifts to children. Police and fire departments have gladly sent out horses and fire trucks to add excitement for these youngsters. The CMP staff felt a little guilt when they trumpeted these events to news media and turned them into public relations displays. Regardless of how adults may use or exploit such exchanges, however, the young participants remained innocent and learned about one another's culture and community while also being entertained.

Journalistic Exchanges

The KAMAC and KACS initiated a journalistic exchange in March 1993, in which a hundred guests—African American and Korean American journalists and concerned citizens—shared their views in a forum discussion and dinner event underwritten by Kraft General Foods. Thirty to forty journalists from both the mainstream and community media arrived to dine on Korean cuisine and to dissect race relations in general and the nature of the African American and Korean American controversy in particular. One panelist from the *Chicago Defender* confessed that evening that it was her first time so far on the North Side. The geographic distance she was referring to was very much symbolic of cultural distance. Approaching the controversy as a problem of urban poverty rather than seeing it as a black/Korean racial conflict was heatedly debated, but the arguments were inconclusive. The forum, however, was a success in that the CMP staff and Chicago's Korean American merchants were able to befriend many African American journalists. Those journalists' subsequent coverage of mediation programming was very hospitable and more informed as a result. African American photographers came out to photograph CMP events, and African American reporters wrote stories and quoted the merchants favorably.

Another cause for beneficial media coverage was the CMP's African American mediator, Karen Gunn, who, as an African American working in a Korean American organization, was an anomaly and therefore newsworthy. She began to receive the attention of both local and national media: representatives of ABC-TV, CBS-TV, PBS's *MacNeil/Lehrer Report*, and the *New York Times* all came to Chicago to write stories and tape interviews with her and other staff members. Although these reporters often turned their stories into personality pieces rather than focusing coverage on the mediation program itself, Ms. Gunn competently and eloquently spoke on behalf of the Korean American merchants in Chicago. Had there been no African American mediator on staff, the CMP would have received much less media attention.

Community Policing

The KAMAC and KACS leadership has devoted much time to positioning the organization as a liaison between the police department and Chicago merchants. By strengthening this relationship with police, Korean American merchants have learned how to most effectively access timely police protection, while helping area police departments become more sensitive to the needs of the merchants. Shopkeepers have also benefited from safety workshops and meetings with police district commanders and neighborhood relations sergeants. Previous experiences of crisis management during times of rioting or unrest enabled the KAMAC and KACS to bring about strengthened police protection during the 1993 NBA championship series and to help merchants rigorously network with community residents for their common safety.

The Consulate General of the Republic of Korea, in addition to offering financial contributions to KAMAC programs and a scholarship fund for the Kennedy-King College, has played a significant role in enhancing the business safety of the merchants. Consul Choi Sung Ho, a law enforcement attaché, advised merchants to frequently visit police stations and follow up on commanders' promises, and he diligently accompanied merchants to police stations in order to do so. Whenever a new district commander was assigned, the consul would kindly call the KAMAC officers and CMP staff to invite them together for a courtesy visit. At his request, merchant leaders attended virtually all police banquets and retirement parties arranged by local district stations and downtown headquarters.

Through the consul's initiatives, the Consulate General sponsored a couple of banquets for police commanders and local merchants in appreciation for the improvements in community policing. Prior to the Bulls' 1992 and 1993 play-off series, he visited all ten police stations on the South and West Sides and requested more protection for Korean American stores. The Consulate General is very much an integral component of the CMP, and through its help and contributions the usual awkwardness between a motherland's government and its emigrants disappeared. Professional affinity and friendship between African American police commanders and the consul, despite the fact that he was a bureaucrat of a foreign government, were decisive factors in improving police protection and saving virtually hundreds of Korean American stores. Commanders deployed a sizable number of police officers, who marched in rows near strips of Korean American stores and blocked off some areas with squad cars and police dogs. Potential looters had no room to penetrate.

Workshops and Seminars

The CMP staff has planned and implemented forums to educate Korean American merchants on a wide range of topics including, but not limited to, basic American business laws and practices, appropriate treatment of and behavior toward consumers, community race relations, crime prevention and security, business insurance, and small business loan packaging. It has always been difficult to draw merchants' participation, especially during peaceful times. In the middle of a boycott or riot, however, cooperation and volunteerism always increased. Even when disturbances were happening in other cities, Chicago merchants called the KACS to inquire about the situation and plan strategies. In any case, the merchant leadership always made hundreds of calls to urge shopkeepers to attend workshops and seminars, especially when high-ranking bureaucrats or politicians were scheduled as guest speakers. Unfortunately, merchant members often had to be coerced in order to produce a respectable turnout and save the image of the KAMAC. Regardless, these events enabled the participating merchants not only to gain practical information but also to network with African American leaders and display an image of their collective strength to guests and news reporters.

Politics and Public Relations

In order to enlist the help of politicians and bureaucrats as buffer figures, Korean American merchants have been forced to participate in politics. Local politicians have often initiated contact with merchants in order to solicit possible donations to their campaigns. The KAMAC encourages its members to reserve a table for ten at fundraising dinners for the area's alderman. Korean merchants have also supported candidacies of African Americans in city and state elections. Such participation in political fundraising does not directly translate into an immediate asset, but the KAMAC leadership considers it an insurance premium and an investment in the future. In response to the KAMAC's contribution to her U.S. Senate campaign, Carol Moseley-Braun promised to hire a Korean American on her staff, a promise that she kept after the election.

At the KAMAC's annual meetings, recognition plaques are presented to African American and white politicians, bureaucrats, and ministers for their contribution to the CMP. The KAMAC has also arranged for many

African Americans to receive plaques of honorary membership in the Korean American Association of Chicago. In conjunction with the Consulate General, the KAMAC encouraged the Municipal Council of Seoul to invite two aldermen from the Chicago City Council to take a trip to Korea. The KAMAC leadership and CMP staff have also been recognized with medals, awards, and plaques from the Republic of Korea, the City of Chicago, and various community organizations on many occasions.

The contribution of such recognition efforts (whether the KAMAC is being recognized for excellence or, alternately, recognizing excellence in others) is indeed substantive and tangible. Though motives of soliciting contributions and investments were undeniably involved, these public relations efforts lubricated the process of networking with resource persons.

Merchant Leadership and Fundraising

When terms for membership in an organization are clearly defined, such as ownership of a store in the inner city area, and the membership is small, say, less than five hundred, the role of leadership is perhaps the most critical variable in determining the success of that organization. When an organization represents an interest group and its members encounter crises from time to time, those members come to greatly rely on their leadership; they will cooperate with leaders and will be very reluctant to dissent. The KAMAC's leadership epitomizes these general statements.

The founding president, Chang Kun Kim, was given a few nicknames by the CMP staff: they called him *Quarterback* because of his talents in mobilizing community resources and assigning tasks according to one's character and ability; *Godfather* because he was the very first Korean American merchant to start a retail shop on Chicago's South Side; and *Fireball* because of his quick temper. This man demonstrated the political skills, good judgment, passion for work, and the wealth necessary to weave together different factions of the community, to maneuver African American leaders, to contribute to and befriend political candidates and use them as resource persons, to raise program money within his circle of affluent friends, and to personally donate the largest amounts of energy and money to the project. Though people disagreed with him from time to time, he possessed such charm and charisma that opponents could not hate him. It was the sheer power of his personality and his leadership that created the resource networking masterpiece illustrated in Figure 10.1.

This seems to suggest that personal ties are perhaps much more

FIGURE 10.1 Network of Resources

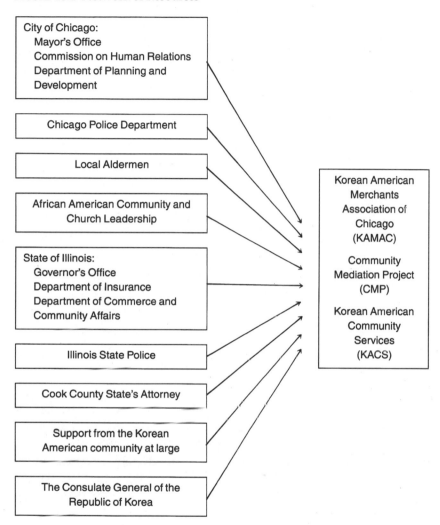

important than issues when it comes to implementing a community program. The significance of issues involved in black/Korean tension can help unite the community, but such causes alone do not result in community action. Organizational apparatus without passionate leadership lacks the spark necessary to energize the operation.

From antiquity, adventurous merchants, along with soldiers and religious seekers, have been the pioneer itinerants in any foreign land. This intrinsic nature of merchants, who are not afraid to venture into new

TABLE 10.2 Intraorganizational and Community Fundraising

Annual Dues and Food Basket Contributions	
December 1990	$24,113
December 1991	$22,415
December 1992	$39,298
December 1993	$46,519
Subtotal	$132,345
Scholarships	
June 1991	$1,950
June 1992	$3,450
June 1993	$4,100
June 1994	$3,450
July 1994	$9,846 (Scholarship Benefit Golf Outing)
Subtotal	$22,796
Political Campaigns	
February 1983	$30,000 (Harold Washington's Mayoral campaign)*
October 1992	$25,000 (Carol Moseley-Braun's U.S. Senate campaign)
Subtotal	$55,000
Total	$210,141

Source: KAMAC Annual Reports 1991–95
*Personal conversation with Chang Kun Kim.

markets, can be seen in Korean Americans who choose to act as pioneer businessmen in the inner city. These merchants were bold enough to trade in high-risk areas for profits, and the KAMAC's officers knew how to harness such courage in order to carry out good teamwork in high spirits and how to respect and build intraorganizational solidarity. Like any group of pioneers, the CMP staff appreciated and enjoyed their coarseness, boldness, simplicity, and most of all, their friendship. One staffer commented, "working with the *Fireball* is more fun than tackling the issue itself."

The KAMAC has been quite successful in its fundraising over past years. Although the United Way provided funding for CMP staff salary, administrative expenses, and office supplies, most of the money for programming was raised by the KAMAC. The emerging organization raised nearly $200,000 during the years 1990–94. Although the members paid their membership dues, a bigger portion of the budget came from the

KAMAC officers and the community at large. Upon assuming the presidency, every one of the three KAMAC presidents thus far has hired a manager from his shop to become a full-time volunteer leader.

The Attitude of Korean American Merchants

There certainly does exist a vicious cycle between the merchants and consumers in inner cities. The merchants complain, "Many customers are shoplifters." The customers complain, "They don't treat us right." "You are all lazy bums," the merchants respond. "You bloodsuckers, we don't want you in our neighborhoods," the customers shout back. The community mediation in Chicago has endeavored to break this vicious cycle. Although it is difficult to measure how successful the program has been, it appears that some degree of change in behavior, though not necessarily in intrinsic attitude, has occurred.

In October 1992, the CMP staff asked Chicago's Korean American merchants some questions on their business attitudes toward and perceptions of African Americans. These questions were intentionally pedagogical to inspire self-reflection, designed to encourage merchants to recognize in themselves the need for a change in attitude and to see the positive attributes of African Americans rather than the negative ones. The survey revealed that after the L.A. riots and NBA play-off disturbances in Chicago, the merchants' perceptions of African Americans and their business attitudes virtually remained the same, although some merchants became more bitter toward African Americans and noticed African Americans turning wilder than before. It is a positive sign, however, that 21 percent of the merchants said they were greeted with sympathy from their customers after the riots. Although the majority of Korean American merchants (57.4%) were pessimistic about their own efforts to ease the tension, they demonstrated a consensus that the mediation program efforts and their contributions to the African American community should be continued. A comparable majority of the merchants also tacitly acknowledged flaws in their attitudes, agreeing with the question, "Is there anything that we should change in order to enhance our understanding of African Americans?"

Almost all merchants stated that their customers should be greeted and treated more respectfully and they should be more understanding and grateful to African Americans rather than condescending and contemptuous. Most of them also all agreed with the following ten points:

TABLE 10.3 Business Attitudes toward and Perceptions of African Americans
n=162

After the L.A. riots and Bulls' riots, how do you perceive of the attitude of African Americans?

Sympathetic to Korean American merchants	4	2.5%
Wilder	38	23.5
Same as before	109	67.3
No answer	11	6.8

Did any African American customers sympathize with the agony that you went through during the riots?

Yes	34	21.0%
No	120	74.1
No answer	8	4.9

After the L.A. and Bulls' riots, how did your attitude towards African Americans change?

More understanding	12	7.4%
More bitterness	30	18.5
Same as before	107	66.0
No answer	13	8.0

If we Korean American merchants try, will the black/Korean tension be eased?

Yes	57	35.2%
No, it is a socio-economic problem	93	57.4
No answer	12	7.4

Even if black/Korean tension is a societal problem, shall we continue to try our programs, though the results may be meager?

Yes	139	85.8%
No	4	2.5
I don't care	8	4.9
No answer	11	6.8

Should we continue to contribute to African American community?

Yes, cheerfully	85	52.5%
Yes, because we have to	60	37.0
No	1	0.6
No answer	16	9.9

Is there anything that we should change in order to enhance our understanding of African Americans?

Yes	144	88.9%
No	5	3.1
No answer	13	8.0

Source: KACS 1992

1. African Americans are affective, feeling-oriented people.
2. I feel natural affinity towards African Americans because we are all on the same boat as minorities.
3. I feel grateful to black customers who make my living possible.
4. I hate shoplifters.
5. Racial discrimination and the persisting history of slavery are still oppressing factors for African Americans.
6. We should greet our customers kindly by saying "hello," "how are you," etc.
7. We should participate more in community meetings, despite language barriers.
8. We should give out change in a good manner.
9. We should hire more African Americans whenever help is needed.
10. We should avoid using derogatory terms for African Americans.

Written comments of the merchants were also all moving and authentic.

— It hurts the business to look down upon all African Americans for a few bad customers.
— The customers are kings. Better service!
— Customers should be treated as guest to stores.
— Persuasive dialogues, not physical fights, are what we need.
— As we get refunds and exchanges from Marshall Field's, we should do exactly the same for black customers.
— "It is because of me," we should tell ourselves. We shouldn't deceive the customers with imitation and cheap products.
— Employers and employees are all equally human beings. Black employees should be treated fairly. They aren't slaves!
— Yes, there are shoplifters, but doesn't every race or nation have good guys and bad guys? We shouldn't generalize based on a few examples.
— We should realize that Koreans and blacks are all minorities. Getting rid of distrust, we should share more time to reaffirm our togetherness.
— Whenever possible, I try to think from the customers' side and listen to their requests.
— We are making money from black neighborhoods. We should try to create the image that we are friends of black people.

For future study, it would be beneficial for researchers to revisit these merchants several years later to find out how much of their genuine concerns were translated into actual attitude and behavioral changes. In the aftermath of the Los Angeles riots and Chicago NBA play-off riots, however, it is clear that the merchants deeply felt their attitudes must change in order to survive.

Business Insurance

Carrying business insurance can give a merchant psychological and economic relief, protecting his business in cases of damage or incidents

TABLE 10.4 Business Insurance

Do you have business insurance?		*n*=162
Yes	99	61.1%
No	59	36.4
No answer	4	2.5
Types of insurance:		*n*=99*
Fire	98	99.0%
Theft	33	33.3
Liability	76	76.8
Time purchased insurance:		*n*=99
Before the 1992 Bulls' riots	84	84.8%
After the 1992 Bulls' riots	6	6.1
No answer	9	9.1
Premium:		*n*=99
Over $3,000	11	11.1%
Over $2,000	18	18.2
Over $1,000	36	36.4
Less than $1,000	22	22.2
No answer	12	12.1
Insurance carriers:		*n*=99
State Farm	38	38.4%
Allstate	5	5.1
Others	44	44.4
No answer	12	12.1
Reasons for not yet having business insurance:		*n*=59*
Too expensive	37	62.7%
Tried but rejected	26	44.1
Waste of money, why bother?	7	11.9

Source: Korean American Community Services 1992
*Some merchants checked multiple answers

like arson. Business insurance is also one indicator of stability, in that only the more established merchants can afford to pay the premiums. Many inner-city merchants say, half in jest and half seriously, that it is cheaper to replenish their stolen goods than to carry theft insurance. According to the 1992 CMP survey, ninety-nine merchants (61.1%) had some type of business insurance, whereas fifty-nine of the respondents (36.4%) did not have any insurance at all. The majority of those merchants with insurance paid an annual premium of more than $1,000, much higher than premiums in low-risk areas. Most of their insurance policies, however, only covered fire damage, and just one-third of those merchants with insurance—or 20.4 percent of all merchants surveyed—carried theft insurance. Of those fifty-nine merchants who had no insurance, many had considered the premium too expensive (the problem of affordability) or had tried to purchase insurance but were rejected by companies (the problem of accessibility), or both. Only 43.5 percent of the insured merchants were covered by major companies, that is, State Farm and Allstate (the two largest companies in Illinois). The remaining respondents, 44.4 percent, were insured by pipeline companies, small and headquartered outside Illinois. Even after the agonizing experiences of the Los Angeles and Bulls' championship riots of 1992, however, only six more merchants obtained insurance after June 1992.

The KAMAC and KACS are currently working closely with the Illinois State Department of Insurance to make business insurance more accessible and affordable to merchants on the South and West Sides. Once the planned Market Assistance Program is implemented by the Department of Insurance, which regulates and licenses all Illinois insurance companies, major companies will be mandated to insure inner city merchants at a reasonable premium. If successful, this program will significantly decrease the percentage of inner-city Korean American merchants with no business insurance.

Some Suggestions

Community empowerment and economic empowerment are closely linked issues for Chicago's inner-city Korean American merchants. As they encounter boycotts and consumer disputes, they become increasingly aware of the necessity of networking with African American leaders. As long as Korean Americans desire to trade in the inner city, it will be requisite to continue to maintain and expand this network. This networking, however, must always be with legitimate leaders and organizations. Any connections to illegitimate organizations, however powerful they may be, can be detrimental in public relations with the legitimate African American community and dominant white majority.

Chicago's Korean American merchants were approached by 21st Century Voices of Total Empowerment (VOTE), a local organization allegedly linked to gangsters, in late 1993. This group then led a boycott on December 28, 1993, after the merchants did not give in to their requests. The CMP staff, in consultation with the area merchants, immediately asked prominent African American leaders to mediate. On August 2, 1994, the 21st Century VOTE was approved for a $45,000 Community Development Block Grant by a 7–2 vote at the finance committee of the Chicago City Council; they were hired as a subcontractor to the Chicago Urban League to negotiate with unions and refer jobs on public works projects in the city. On August 3, 1994, however, the entire council overturned the funding proposal by a 34–6 vote (*Chicago Tribune*, 3–4 August 1994). Hoping to capitalize on the mobilizing strength of this gang-related organization for his upcoming mayoral campaign, Mayor Richard M. Daley of Chicago had initially engineered the support of the committee, but he switched his position the next day and the proposal was turned down. Had the merchants originally agreed to the 21st Century VOTE's demands in December 1993, it certainly would have been reported by mainstream media and could have been a fiasco for the CMP efforts with the legitimate black and white population.

Where should inner-city merchants go from here for economic empowerment? They can at least implement the following changes immediately: conform behaviorally to what is acceptable to African Americans, as long as their demands are justifiable; realize community participation as a part of business operation—a mercantile responsibility, not an extra-mercantile option—and contribute monetarily as a group; secure business insurance; purchase buildings and renovate them; and file income tax returns properly, in order to more easily obtain bank, city, state, and federal government loans.

Franchising may be another option for some merchants to leave the inner city and diversify their business. It may help merchants structure or formalize their operation, relieve them of the stress resulting from frequent shoplifting and threats to personal safety, and add prestige to their status. Franchising is regarded as a safe venture: less than 5 percent of new franchises fail, while 65 percent of new nonfranchise businesses fail within five years. Many Korean American merchants are economically capable of thriving in this arena; average total investment per franchise is approximately $147,000 (Lewy and Choi 1994). In conjunction with Columbia College, Chicago, the KAMAC and KACS and other community organizations explored this option through a two-day seminar on franchise business and a trade fair.

These business activities signify that what started as an organization focused on race relations efforts is now shifting gears to incorporate something other than what was originally intended in the program. No doubt, race relations begot the merchant organization, but that apparatus can now be used to achieve multiple goals. The merchants will increasingly conceptualize race relations as a subset of their economic pursuit. Therefore, the organization or community program representing them must also satisfy their economic needs; race relation efforts alone are unlikely to sustain its membership in the future.

The components of Chicago's programming experience have frequently been replicated in other major cities. Chicago is perhaps distinguished from other cities by three factors: (1) the presence of one single, centralized, funded apparatus that monopolized the issues related to black/Korean conflict; (2) strong and experienced leadership capable of mobilizing all possible resources of the mainstream society, the Korean American community, and the African American community; (3) full-time mediation specialists, including an African American, who worked with the merchants to develop the best possible ways to ease the tension. Our evaluation of the CMP is quite ambivalent, because we are skeptical about the merchants' inner attitudes toward African Americans, on the one hand, and yet, on the other hand, we are confident about the CMP's capacity to contain the tension by educating merchants on behavioral expectations and utilizing the intracommunity and intercommunity networks built in past years. The clustering of Chicago's Korean American stores in two- to three-block shopping strips perhaps makes merchant cooperation easier than would be possible in places in which stores are widespread, such as South Central Los Angeles. This dense grouping of stores was also one of the key factors that brought about the successful police protection during the Bulls' NBA championship crises.

Conclusion

The world is gray, not black and white. While students of social sciences may have spirit and passion for the improvement of their communities, they are primarily called upon to understand and interpret broad social phenomena. Their contributions often lie in helping leaders and masses alike in their quest for something both *ideal* and *possible* (Suttles 1990). The ideal alone, which cannot translate into collective praxis, is not of much value to earthly mediators. To pursue the impossible and improbable ideal may happen in a realm that belongs to individual religious virtuoso. Being reminded of such ideals, however, will help outline what is both virtuous and possible. Academic social scientists and community activists are called on to search for the possible good, while envisioning, though oftentimes discarding, the impossible better.

It may be ethically debatable to manipulate, if not exaggerate, the perception that Korean Americans are wholly genuine and selfless in their efforts to improve race relations. It could also be considered vanity to boost one's ego with plaques, trips, and banquets, to make campaign donations to local politicians, and to propagandize an organization's good programs and noble intentions. These public relations are, however, indispensable and an integral part of community mediation. We have nothing to offer in defense of such practices, except to confess that the people involved in Chicago's mediation efforts are not dreamers, they are very much down-to-earth realists. Although many components of the CMP were intended to generate a *perception* of interracial friendship rather than to create such an authentic friendship, the KAMAC and KACS leaders and CMP staff felt their share of gratification from the success of the project, and they deeply believe that something is much better than nothing. They would assert that their efforts to help the merchants were always noble, especially when interethnic disputes and crises endangered not only Korean American merchants but also the community at large. Tears, sweat, smiles, and humor have all congealed into the CMP. This project painted a self-portrait using gray as its primary color, mixing black and white equally. The ideal and the real, authenticity and hypocrisy, virtue and vice, substance and theatrics, all have played a part in this performance, which, in the end, was a smashing success.

REFERENCES

Korean American Merchants Association of Chicago. 1991–1995. *Annual Reports.*
Korean American Community Services. 1992. *The 1992 Korean American merchants survey.* Chicago.
Lee, Yoon Mo. 1994. Perception and reality of the relationship between Korean Merchants and African-American customers. Chapter 14 in *Korean Americans: Con-*

flict and harmony, edited by Ho-Youn Kwon. Chicago: North Park College and Theological Seminary.

Lewy, Thomas, and InChul Choi. 1994. *The Korean American entrepreneur's guide to franchising*. Chicago: Columbia College, Chicago, and Korean American Community Services.

Suttles, Jerald D. 1990. *The man-made city: The land-use confidence game in Chicago*. Chicago: University of Chicago Press.

11 Identity Politics: Chicago Korean-Americans and the Los Angeles "Riots"

Jung Sun Park

THE LOS ANGELES "RIOTS," WHICH BROKE OUT ON APRIL 29, 1992, were crucial "social dramas"—that is, "public episodes of tensional irruption" (Turner 1974: 33)—in contemporary American history. Through the looking glass of the large-scale, violent social dramas, which brought the "fundamental aspects of society, normally overlaid by the customs and habits of daily intercourse, into frightening prominence," (Turner 1974: 35) we were, once again, painfully reminded of lingering racial prejudice and exacerbated economic inequality. This time, however, the topography of tensions and conflicts between groups diverged from the old black-white dichotomy and took on a more diverse shape. The visible involvement of Asian Americans and Latino Americans along with African Americans and European Americans in the "riots" as both assailants and victims indicated that new types of interethnic and interracial relations were emerging. Signifying the transformation of intergroup relations in urban America, the social dramas were thus labeled as the nation's first "multiethnic riots."

Although the unique characteristics of the Los Angeles "riots" triggered growing interest in the new forms and arenas of intergroup relations, our knowledge and analyses of the emergent trends have remained limited. The complex interplay of race, ethnicity, class, and nationalism embedded in the new trends obfuscates our analyses of the new phenomena. At the same time, however, our lack of information and understanding about those "new" groups, such as Asian Americans and Latino Americans, prevents us from comprehending these changes. As minorities, especially as politically powerless minorities, those groups have long remained invisible and silent in public discourses. Consequently, their voices and views have largely remained unheard or underrepresented, even in the context of the "multiethnic riots"; this has resulted in a partial and biased understanding of the 1992 "riots." Thus, if we are to fully understand the changing characteristics of intergroup relations, it is critical that we incorporate the perspectives of those new players who have been neglected thus far. By doing so, we can gain better insight into the junctures where the complicated agendas and interests of diverse groups intersect, compete, and cooperate—which, in turn, will shed light on the trajectories of the transforming interethnic and interracial relations in late-twentieth-century America.

As a step toward gaining a more comprehensive understanding of the new intergroup relations revealed during the Los Angeles riots, I will bring forward the stances and perspectives of one of the most visible, yet one of the most silenced new players: Korean-Americans. In particular, based on a Chicago Korean-American case, I will analyze the ways in which the riots affected a regional Korean-American population's sense of collective identity and their views on, and practices of, intergroup relations. More specifically, I will first examine how Chicago Korean-Americans' ethnic identity has become (re)constructed and politicized in the context of the riots, through an analysis of mainstream media coverage and the Korean-American population's reactions to it. Then I will discuss how this politicized ethnicity reshaped Chicago Korean-Americans' positionality and relations vis-à-vis other groups.

By exploring the riots through the eyes of Chicago Korean-Americans, who were not directly exposed to the incident, I intend to draw attention to two important but overlooked aspects of Korean-Americans' experience of the incident: the broader implications of the riots on Korean-Americans who live in places other than the Los Angeles area; and the effects of local socioeconomic and political contexts on the responses of particular regional Korean-American populations. So far, our understanding of Korean-Americans' experience of the riots has almost exclusively relied on the Los Angeles Korean-American case. Considering the immediacy of their experience, there is no doubt that the main analytical focus should be placed on the local population. However, the centrality of the Los Angeles case was overemphasized to the extent that, implicitly and explicitly, it was taken to represent the entire Korean-American experience of the incident. Other Korean-American populations' experience of, and responses to, the riots were almost completely ignored.

Yet, the riots had overreaching repercussions on Korean-Americans elsewhere, beyond the geographical boundaries of Los Angeles, and these diverse Korean-American populations' experiences were both similar to, and different from, those of their co-ethnics in Los Angeles. The commonalities are related to the overreaching impact of the riots on Korean-Americans as a collectivity. During the course of the riots, Korean-Americans were, both voluntarily and involuntarily, bound together as a collectivity through their shared ethnic background, their structural sociopolitical position, and the larger society's framing of them as a group. Thus, based on their membership in the collectivity, Korean-Americans elsewhere empathized with and were connected to their co-ethnics in Los Angeles, symbolically, if not practically, going through the experience of the riots together.

Yet the repercussions of the incident varied considerably among individual Korean-Americans and local Korean-American populations. For example, as I argued elsewhere, perspectives and positions of individual Korean-Americans varied widely, depending on their socioeconomic status, generation, and political views (Park 1992). Local-level collective responses, my focus in this chapter, were less diverse than individual ones, but they too differed because the specific social, economic, and political positions and contexts of local Korean-American populations influence the local Korean-Americans' particular perspectives and agendas. For example, the history and patterns of a local Korean-American population's relations with other ethnic and racial groups, their occupational niche, and their political power are all factors that differently affect local experiences. Since both the generality and particularity across regions are integrated parts of Korean-Americans' experience of the riots, our understanding of the significance and implications of the riots for the Korean-American population will remain partial unless we incorporate the views and voices of diverse local Korean-American populations. By introducing a Chicago Korean-American case, I hope to lay the groundwork for a broader comparative analysis of Korean-Americans' experience of the 1992 riots.

Victor Turner argues that in the unfolding processes of a social drama, "the scope and range of the field will have altered; the number of its parts will be different; and their magnitude will be different. More importantly, the nature and intensity of the relations between parts, and the structure of the total field, will have changed" (1974: 42). The changes that the Los Angeles riots generated in Chicago Korean-Americans' social fields are most noticeable in the transformation of their collective identity and their structural repositioning in relation to other groups. These changes all began with Korean-Americans' painful realization of their position in the United States. Through a series of incidents and conditions, such as the massive destruction of Korean-American businesses, the lack of proper police protection, and the biased media portrayal, Chicago Korean-Americans clearly saw where they, as a collectivity, were situated in the social and cognitive matrices of their adopted country. To their dismay, Korean-Americans realized they were powerless, voiceless, and marginal "others," whose membership in U.S. society was often questioned and denied. Korean-Americans' marginality and powerlessness stemmed, in a way, from their structural positionality as "in-betweens."

At the same time, the larger U.S. society's ideological construction of who Korean-Americans are and where they belong also has played a pivotal role in their peripheralization. For example, throughout the course of the riots, Korean-Americans were frequently categorized as "foreigners." The categorization was quite powerful and effective in undermining Korean-Americans' position in the society: it negated the very foundation of their existence here. In other words, by completely excluding Korean-Americans from the category of "we Americans" and relegating them to the "foreigner" category, the dominant society left no room for Korean-Americans' membership and belonging. Although this extreme "otherization" of Korean-Americans was a predominant force in generating their marginality, other ideological categorizations also influenced their status. Most notably, based on their real and putative resemblance, Korean-Americans were linked to the Asian American population as a whole. Korean-Americans then became burdened with certain historical legacies of Asian American experiences, such as invisibility and stereotyping. Thus, mainly through the lens and voices of the media, the larger society's disciplinary and controlling power over Korean-Americans was discursively articulated, imposed, and disseminated, binding Korean-Americans within multiple layers of unequal power relations.

Realizing their marginality and its sociopolitical implications, Chicago Korean-Americans consciously engaged themselves in the (re)construction and politicization of their collective identity as a way to challenge the situation. Led by community political leaders and activists, Korean-Americans began the process of negating their otherness through the advocation and mobilization of their ethnic identity, that is, their Korean-American identity. As a way of classifying group relationships, ethnicity basically operates through the logic of inclusion and exclusion, a "we" and "they" dichotomy (see, for example, Barth 1969; Vincent 1974;

Wallman 1981; Eriksen 1993). Hence, by declaring their ethnic American identity, Chicago Korean-Americans claimed their inclusion as "one of us," as opposed to the larger society's exclusion of them as "foreign others." The political connotations of such inclusion could provide Chicago Korean-Americans with grounds on which to protect their rights and participate in the U.S. sociopolitical system as equal members.

The flip side of this inclusion entails a contradictory outcome, however, owing to intrinsic characteristics of ethnicity. According to John and Jean Comaroff, "The emergence of ethnic groups and the awakening of ethnic consciousness are . . . the product of historical processes which structure relations of inequality between discrete social entities" (1992: 55). So they claim that "ethnicity has its origins in the asymmetric incorporation of structurally dissimilar groupings into a single political economy" (54). In other words, Chicago Korean-Americans' articulation of their ethnic identity placed them into another field of asymmetrical power relations. It meant they were now more systematically incorporated into America's strictly formulated racial and ethnic hierarchy. In this sense, the identity politics in which Chicago Korean-Americans were involved differ from the prevalent type of identity politics, which highlight difference. In this prevalent type of identity politics, differences are used as a means by which individuals and groups can "multiply the source of resistance to particular forms of domination" (Jana Sawicki, quoted in Gregory 1993: 402). However, in the case of Chicago Korean-Americans, the fundamental cause of their powerlessness lay in the total denial of their membership in this land. Thus their identity politics were constructed and imagined, and took the form of a politics of "similarity," emphasizing inclusion based on their similarities to the rest of the society. A celebration of Korean-Americans' differences and claims of their rights and entitlement based on such differences could only begin once the basic inclusion in society was accomplished.

The transformation of Chicago Korean-Americans' collective identity from a foreign immigrant group to an incorporated ethnic group inevitably brought about changes in their positions and relations relative to other groups. Since Korean-Americans are transnationals who are "fully encapsulated neither in the host society nor in their native land but who nonetheless remain active participants in the social settings of both locations" (Glick-Schiller and Fouron 1990: 330), the shifting positionality of Chicago Korean-Americans entailed changes in their intergroup relations not only within the United States but also across borders, specifically, in relation to their homeland. Thus, their views on the roles and

meanings of their homeland underwent critical reevaluation. Furthermore, this changing meaning of homeland altered the ways in which
Korean-Americans related to other Korean diaspora populations. Since
the centrality of their homeland had diminished, their relations with
other overseas Koreans were also reconsidered. Overall, these changes
imply a major structural reorganization of Korean-Americans' positions,
as well as transformation of their reference points and social fields. In the
following section, I discuss the impact of the Los Angeles riots on Chicago Korean-Americans, focusing on the identity politics engendered by
the incident and its consequences for intergroup relations.

KOREAN-AMERICANS IN CHICAGO

Korean immigration to the United States dates back to the turn of the
century, yet it was not until the 1965 Immigration and Nationality amendments became effective that Koreans started coming to America in large
numbers (I. Kim 1981; Kraly 1987; Takaki 1989). According to the 1990 U.S.
Census, 798,849 Korean-Americans are currently living in the United
States, and Chicago has the nation's third largest Korean-American population, after Los Angeles and New York. Of 36,189 Korean-Americans in
the Chicago area, some 22,326 reside in various suburbs, whereas the remaining 13,863 live in the City of Chicago (*Chicago Tribune* April 26, 1992).[1]

In general, the Chicago Korean-American populations are residentially dispersed, with a relative concentration in the northwestern and
western suburbs. A considerable number of Korean-Americans also
live in a northwestern neighborhood in Chicago called "Koreatown" by
Korean-Americans.[2] Sharing similar traits with their co-ethnics elsewhere in America, a large proportion of Chicago Korean-Americans are
engaged in small business, many of which are within two major business
sections in Chicago: the northwest side and the South Side. The former is
located in the Koreatown area and attracts mostly co-ethnic clientele.
Compared to Los Angeles's Koreatown, Chicago's Koreatown is smaller
and less conspicuous; it is situated in a multiethnic neighborhood and
covers one long business strip extending over several blocks. The South
Side business section is, on the other hand, established in predominantly
African American neighborhoods and serves African American clientele.
Those businesses are major sites of Chicago Korean-Americans' interethnic and interracial conflict. However, because they are located far
away from both the Koreatown area and the majority of Chicago Korean-
Americans' working and residential areas, what happens in the South

Side area has little immediate physical resonance for the general Chicago Korean-American population.

These locations of Chicago Korean-American residences and business expose Korean-Americans to contact and interaction with other groups as an integrated part of their everyday lives. However, as a first-generation-dominated, relatively recent immigrant population, Korean-Americans' interactions and socialization across racial and ethnic boundaries tend to remain minimal, and such interaction is usually limited to the workplace.[3] In the private domain, most first-generation Chicago Korean-Americans' social worlds are constructed within ethnic boundaries based on family networks and ethnic institutions such as churches.

As mentioned earlier, Korean-Americans are transnational. Not surprisingly, therefore, the connections between many Chicago Korean-Americans and their homeland (particularly South Korea) are still intact; indeed, through business transactions, frequent visits, and other contact, as well as a broad range of cultural consumption, Chicago Korean-Americans maintain strong socioeconomic and familial relationships with their country of origin. This lingering transnational linkage is, in a way, rooted in Chicago Korean-Americans' sense of primordial ties and established socioeconomic networks. On the other hand, it is also reinforced by their marginal status and experiences of discrimination in America.

As phenotypically and culturally distinctive people who are not completely proficient in the English language and have insufficient knowledge of "mainstream" American society, Chicago Korean-Americans (especially the first-generation immigrants) tend to, voluntarily and involuntarily, isolate themselves from the larger society. Heavy reliance on ethnic social and economic networks, combined with the significance of Korea as a shared main reference point, contributes to Chicago Korean-Americans' strong tendencies to hold onto their Korean identity as a primary identity and to view the world through a clear "we" versus "they" dichotomy. For example, Chicago Korean-Americans often call the Korean-American community "*gyoposahoe*" ("our countrymen's society") and the larger society "*migugsahoe*" ("American society"), reflecting the social and psychological gap between the two (I. Kim 1981: 181). However, the Los Angeles riots cast a critical question about the validity and meaning of such boundary demarcation to Chicago Korean-Americans, thereby initiating a crucial structural transformation.

Approximately seven hundred stores, about half of the total Korean businesses in Chicago, are located in African American neighborhoods on the South Side.[4] Compared with their counterparts in other major American cities such as Los Angeles, New York, and Philadelphia, Chicago's Korean-American businesses in those areas have had relatively less overt conflict with their clients; however, the location of these businesses inevitably engenders some conflict between Korean-Americans and African Americans. This conflict has manifested itself as boycotts and small-scale incidents of looting over the years. The looting incidents, the first of which took place in 1991 after the Chicago Bulls' NBA championship victory, became a particularly deep concern of the South Side's Korean-American merchants: each time the Bulls won the NBA championship (which they did consecutively in 1991, 1992, and 1993), there followed incidents of looting and attacks, though these varied in scale.[5]

Hence, each year the Korean-American merchants have anticipated this disturbance and tried to prevent it or at least reduce its impact by lobbying local politicians and police and by communicating with local African American leaders and organizations. By and large, these efforts to mitigate tension have been successful, building Korean-Americans' know-how about cooperation with local police as well as residents. However, when the Los Angeles riots broke out, Chicago Korean-Americans became worried; they were especially concerned because of the anticipated negative effect of the much-publicized "black-Korean conflict" rhetoric. Adding more anxiety to their situation, the Bulls seemed likely to win the championship again in 1992 (the team was advancing in the playoffs and eventually did win the championship), so there was a growing sense of immediacy and concern over another outbreak of riots in Chicago.

Although merchants on the South Side felt the immediacy of the riots most keenly, many other Korean-Americans were also concerned about the riots' general impact on the Chicago Korean-American community. Furthermore, Chicago Korean-Americans' empathy with their co-ethnics in Los Angeles was not simply grounded in their concerns about another outbreak of violence in Chicago. It was also rooted in their sense of collectivity drawn from shared blood, culture, and, most of all, their similar experiences and fate as immigrants. Cathy Lee, a 1.5-generation professional, explained the sentiment this way[6]:

> You know, when L.A. happened, I don't think there was one
> Korean-American who felt that was just [an] issue of the merchants.
> I think every one of us felt that was our issue, I mean, we saw it, we
> were pained by that whole imagery that we saw on television, you

know. It's like . . . we saw our twenty, thirty years of dreams being
burnt away through sound bites and film clips. . . . . That was a very
painful process, and, because of that, merchant issues became more
mainstream Korean community issues. It wasn't just their problem—
it sort of became our whole community problem.

The televised burning down of this "American dream" was probably
what had connected Chicago Korean-Americans with their co-ethnics in
Los Angeles in the first place, for, whether they were merchants or not,
they had also worked so hard to make their "American dream" come
true. Sharing the experiences of hard work and hardship in a foreign
land, Chicago Korean-Americans could understand, from their heart,
what it was like to lose a lifetime of work and dreams. Moreover, the
danger of violence was a possibility for them, also. The televised images
of violence and destruction conjured up the potential danger lurking in
their own lives—like their counterparts in Los Angeles, they, too, could
find themselves "in the wrong place at the wrong time" and lose everything in a moment. Chicago Korean-Americans' fear, and its foundations,
largely stemmed from their awareness of their "in-between" position in
the U.S. socioeconomic structure. As a minority group in the middle, they
are located in the "buffer zone" between races and classes, and could
become a proxy and an alternative target in such conflicts. A second-
generation professional, David Park, described the situation in the context of the Los Angeles riots:

> I think from the black viewpoint, they viewed it as more American
> society in general vs. blacks. And I think, for that reason, when they
> decided to fight back and rage against the society, I think, for them it
> made just as much sense to rage against the Koreans. I also think that,
> in many respects, the Koreans to them represented the white society
> or dominant society. And economic forces and economic opportuni-
> ties that they feel denied. And so, for that reason, we were positioned
> to be scapegoated. And when the time came for rioting, I think, that's
> why what might have seemed a black vs. white thing, the Rodney
> King case itself, turned out to be sort of black vs. dominant society, of
> which Koreans were the visible and nearby representative.

In addition to Korean-Americans' structural position, the larger society's categorization of Korean-Americans as a collectivity constructed the
incident as a collective crisis. In public discourses regarding the incident,
variety within the Korean-American population was mostly ignored; in-

stead, skewed images of a Korean-American collectivity, drawing mainly on the stereotypes about, and experience of, Korean-American merchants, were emphasized and disseminated. In other words, the characteristics of the Korean-American population were circumscribed and represented within the frame of the merchant experience. The media, in particular, played a pivotal role in constructing, reinforcing, and circulating such biased images. Through the media imagery, the Los Angeles "merchant problem" was transformed into a "whole community problem" for Chicago Korean-Americans, and the media has become a major reference point against which new definitions and images of the Korean-American collectivity were constructed.

"Others" on the Periphery: Korean-Americans in the Looking Glass of the "Mainstream" Media

During the course of the Los Angeles riots, three images of Korean-Americans prevailed in the media. A film titled *SA-I-GU* (*April 29*), which documented the feelings and perspectives of some Korean-American women whose lives were directly affected by the riots, succinctly summarizes these images:

> The three main media images of Koreans before, during and immediately after the "riots" were one, of a Korean shopkeeper shooting a black teenager [Latasha Harlins] in the back of the head, from a store videotape and that was the second most shown video during the one week following April 29, 1992 on L.A. commercial news, usually shown together with the beating of Rodney King. And two, screaming, begging, crying, yelling, inarticulate—not speaking but just hysterical—mostly female shop owners who were begging people not to destroy their stores, who were lamenting over their stores having been destroyed. And three, the footage shown over and over again of Korean—mostly male—merchants on the roof with guns, apparently ready to shoot anybody and through with the implication that they only cared about their property, that they didn't care about human life or the communities—the people in the communities where they were . . . where their stores were even located (Elaine Kim in *SA-I-GU*).

Needless to say, all these media images were shocking and distressful to most Chicago Korean-Americans. For them, it was surprising and discomforting enough to see their co-ethnics being portrayed on national network television as somewhat like outlaws in the Wild West, shooting aimlessly in the air and frantically defending their property, perhaps at the expense of others' lives.[7] More troublesome than the image of Korean-American vigilantes, however, was the juxtaposition of the Latasha Harlins footage with the Rodney King case. The videotape showing the killing of Latasha Harlins, an African American, by Soon Ja Du, a Korean-American merchant, after a dispute over a bottle of orange juice was aired repeatedly, sending a strong message of just how "ruthless" and "blood-sucking" Korean merchants are. The media continually played the scene showing Du shooting Harlins in the back, highlighting "Korean" merchants' brutality and supporting the media's notion that Korean-American merchants are "cold-blooded" murderers who deserved what happened to them during the riots. Considering that the Harlins shooting had taken place on March 16, 1991—about a year before the Los Angeles riots—and the verdict came out almost six months before the incident, the media's continuous juxtaposition of the two cases raises a question about the media's intention. Utilizing various examples of "black/Korean conflict," the media disproportionately emphasized the conflictive aspects of the two groups' relations, strongly implying that Korean-Americans had been asking for this kind of looting and destruction due to their repugnant relations with African Americans.

Chicago Korean-Americans with whom I spoke criticized and refuted the media's framing of "black/Korean conflict" in various ways. For example, a 1.5-generation South Side merchant, Mark Lee, argues that "instead of making the issue black against white, they [whites] divert it into Korean against black through the media." A second-generation professional, David, shares Mark's opinion and interprets the reason to be that "it's easier, and it's more interesting. The audience is going to be more interested in hearing that it's Koreans and blacks fighting against one another than the same old 'the system is wrong and racism is a problem.' I think this was a sort of selfish kind of motivation." Another second-generation student, James, attributes the roots of this "selfish motivation" to economic factors:

> It's really shameful. The media is always out there to sell a story. No matter what they do, they are going to try to sell the most shocking, most controversial story they can sell. It's all sensationalized. [Q: Why did they do it?] To sell a story, make money. Money is everything in this country. It's sad to say. . . . The media is like any other business—they want to make money.

Some even claimed that it was a classic example of "divide and conquer" in order to pit two minorities against each other. Although diverse interpretations were given as to the hidden motivation of the media, there was a general consensus about the harmful impact of the "black/Korean conflict" rhetoric. It was not, however, the emphasis on conflict alone that negatively pigeonholed Korean-Americans' place and status in the United States. What jeopardized Korean-Americans' position even more seriously was the depiction of them as "foreigners." The media frequently showed glimpses of the emotional and helpless victims, who could not express their feelings and opinions in English even at that critical moment. Hysterically crying out and shouting in their mother tongue, incomprehensible to the general public, the images of these victims were, indeed, strong and effective enough to inscribe Korean-Americans' "otherness" in the general public's mind.

The cultural construction of Korean-Americans as foreigners was not limited to television coverage. Print media also took an active part in portraying Korean-Americans as "others." For example, while using the "politically correct" term *African Americans, Newsweek* magazine nevertheless referred to Korean-Americans as *Koreans* and *new immigrants* in its article on the Los Angeles riots, reinforcing the false idea that they were not citizens or somehow did not belong in America (*Newsweek*, May 18, 1992). Despite some variation, other magazines and newspapers also used the terms *Korean* and *Korean-American* interchangeably, relying on the former more frequently and thereby projecting a feeling of "foreignness" (see, among others: *Newsweek*, May 11, 1992; *U.S. News and World Report*, May 11, 1992; *New York Times*, May 16, 1992; *Time*, May 11, 1992; *Village Voice*, June 9, 1992; *Chicago Tribune*, May 8, 1992). In that context, even some of the more sympathetic coverage of Korean-Americans' "foreign" cultural practices and behaviors, such as the *Kye* (a rotating credit system) and the avoidance of eye contact and touching (alleged sources of black / Korean misunderstanding), ended up highlighting the "otherness" of Korean-Americans, perhaps contrary to the reporters' intentions.

Discussing the television news media's coverage of the Los Angeles riots, Erna Smith (1993) argues that the practice of "framing" in the media has resulted in a biased portrayal of the incident. According to Smith, "A news 'frame' is a theme or story line that organizes the facts in a news report and gives them meaning" (1993: 6). Since a news frame is "routinized" by "journalistic norms and practices" in terms of where to get information, financial resources, what kinds of news to cover, and who the target audiences are, the result is a "selective emphasis of facts" and skewed portrayals of these facts and realities (1993: 8–9). In addition, frames are "frequently drawn from shared cultural narratives and myths" (Gamson, quoted in Smith, 1993: 9); thus they reinforce and reassert already existing stereotypes and biases.

The core of this frame of Korean-Americans' "otherness" lay in two elements of America's racial ideology: the fundamental distance America feels toward Asia and the lack of distinction between Asians and Asian Americans. As a quintessential "other" to the West, the East holds both a certain ideological and emotional burden and a fascination for the West. Historically, the division between the East and the West has shaped the ways in which America perceives and treats its people of Asian origin. For example, from the very beginning of their immigration history, Asian Americans have always been treated as exotic "others" who are "inassimilable"; numerous systematic efforts to exclude, control, and contain them have been made (see Hing 1993). Even now, after 150 years of immigration history, their belonging in this country is, more often than not, questioned, denying their full-fledged membership in American society. The internment of Japanese Americans during World War II and the killing of Vincent Chin, motivated by anti-Japanese sentiment, are just some examples of the lingering and profound discrimination against Asian Americans and the blurred boundary between Asians and Asian Americans (see *U.S. Commission on Civil Rights* 1992). In this sense, the "otherization" of Korean-Americans can trace its genealogy to America's longstanding racial ideology with regard to Asians and Asian Americans.

Korean-Americans' connection with the historic legacy of Asian American experiences can also be found in their underrepresentation and misrepresentation in the media. Indeed, Asian Americans have suffered from their invisibility and stereotypes throughout their history. It has been the case that either their voices and perspectives are virtually absent, or, when they are portrayed in the media, they are represented through coded stereotypes. So images of vicious villains like Dr. Fu Manchu or of mysterious and subservient men and women, such as the obedient and exotic female characters and the quiet, loyal male servants commonly portrayed in movies and television series, have shaped the general public's imagery of Asians and Asian Americans.[8] Burdened with this historical legacy, Korean-Americans' voices were underrepresented during the riots, as David Park argues:

> I don't think that the Korean viewpoint was—just in terms of media coverage and discussion of the event—I don't think it was fairly por-

trayed. Media images, I remember most were of . . . we were victims and vigilantes. And, I agree there were many of those, but there was a noticeable lack of Korean viewpoints expressed in much of the discussion and analysis of what happened. A lot of people on the black side spoke of their view of black-Korean tensions. A lot of white commentators spoke of their opinions about why these two groups were against each other. Yet, as for Koreans themselves actually speaking out from their viewpoints and experiences—this aspect was lacking.

Although the stereotypical images and otherness of Korean-Americans are intertwined with the historical legacies of other Asian American populations, Korean-Americans' recent immigration history and economic niche in small business also adds unique dimensions to their experience. For example, the association of Korean-Americans with small business is so prevalent that in everything from scholarly accounts (see Light and Bonacich 1988; Waldinger 1989) to popular culture (for example, movies such as *Do the Right Thing*) Korean-Americans' characteristics are portrayed in conjunction with their economic niche. In fact, the images of Korean-American merchants who conduct business in African American neighborhoods, and of the periodic manifestations of tension and conflicts between these two groups in the form of boycotting and looting, have been the aspects of Korean-Americans' lives and experiences most frequently depicted in the media (see, among others, *Chicago Tribune*, November 28, 1991; *New Republic*, July 2, 1990; *New York Times*, September 22, 1990; *Los Angeles Times*, May 30, 1991; *Washington Post*, November 29, 1991). These images have been so prevalent and strong that movies such as *Do the Right Thing*, *Falling Down*, and *Menace II Society*, as well as songs such as Ice Cube's *Black Korea*, have all depicted Korean-Americans as greedy foreign merchants. In the media coverage of the Los Angeles riots, these stereotypes and preconceptions became crystallized and infused an assumed meaning into the media's use of terms such as *Korean merchants* and *Korean shopkeepers*. Indeed, these terms were so prevalent in the media that it seemed as if *Korean* as an adjective was almost automatically associated with the noun *merchant*, symbolizing the conflation of ethnicity and occupation.

The exclusion and marginalization of Korean-Americans during the riots also took a form other than that of the selection of a linguistic marker. In this case, it was more of a structural definition and distancing, which was disclosed through an emphasis on the close links between the

"Korean immigrants" and their motherland. For example, a *Los Angeles Times* article reported the "the speaker of the South Korean Parliament said Saturday that the U.S. government should compensate Korean-Americans for damage done to their businesses in the Los Angeles rioting" (May 3, 1992). A *Wall Street Journal* article also reported that "a South Korean delegation headed by Deputy Foreign Minister Ho Seung will fly here today to meet with California Gov. Pete Wilson and other officials to discuss rebuilding. Overseas financial aid could include emergency funds and interest-free loans for affected businesses" (May 4, 1992). These articles' emphasis on the governmental involvement of South Korea was critical in that it fundamentally challenged Korean-Americans' position in the United States in a legal sense. If they were under the active protection of the South Korean government, as the articles implied, then Korean-Americans were still the political subjects of South Korea. The direction of such an argument would lead to the conclusion that Korean-Americans do not belong in this country either legally or culturally; therefore, they lack any basis on which to claim their rights and entitlement here.

A later *Wall Street Journal* article stated the denial of Korean-Americans' membership in America in a different manner. Its title read, "Koreans Slow to Aid Korean-American Victims of Riot" (May 20, 1992). The article said that "the general lack of interest in helping" Korean-Americans is "surprising." But why did the reporter take Korea's assistance of Korean-Americans for granted? Perhaps the strength (or lack of) of primordial ties was what the article primarily intended to convey, but the underlying assumption was that Korean-Americans do not fully belong in America and that, therefore, they should seek and expect support from Korea. *U.S. News and World Report* was even more direct about stating its opinions regarding this matter. Its article asserts: "Koreans also maintain closer ties to home than *most other immigrant groups*" (May 18, 1992, emphasis added).

Taking into account the fact that there are many other transnational immigrant groups that maintain close ties with their homeland, including those who even regularly migrate back and forth between their homeland and the United States, (such as the Mexican American population in California)[9] this was clearly a biased and unsubstantiated statement. Yet, as political rhetoric, the factual ground of the statement is secondary to the ideological message it intended to deliver. In this case, the statement had strong persuasive power since it corresponded to the prevailing perception of Korean-Americans' "otherness," which was already ingrained in public discourses.[10]

In response to this ideological marginalization, Chicago Korean-Americans firmly maintained their position as members of U.S. society. First-generation merchant Youngsoo Ku explains: "I oppose the Korean government's intervention in this matter. It is not that I oppose the intervention itself; it's that the more the Korean government intervenes, the more we are going to be isolated in the U.S. As long as we live in this country, we have to fight against the U.S. government on our own, as U.S. citizens."

In order to redefine where they stand, Chicago Korean-Americans have made conscious efforts to reconstruct and politicize a collective identity that enables their inclusion in America. The following section is an account of these processes.

(Trans)formation and Politicization of Ethnic Identity

During and immediately after the riots, many Korean-Americans were too shocked and dismayed to know how to react to the situation or what to ask of the larger society, which they believed was responsible for the situation. A shop owner who lost her property during the riots and was featured in the film *SA-I-GU* stated, "Right now, I'm angry at everybody. Or on contrary, I'm angry at myself. Because I don't know to whom, to where I should be angry at. I am totally confused . . . totally confused." At that time, these feelings of confusion, anger, and frustration were probably the most prevailing sentiments among many first-generation Korean-Americans in Chicago as well. A first-generation professional told me, "America has a 300-year history of racism, and we only have twenty years of immigration history here. How come the result of racism fell upon us?" Aside from the immediate emotional reactions, many also raised more fundamental questions and thoughts with regard to their immigration experience: Why are we here in the first place? Who are we? And what should we do for the future? First-generation professional Yoonshik Park remarks,

It [the riots] raised the question of reevaluating the Korean-American identity. The new phenomenon taking place in the Korean community is that people who stay outside of the community, especially the second and third generation, are reevaluating their

Korean-American identity, and come out and get involved in the Korean community. So, the riots provided momentum for the achievement of Korean-American solidification, and brought up the question of the search for identity. In addition, we still don't know the answer yet . . . but it made us think about survival tactics. . . . Many people are not aware of that yet.

As Mr. Park points out, the dismantling experience of the Los Angeles riots triggered in many Korean-Americans a search for their identity, as well as for their future direction and empowerment strategy. In Chicago, it was the younger generation (the 1.5 generation and the second generation) who took the lead in guiding and disseminating this newly sought direction.

When the riots broke out in Los Angeles, first-generation Chicago Korean-American community leaders, who lacked English-language ability and knowledge about the larger society, actively sought the younger generation's participation and help in dealing with the situation. As a consequence, the younger generation energetically began to get involved in the preparation of a more organized response to the incident, thereby becoming influential in the decision-making processes of community affairs more than ever before. For example, the younger-generation Korean-Americans prepared a press release representing the official position of the Chicago Korean-American community concerning the Los Angeles riots (it was sent out under the aegis of the Korean-American Association of Chicago, which functions as the representative organization of the Korean-American community in Chicago). Not surprisingly, this statement was not printed in any of the newspapers in the Chicago area, further supporting the fact that Korean-Americans' own voices were not reflected in public discourses during the course of the incident.

Despite such discouragement, some active and devoted younger-generation Korean-Americans continuously engaged themselves in delivering Korean-American voices to the "mainstream" society and other groups. For instance, 1.5-generation community activist Cathy Lee made frequent public speeches at university campuses and organizations in the Chicago area explaining and representing Korean-Americans' perspectives. At a forum held at Northwestern University on May 21, 1992, she emphasized the socioeconomic reasons for Korean-Americans' presence in urban ghetto areas, the cultural differences between Korean-Americans and African Americans, and the need for peace and harmony between the two groups. In her speech, Lee also criticized the "model minority" myth as a device of the larger society to "divide and conquer" the minorities and extended her arguments to the impact of Japan-bashing on exacerbating "xenophobic feelings" toward Korean-Americans, claiming that the Los Angeles riots were "hard-core economics and hard-core politics." Her perspectives on the role of various socioeconomic and political variables in shaping the Korean-American experience, indeed, reflect a shared sentiment and viewpoint among the younger generations of Korean-Americans in Chicago, and, consequently, they set the tone and direction of the collective responses of the population.

One of the most striking features in the younger generation activists' efforts to represent Korean-American voices in public discourses was their deliberate and consistent use of the term *Korean-American*. Given the circumstances, this is the best possible identifier to enable Chicago Korean-Americans' empowerment and entitlement. Yet political message aside, the term also carries psychological implications, especially for the younger generation, whose home and main reference points are the United States. My brief conversation with David, a second-generation professional, illustrates what the term means to young Korean-Americans.

INTERVIEWER: What do the terms *Korean* and *Korean-American* mean to you?

DAVID: *Korean* and *Korean-American* mean the same to me. Well, also, especially when you talk, to other Korean-Americans, a lot of times, you just don't bother with the American part because it's just extra work.

I: What about the non-Koreans?

D: Then I'm definitely more conscious remembering to say that [Korean-Americans].

I: Why?

D: Because defining yourself as an American is more important when dealing with those outside your group.

I: In what respect?

D: It's important for members of an outside group to remember that I am not a foreigner.

I: Do you feel that you are a foreigner?

D: No.

I: Have you ever felt you are a foreigner?

D: I've often been treated that way and made to feel that way.

I: In what context?

D: Throughout life.

Identity is constructed in the dialectical processes of self-ascription and ascription by others, and the unequal power relations embedded in these naming and boundary-making processes influence the trajectories of identity formation. In Korean-Americans' case, ascription by others generally entails exclusion and otherization of them, so their self-ascription tends to be formulated as a reaction to this imposed category. In the context of the riots, the need to construct a category that would effectively refute the denial of their place in America became greater than ever. Thus, in response, the politicized notion of Korean-Americanness was highlighted and articulated. Aware of its political connotation, the younger generation has utilized the term to its fullest in public speeches and writings. For example, when community activist Cathy Lee was interviewed by a mainstream local newspaper, she self-consciously and consistently used the term *Korean-American* (see the Q & A section in the *Ravenswood/Albany Park News Star*, May 13, 1992). Some others even claimed that they should use the term *Korean American*, without a hyphen, symbolizing their full-fledged membership in the U.S. society. The official press release of the Chicago Korean-American community mentioned earlier, as well as numerous other written materials regarding the Los Angeles incident sent to politicians and institutions, also persistently used the term. A statement prepared by a group of Korean-American students at the University of Chicago contained the term as well (*Chicago Maroon*, May 12, 1992). The younger generation intentionally made the term a critical political rhetoric for their empowerment in public.

The continual use of the term *Korean-American* by the younger generation had an immediate impact on the first generation, who soon realized the political significance of the designation. Despite their diverse individual ethnic identities, the first generation (especially the political leaders who are active and visible in the community activities) began using the term as a marker for their collective identity in public discourse. In October 1992, a group of political leaders of the Chicago Korean-American community held a fundraising party for then-senatorial candidate Carol Moseley-Braun. The party was mainly sponsored by the Korean Merchants Association, an organization of merchants who conduct business on the South Side and whose primary interest is the improvement of relationships with the African American community. All of the speakers from the host Korean-American community unequivocally referred to themselves in their speeches as Korean-Americans. One emphasized that "Korean-Americans consider ourselves to be Americans." The slogans of the event were "Korean-Americans salute Carol M. Braun" and "Korean-

American Merchants Support Carol Braun." Similar rhetoric was used in December 1992, when the Korean Merchants Association held its annual food basket program on Chicago's South Side as a way of returning something to the African American community. The event was advertised as "Korean-American and African-American Relations Effort: Christmas Food Basket Program."

Raymond Williams (1977) explains language as a mechanism that grasps and articulates social reality; thus, it most effectively captures the sociostructural conditions and social meanings embedded in group relations. Chicago Korean-Americans' conscious articulation of their politicized collective identity, then, stemmed from their assessment of the social environments and conditions that shape them. Although Chicago Korean-Americans had been aware of their marginal status in the United States, it was not until they peered through the looking glass of the Los Angeles riots that they could immediately and clearly face the bleak reality of racialized and ethnicized America. As a coping response, Korean-Americans articulated and mobilized a collective identity that best suited the situations in which they were bound. Michael Omi and Howard Winant put this process as follows:

> Social movements create collective identity by offering their adherents a different view of themselves and their world; different, that is, from the world view and self-concepts offered by the established social order. They do this by the process of re-articulation, which produces a new subjectivity by making use of information and knowledge already present in the subject's mind. They take elements and themes of her/his culture and traditions and infuse them with new meaning. (Omi and Winant, quoted in Apple 1993: 35)

Rearticulation of identity is also a process of producing meanings. Through the creation of meanings that can make sense of changing environments and relationships, individuals seek to establish some kind of "accountability."[11] In the Chicago Korean-American case, that accountability is still in the process of construction, a stage Williams calls "structures of feeling." According to Renato Rosaldo, the "structures of feeling differ from such concepts as 'worldview' and 'ideology' because they are just emerging, still implicit, and not yet fully articulate" (Rosaldo, 1993: 106). Simultaneously challenging and accommodating the structural constraints and unequal webs of power relations surrounding them, Chicago Korean-Americans have, thus, been engaged in the processes of constructing self and meaning.

Shifting Positions and Changing Group Relations

The public advocation of *Korean-Americanness* indicates that some fundamental changes regarding selfhood and the meanings attached to it are currently taking place in the Chicago Korean-American collectivity. As Abner Cohen argues, "selfhood is recreated in terms of the symbolic forms that articulate the changing organizational needs of the groups" (1979: 105). The organizational needs of Chicago Korean-Americans in the context of the Los Angeles riots were, most of all, to find a firm basis for their membership in U.S. society, and this was sought through the articulation and politicization of an ethnic identity. The symbolization of the Korean-American identity as a new "categorical imperative" (to borrow Cohen's term) to redefine their selfhood generates the conceptual and structural repositioning of Chicago Korean-Americans vis-à-vis other groups. Structurally situated "in-between," both at local- and global-level group relations, Chicago Korean-Americans' repositioning processes take place on multiple levels: in relation to their country of settlement, in relation to subgroups within that country, in relation to their country of origin, and in relation to other diaspora communities of Korean descent.

First, Chicago Korean-Americans' repositioning begins with a transformation of relationships with the larger U.S. society. Through the much-mobilized and politicized rhetoric of Korean-Americanness in public discourses, Chicago Korean-Americans claim their full-fledged, equal membership in the society. While the major target audience of Korean-American rhetoric is the "mainstream" society, Chicago Korean-American community leaders are also aware of the need to generate a subjective boundary shift within themselves and to change the ways in which they understand their selfhood in the United States. As a result, some campaigns calling for an increase in *chuinuisik* ("host mentality") in the United States have been initiated; these range from increased interest and commitment in recording Korean-American immigration history to more direct political campaigns such as voter registration drives.

The new construction of social meanings facilitated by the English term *Korean-Americans* is also well manifested in the change of the Korean term referring to the larger U.S. society. The old Korean term referring to the larger society—*migugsahoe* ("American society")—is now often juxtaposed with, and is being gradually replaced by, a new term—*churyusahoe* ("mainstream society")—in public discourses. Compared to the broader, nationality-based dichotomy between "American society" and "Koreans," the distinction between mainstream society and Korean-Americans' nonmainstream position implies that Chicago Korean-Americans have begun to think about their position within the American context. At the same time, however, the hierarchy and distance between the larger society and the Korean-American population are still conveyed by the new term. That is, the Korean-American population is situated on the periphery—thus indicating its powerlessness and situation of inequality. Compared to the more politicized and rhetorical English term, "Korean-American," which emphasizes an equal membership in America, the Korean term *churyusahoe* more directly illustrates and reflects the perceived social reality of inequality. If we are to agree with Raymond Williams's notion of language as "living evidence of a continuing social process" (1977: 37), these shifting terms, both Korean and English, indicate where, how, and to what extent the change of positions is taking place in relation to the larger society.

Second, Chicago Korean-Americans' membership in U.S. society has caused them to redefine themselves in relation to other groups in the society. As a racially and ethnically distinct group, Korean-Americans are bound to become a minority group in the United States. The layers of identities imposed on Korean-Americans by the larger society's hierarchical social structure and racial ideology connect Chicago Korean-Americans with other Asian American groups. This arbitrary category called *Asian Americans*—which encompasses a very broad range, from people of East Asian descent to those of Indian origin (in other words, incorporating a slightly altered notion of the "Orient" as ascribed by the West)—may not have immediate appeal to Chicago Korean-Americans. Yet as a political category, it carries a certain significant meaning for Chicago Korean-Americans. In particular, the experiences of discrimination suffered by Chinese Americans and Japanese Americans have become reference points by which Chicago Korean-Americans can compare and understand their own experience of the collective crisis. During the course of the Los Angeles riots, other Asian American groups supported Korean-Americans and expressed their concern and sympathy. Some members of the more established groups, such as Chinese Americans and Japanese Americans, even functioned as de facto "voices" of the Korean-American community, whose voices and perspectives were obviously lacking in the public discourse. Through these experiences, Chicago Korean-Americans have developed closer relationships with other Asian American groups, with whom they continue to work together in coalitions.

What appears to be a noticeable change in Chicago Korean-Americans' intergroup relationships is their shifting perspectives toward African Americans and Latino Americans. Korean-Americans' troublesome relationships with these groups (especially with African Americans) have been much written about and much discussed even before the riots. During the riots, then, African Americans and Latino Americans became the two major forces behind the destruction of Korean-American businesses. Meanwhile, the prevailing rhetoric of the "black-Korean conflict" reified Korean-Americans' relationships with African Americans. Hence, misconceptions, accusations, and resentment have been embedded in Korean-Americans' relations with these groups, and a clear line that cannot be crossed seems to have developed. Despite this common perception and the history of relations between the groups, what was expressed by Chicago Korean-Americans during and immediately after the riots was quite surprisingly different. The majority of the people I interviewed immediately after the riots told me that Korean-Americans should improve their relationships with African Americans and collaborate with them on political issues as fellow minorities. A 1.5-generation college student, Peter Kim, puts it this way:

> I think the next twenty years are going to be very interesting for
> America, because the different minorities are really going to have to
> work it out in order to survive. I really don't want to see it as a mini-
> ature competition between the Hispanics, blacks, Koreans, you
> know, Arab Americans, while the white Americans sit on the big
> piece of the pie. I think practically they are gonna have to cooperate,
> but I don't know.

As touched on in this statement, the basic logic behind improving relationships between Korean-Americans and other minority groups is that of survival. The common denominator that binds these contesting groups is their awareness of, and discontent with, their powerlessness in America. The larger and more important issue is the inequality existing between the powerful and powerless—not that existing among the powerless groups themselves. As Chicago Korean-Americans' realization of their minority status grows, their repositioning among other minority groups begins. So Korean-Americans have begun to use labels such as *African American* and *Latino American* instead of *blacks*, *Mexicans*, and *Hispanics*. These rhetorical shifts are important in that, by calling other groups by their proper titles, Korean-Americans deliver a message that they want to be treated likewise—as an equal member of the society.

Moreover, some progressive Korean-Americans even call these other groups "African American brothers" and "Latino American brothers," emphasizing their camaraderie as minorities. All of these terms demonstrate Korean-Americans' intentional political efforts to mitigate the present tension and to improve their relationships with other groups in the future.

Just how much these political messages can cross group boundaries and manage to generate the intended outcome remains unanswered, however. Assessing the degree of acceptance and internalization of this newly vocalized spirit of camaraderie and mutual respect is beyond the scope of this study. Yet, what is important here is the fact that this political rhetoric has been emerging as the sociopolitical relationships between the involved groups undergo change. As Murray Edelman argues, "the economic and social conditions in which people find themselves are decisive influences upon their interpretations of language, and especially of political language" (1988: 107). So, at least for Korean-Americans, these terms signify their revalorization of intergroup relations and their changing position in them.

Third, the transformation of Korean-Americans' position in U.S. society has affected changes in the relationships between Chicago Korean-Americans and their country of origin. While their close link with Korea is still maintained, there has been some intentional distancing from the home country, especially in the political arena. For example, Korean-Americans used to call themselves *gyopo* ("our countrymen"), the term used in Korea to denote overseas Koreans. This term implies that overseas Koreans are still Koreans, if not legally then at least psychologically. Although the term projects a Korea-centered view, it has rarely been challenged or opposed by overseas Koreans. However, since the term holds political connotations regarding the polity and its subjects, it has become contested terrain as membership in America becomes a central issue for Chicago Korean-Americans. Even before the riots, Chicago Korean-Americans occasionally expressed discomfort with the constant use of the term, especially by Korean officials such as the members of the Consulate General. The relationship between the Consulate General, as a representative of the home government, and Korean-Americans has a long history of both accommodation and conflict (see I. Kim 1981). From the Consulate's point of view, the Korean-Americans who are not American citizens are still subjects of Korea, and the terms they use to refer to Korean-Americans, *mijugyopo* or *mijugyomin* (both of which mean "countrymen in North America"), carry such a connotation. In a strictly legal sense, this rather broad application of the scope of the Korean polity abroad should do little more than offend Korean-Americans who are legally American citizens.

Yet as Chicago Korean-Americans' sense of Americanness grows and as structural repositioning begins, the terms, as a symbol of their belonging in and subordination to Korea, have been resisted and questioned by Chicago Korean-Americans, regardless of their actual citizenship status. A new word, *hanin* ("Korean-American"—it literally means "people of Korean descent," but often refers specifically to Korean-Americans in the United States), has been mobilized to counter the existing term, *gyomin*. As political rhetoric, the terms do not need to reflect individuals' actual legal status or internalization of a certain national identity. Instead, the significance lies in the whole range of possible meanings that a term carries, which enables individuals to make sense of their experiences in the complex social fields in which they reside. In this light, the meanings that *hanin* encompasses—such as political independence from Korea and the distinctive characteristics of Korean-Americans—provide Chicago Korean-Americans with some explanatory power regarding their experiences, especially as they try to create a niche in America and incorporate themselves into American society. In the political domain, inclusion in America means exclusion from Korea; by selecting one term over another, Chicago Korean-Americans symbolically imply the shifts in their political affiliation and their references in a global context.

Fourth, the changing global landscape, as well as their growing independence from the country of origin, encourages Korean-Americans to reassess their relationships with other overseas Korean populations. The demise of the cold war and the rapidly increasing exchanges of human and material resources across borders are now generating major changes in the world.[12] Above all, these global restructuring processes affect the ways in which local populations are connected with larger national and global practices. Given these circumstances, agents who can penetrate the interstitial dimensions of social relationships, which can connect not only the local and global but also the diversified and multiple subunits of a particular level, will be in a powerful and influential position as this globalization expands.

Korean-Americans, who are "in-betweens" among nation-states as well as subgroups within a nation, are situated in this kind of unique interstitial position, and they are gradually focusing on ways to participate in the global arena. For example, Chicago Korean-Americans are showing an increased interest in issues such as the reunification of the

Korean peninsula and transnational business. In particular, as the political climate between the Korean peninsula and the United States changes (for example, as a result of attempts to normalize diplomatic relations between North Korea and the United States), Chicago Korean-Americans have begun to seriously discuss their role and position in the changing international political field (see, for example, *Chosun Daily*, November 3, 1994; November 4–5, 1994). Chicago Korean-Americans' growing interest in these newly emerging transnational fields has also broadened their horizons with regard to their relationships with other Korean diaspora communities that are similarly situated. As a consequence, efforts are being made to strengthen the links among diverse overseas Korean groups. The use of the term *dongpo* ("people of the same ancestry") as opposed to *gyopo* ("our countrymen") in this sense reflects Korean-Americans' interests in such links. *Dongpo* has a transcendental quality, which embraces the broad category of other Korean diaspora, whereas *gyopo* carries a national connotation. Thus, Chicago Korean-Americans' adoption of the former term implies the redefinition of yet another social field as they shift their positions.

CONCLUSION

As transnational immigrants who are subordinately positioned in America's stratified ethnic and racial hierarchy, Korean-Americans are bound by complex webs of power relations. In particular, their structural "in-between" position (between countries of origin and settlement as well as between races and classes within the host society), combined with the hegemonic racial ideology of the host society, have carved the trajectories of Chicago Korean-Americans' identity politics. For example, Korean-Americans' in-between position in relation to their country of origin and their new home deprived them of not only their cultural citizenship but also their legal citizenship (at least symbolically) in America. At the same time, their location in the middle, between races and classes in America, situated them to be buffers.

The historical legacies of Asian Americans, such as otherness and invisibility, further exacerbated Korean-Americans' extreme marginality and powerlessness. Encountering various structural and cultural forces that fundamentally jeopardized their existence and location in America, Chicago Korean-Americans began their identity politics by focusing on their inclusion and entitlement. On the one hand, the claim of inclusion empowered them by conferring membership, but, on the other hand, it situated them as part of a different set of unequal power relations—this time, as a systematically incorporated minority in the racial and ethnic hierarchy. In this sense, Chicago Korean-Americans' identity politics was a process of constant struggle and negotiation between "choice and constraints" (Ericksen 1993: 57).

Moreover, Chicago Korean-Americans' structural positionality also brought about changes in intergroup relations beyond their specific locality. Thus the transformation of identity repositioned Chicago Korean-Americans not only in relation to the larger U.S. society and its subgroups but also vis-à-vis the homeland and other diaspora populations. This clearly illustrates that, for contemporary transnational immigrants whose lives span borders, local experiences have global connections and connotations. Through a discussion of Chicago Korean-Americans' identity politics, I have tried to shed light on the complex interplay of structural and cultural forces that shape transnational immigrants' lives and how these populations can cope with the multiple layers of power relations embedded in their lives. The construction and politicization of a collective identity is, in this regard, a group's way of making sense of its members' life experiences and of defining and building their niche in society.

NOTES

1. Many Korean-Americans claim that the census figures seriously underestimate the size of the Korean-American population. They claim that Korean immigrants' lack of linguistic ability, interest, and time makes it difficult for a considerable proportion of the group to participate in the census and therefore prevents the census from reflecting their true number. In Chicago, Korean-Americans commonly quote 100,000 as a representative figure for their population, although some consider this estimate to be exaggerated. One of my informants, who works at a community institution, estimates the real number to be between 60,000 and 70,000 based on his method: he counted the numbers of seemingly Korean last names listed in the Chicago area phone directories and multiplied the sum by four (the average number of persons per household). Lack of reliable statistical data about Korean-Americans generates much confusion in understanding even the basic demography of the group.

2. For the historical changes of Koreatown's location and the concentration of the Korean population in Chicago, see Y. Kim 1991. See also Conquergood 1992 for the changing and multiethnic characteristics of the area called Koreatown.

3. This may not be true for members of the American-born and American-raised younger generation, who tend to socialize across racial and ethnic lines. Since the first generation still dominates the Korean-American community, however, their socializing pattern still represents the general practice of Korean-Americans' interethnic relationships.

4. Personal conversation with a reporter from a Chicago Korean-American

newspaper. According to Choi 1994, the number of stores on the South Side has decreased from approximately 1,200 to 700 in the last three years.

5. See Chapter 11 for detailed information on the scale, damages, and characteristics of looting on the South Side during the consecutive Bulls' championships.

6. All of my informants' names are pseudonyms. The term *1.5 generation* is used among Korean-Americans to refer to first-generation immigrants' children who came to the United States when they were young. The variations within this category are noticeable enough that even more detailed distinctions such as 1.25 generation or 1.75 generation are sometimes used to indicate an individual's degree of Americanization. The evaluation of a person's degree of Americanization is both subjective and objective, and can vary depending on contexts.

7. After scenes of a Korean-American man coming out of a building shouting and shooting a gun in the middle of the street in the daylight (the camera did not show whether he was aiming at a specific target or shooting into the air; viewers saw only a close-up shot of the gunman, who kept firing his gun, with a frantic expression on his face), a white news reporter said, "They are shooting at anybody. They just want to get rid of everybody." From news footage shown at a conference titled *Media, Race and Governance* held at Northwestern University on February 5, 1994. The image and comment obviously carried the message that Korean-Americans would do anything, including kill, to protect their property. Other images included Korean-American men armed with guns defending their stores from the rooftops.

8. See Leong 1991 for a discussion on images of Asian Americans in the mainstream and Asian American media.

9. See Rouse 1989 for a discussion of the "transnational migration circuit."

10. It was not just the media that acknowledged and emphasized the connection between Korean-Americans and their country of origin. For example, Michael Woo, who was then a councilman of the 13th district of the City of Los Angeles, sent a statement to newspapers in Korea outlining his efforts to help the Korean-American victims by cooperating with other politicians as well as by requesting Koreans' help. Although he used the term *Korean-American* when referring to the Korean-American group in Los Angeles, the fact that he sent a statement to their homeland requesting help and emphasizing his political efforts demonstrates that he believed, to some extent, that Korean-Americans are not an integrated part of the United States.

11. Thanks to William Murphy for introducing this concept to me.

12. See Basch, Glick Schiller, and Szanton-Blanc 1994 and Appadurai 1991 for a discussion of transnationalism.

REFERENCES

Appadurai, Arjun. 1991. Global ethnoscapes: Notes and queries for a transnational anthropology. Chap. 10 in *Recapturing anthropology*, edited by Richard Fox. Sante Fe, N. Mex.: School of American Research Press.

Apple, Michael. 1993. Constructing the "other": Rightist reconstruction of common sense. Chap. 3 in *Race, identity, and representation in education*, edited by Cameron McCarthy and Warren Crichlow. New York: Routledge.

Barth, Fredrick. 1969. Introduction to *Ethnic groups and boundaries*, edited by Fredrick Barth. Boston: Little, Brown.

Basch, Linda, Nina Glick Schiller, and Christina Szanton-Blanc. 1994. *Nations Unbound*. New York: Gordon and Breach.

Chicago Maroon. May 12, 1992.

Chicago Tribune. November 28, 1991; April 26, 1992; May 8, 1992.

Choi, Inchul. 1999. Contemplating black / Korean conflict in Chicago. Chap. 9 in this volume.

Chosun Daily (Chicago Edition). November 3, 1995; November 4, 1994; November 5, 1994.

Choy, Christine, Elaine Kim, and Dae Sil Kim-Gibson, producers. 1993. *SA-I-GU*. San Francisco: Cross Current Media.

Cohen, Abner. 1979. Political symbolism. *Annual Review of Anthropology* 8:87–113.

Comaroff, John, and Jean Comaroff. 1992. *Ethnography and the historical imagination*. Boulder, Colo.: Westview Press.

Conquergood, Dwight. 1992. Life in big red: Struggles and accommodations in a Chicago polyethnic tenement. Chap. 3 in *Structuring diversity: Ethnographic perspectives on the new immigration*, edited by Louise Lamphere. Chicago: University of Chicago Press.

Edelman, Murray. 1988. *Constructing the political spectacle*. Chicago: University of Chicago Press.

Eriksen, Thomas. 1993. *Ethnicity and nationalism*. London: Pluto Press.

Glick Schiller, Nina, and George Fouron. 1990. "Everywhere we go we are in danger": Ti Manno and the emergence of a Haitian transnational identity. *American Ethnologist* 17 (2): 329–47.

Gregory, Steven. 1993. Thinking empowerment through difference: Race and the politics of identity. *Diaspora* 2 (3): 401–10.

Hing, Bill Ong. 1993. *Making and remaking Asian America through immigration policy, 1850–1990*. Stanford, Calif.: Stanford University Press.

Kim, Illsoo. 1981. *New urban immigrants*. Princeton, N.J.: Princeton University.

Kim, Youn-Jin. 1991. From immigrants to ethnics: The life-world of Korean immigrants in Chicago. Ph.D. diss., University of Illinois, Urbana-Champaign.

Kraly, Ellen. 1987. U.S. immigration policy and the immigrant populations of New York. Chap. 2 in *New immigrants in New York*, edited by Nancy Foner. New York: Columbia University Press.

Leong, Russel, ed. 1991. *Moving the image: Independent Asian Pacific American media arts*. University of California, Los Angeles, Asian American Studies Center and Visual Communications, and Southern California Asian American Studies Central, Inc.

Light, Ivan, and Edna Bonacich. 1988. *Immigrant entrepreneurs: Koreans in Los Angeles, 1965–1982*. Berkeley and Los Angeles: University of California Press.

Los Angeles Times. May 30, 1991; May 3, 1992.

The New Republic. July 2, 1990.

New York Times. September 22, 1990; May 16, 1992.

Newsweek. May 11, 1992; May 18, 1992.

Park, Jung-Sun. 1992. A wake-up call: The L.A. "Riots" and ethnic awareness among Korean-Americans in Chicago. Paper presented at the annual meeting of the American Anthropological Association. San Francisco, Calif. December 2–6.

Ravenswood/Albany Park News Star. May 13, 1992.

Rosald, Renato. 1993. *Culture and truth*. Boston: Beacon Press.

Rouse, Roger. 1989. Mexican migration to the United States: Family relations in the development of a transnational migrant circuit. Ph.D. diss., Department of Anthropology, Stanford University.

Smith, Erna. 1993. Transmitting race: the L.A. riot in TV news. Paper presented at CUAPR Conference on Media, Race, and Governance.

Takaki, Ronald. 1989. *Strangers from a different shore*. New York: Penguin Books.

Time. May 11, 1992.

Turner, Victor. 1974. *Dramas, fields, and metaphors*. Ithaca, N.Y.: Cornell University Press.

U.S. Commission on Civil Rights. 1992. *Civil rights issues facing Asian Americans in the 1990s*.

U.S. News and World Report. May 11, 1992; May 18, 1992; May 20, 1992.

Village Voice. June 9, 1992.

Vincent, Joan. 1974. The structuring of ethnicity. *Human Organization* 33:375–79.

Waldinger, Roger. 1989. Structural opportunity or ethnic advantage? Immigrant business development in New York. *International Migration Review* 23:48–72.

Wallman, Sandra. 1981. Refractions of rhetoric: Evidence for the meaning of "race" in England. Chap. 7 in *Politically speaking*, edited by Robert Paine. Philadelphia: Institute for the Study of Human Issues.

Wall Street Journal. May 4, 1992; May 20, 1992.

Washington Post. November 29, 1991.

Williams, Raymond. 1977. *Marxism and literature*. Oxford: Oxford University Press.

12 Conclusion

KWANG CHUNG KIM

THROUGHOUT THIS BOOK, ONE THESIS EMERGES CLEARLY: KOREAN and African American conflict in the second half of the twentieth century is a *multiracial*, not *biracial* conflict, even though only two groups are specified. Since the 1965 revision of the U.S. immigration laws, America has been transformed into a multiracial and multiethnic society. Racial and ethnic group relations in the United States must therefore be analyzed within this multigroup context. Perceiving Korean and African American conflict as a multigroup conflict forces one to investigate the structural position of Korean merchants in low-income urban neighborhoods. This perspective could also create a quandary for scholars: What is a good theoretical framework to deal with the multigroup conflict? Several authors in this book find the middleman minority theory useful in this respect. Yet, the theory needs several refinements in order to be appropriately applied to interminority group conflict involving Koreans and African Americans in modern-day America.

Many authors point out that Korean American perspectives have been ignored both in the mass media coverage and in some academic discussions of the conflict. On the surface, this neglect appears to be somewhat ironic because Korean Americans are one of the groups named in the conflict. There are, on closer examination, some possible explanations for the lack of Korean American perspectives and the biracial framing of this issue: It could be a simple matter of societal lag—our perceptions and beliefs have not caught up with the changing reality. It could be an intentional act by some powerful players—a rational choice by media sources, activists, political players, or others. Or it could be the nature of the topic, which easily lends itself to sensationalization. Whatever the reasons, the fact remains that Korean American perspectives have been neglected.

This book is the result of conscious efforts to present Korean American perspectives on the interminority group conflict between Korean Americans and African Americans in the multiracial and multiethnic American society, and it attempts to juxtapose Korean experiences of the conflict in three major cities. This comparison significantly enhances the refinement of the middleman minority theory as it applies to Korean American merchants in the inner city, and it also allows systematic analyses of the three overt forms of Korean and African American conflict.

The mass media has not helped resolve the conflict. It is argued that the media rather hindered efforts at resolution by constructing the conflict narrowly, as a biracial conflict. Nonetheless, the incomplete and biased media coverage had some beneficial impact. For example, through the painful experiences of the conflict Korean American identity has transformed from an uncertain or reluctant one, known usually as *Koreans in America* to an entitled and entrenched group that calls itself *Korean Americans* in spite of the media's focus on Korean merchants' foreignness and limited Americanization (Chap. 11). Intercity comparison reveals another problem with the media coverage, namely, its unevenness. Reports and sensational coverage of the 1992 Los Angeles racial disturbance conspicuously failed to prevent or reduce destruction.

In contrast, efforts at curtailing violence and conflict in the Chicago case were a moderate success. It was, however, the Los Angeles case that drew so much media attention, while the Chicago experience was virtually ignored at the national level. This filtering of information and the focus on a biracial frame have contributed to the current inept and fallacious social reality of Korean and African American conflict. If the Chicago experience had been widely reported at the national level, the Korean and African American conflict would have been projected to the American people in a radically different way.

The structural position of Korean merchants is that of middleman entrepreneurs. Intercity comparison provides several avenues for the refinement of the middleman minority theory in terms of the nationality of suppliers, the ethnicity and class of customers, and the dominant group's response in times of crisis. Pyong Gap Min and Andrew Kolodny (Chap. 8) divide Korean merchants in urban poor minority communities into two groups, based on the type of goods they handle. Prototype middleman businesses deal with fruits and vegetables, grocery products, fish, liquor, or gasoline. Producers and wholesalers of these goods are usually American corporations. When Korean merchants obtain these consumer goods from white-dominated American corporations and sell them to African American or Hispanic customers, they play the role of typical middleman merchants. Another group of Korean merchants handles fashion items and accessories usually directly imported from South Korea and other Asian or Latin American countries. Since manufacturers and wholesalers of these products do not belong to the white dominant group, it raises the question of whether to consider the Korean merchants who handle these imported goods middleman merchants. Min and Kolodny characterize their business as middleman business "in a limited sense."

This approach classifies Korean merchants in terms of the degree to which they fit the characteristics of middleman merchants, implicitly assuming that in the analysis of Korean merchants, the middleman minority theory limits its focus on members of different racial, ethnic, or status groups who play different economic roles within a national boundary. The second chapter suggests another way to revise the definition of middleman minority theory in order to fit the age of globalization: the concept of the dominant group could be broadened to transcend national boundaries and include those who control corporations and the manufacturers in Asian and Latin American countries. Either one of these methods of revising the middleman theory may be utilized in defining the structural position of Korean merchants in Los Angeles and New York City. The revision suggested in Chapter 2 may be more useful for the case of Chicago, however, because most Korean merchants on the South Side of Chicago deal with imported consumer goods such as clothes, shoes, wigs, jewelry and other personal accessories.

Intercity difference is also observed in the ethnic composition of customers. In South Central Los Angeles, African Americans and Hispanics are residentially mixed and members of these two minority groups patronize Korean merchants. Korean merchants' relationship with customers is then inevitably influenced by a tense relationship between the two customer groups (Chap. 3). To some extent, the same approach is applied in the analysis of many Korean merchants in New York City, where Korean merchants' customers include Hispanics, African Americans, and Caribbean Americans. These findings suggest that the middleman minority theory now has to take into account the reality of different consumer groups and their delicate intergroup relationship. In Chicago, since African Americans and Hispanics are, for the most part, residentially segregated, Korean merchants often serve mainly one minority customer group. As a result, Korean merchants in Chicago are relatively free from the compounding influence of customer-group relationships.

The lack of adequate police protection during the 1992 Los Angeles disturbance empirically demonstrated a major point of the middleman minority theory: In times of crisis, the dominant group tends to abandon the middleman minority. Meanwhile, over the years 1991–93 in Chicago, the police responses to mass violence were gradually stepped up to be swift and effective. The contrasting police responses in these two cities suggest that the middleman minority theory may be refined by exploring the conditions that explain these different patterns of police response. For example, mass violence on the eve of the Chicago Bulls' championship celebration was anticipated, allowing police to develop a plan of action. Also, due to the limited scale of mass violence, the police in Chicago may have been better able to protect both white and Korean merchants simultaneously.

Conflict experiences in the three cities reveal intercity differences both in the scale of conflict and the dominant form of conflict observed. First, the scale of mass violence and boycott observed in Chicago has been much smaller than the Los Angeles riots or the New York City boycotts. One possible explanation is the racial homogeneity of customers in Chicago in contrast to the racial diversity of customers in Los Angeles and New York City. A tense relationship between the different customer groups is said to have escalated Korean and African American conflict in South Central Los Angeles and to have delicately affected the course of the New York City boycotts (Chaps. 3 and 6).

Another explanation can be found in the types of Korean stores prevalent in each city. In Chicago, very few Korean merchants handle liquor—in sharp contrast to Los Angeles and New York City (Min 1996; Park 1995–96). Korean liquor stores were a focal point of local residents' antagonism and were explicitly targeted during the Los Angeles riots; the limited number of Korean liquor stores might have helped alleviate the intensity of Korean and African American conflict in Chicago (Chap. 3; Min 1996). Still another explanation is the number of Korean stores. Relative to New York or Los Angeles, there is a lower concentration of Korean merchants on the South Side of Chicago. Additionally, the effective leadership of the Korean merchants' association and well-planned police responses greatly contributed to contain the incidents of conflict in Chicago.

Why did Los Angeles encounter mass violence more destructive than in any other city, and why did New York merchants suffer a longer boycott than in any other city? To mobilize a community in which there is widespread discontent, an incident must occur to ignite local residents' indignity and instantly bring them together in large numbers. The verdict in the Rodney King trial was this incitant event in Los Angeles; it was an essential factor in producing the swift and large-scale mass violence there. While boycott activity was also observed on several occasions in Los Angeles, it would seem extremely difficult to have an organized and prolonged boycott there like the one in New York City. Min and Kolodny (Chap. 8) contend that, in addition to the discontent and highly deprived social conditions of African Americans in the inner city, a boycott requires the existence of a well-established African American nationalism. African American nationalism has been historically much stronger and better established in New York African American communities than in other cities.

Intercity comparison allows an identification of the major features of the three observed forms of Korean and African American conflict—mass violence, boycott, and interpersonal dispute—which exhibit both commonalities and diversities. Four common features are usually observed in these forms of conflict. First, all three forms occur across a clear group boundary. Korean merchants are distinguished from African American residents both racially and culturally. They are also usually residentially separated. At the same time, the two groups play different economic roles—Korean merchants as sellers and employers and African American residents as customers and employees. The combination of these economic (class) and racial-ethnic differences, in a relationship that offers little chance of permeability of group boundaries, tends to escalate Korean and African American conflict and tempts Korean merchants and African American residents to resort to violence or other forms of coercive tactics instead of persuasion and reward (Kriesberg 1982).

Second, the three forms of Korean and African American conflict generally take place in noninstitutionalized settings. Social conflict should, in the best of circumstances, occur in an institutionalized setting in which established rules, practices, moral principles, laws, and other structural constraints could regulate and control the conflict process. Korean and African American conflict, however, occurs with little regulation or constraining influence from institutionalized control mechanisms. In such an anomic situation, what regulates and influences the process of conflict are the highly situational interpersonal or intergroup dynamics, the feelings and aggressions of individual Korean merchants and African American residents, and the naked power plays of numerous groups associated with the two contending parties.

Third, because the conflict plays out in noninstitutionalized settings, a considerable number of unexpected factors are involved—factors not directly related to the original conditions of the conflict. The ultimate source of poor African Americans' deprived living conditions and their related sense of anger and frustration is the historical and contemporary patterns of white segregation and racism. When the target of African Americans' anger is shifted to Korean merchants, as demonstrated by the Rodney King verdict and subsequent rioting, several unrelated and unpredictable factors can become involved in the conflict. Personality factors of Korean merchants and African American customers and boycott leaders' political positions in inner-city African American communities are examples of seemingly unrelated factors that impact the Korean and African American conflict.

Fourth, the injustices and harm experienced by both sides of the conflict are likely to be exaggerated. When African American residents choose Korean merchants as a target of their aggression and Korean merchants blame all African American residents for the negative or hostile activities of a number of African Americans, both Korean merchants and African American residents have to justify their positions. This situational necessity is likely to compel them to exaggerate the negative aspects of the other side. Each contending party demonizes the other side in order to justify its own position. This necessity shifts the focus of both groups to the narrow biracial situation of the Korean and African American relationship, losing the multiracial perspectives. As a result, their focus gradually turns away from the original structural source of Korean and African American conflict, as hatred and ethnic stereotyping escalate.

Interpersonal dispute at the store level is found to be fundamentally different from the intergroup conflict in two significant ways. First, interpersonal dispute develops in the private or isolated setting of a particular store. Consequently, the interpersonal conflict seldom gets public attention and usually remains a private event without any third party's knowledge or involvement. However, if an interpersonal dispute results in the physical injury or death of one of those directly involved, it can be publicized and framed in the context of intergroup conflict.

In contrast, the events of intergroup conflict often fascinate mass media and usually receive local or national media attention. Such media attention tends to facilitate the intervention of concerned third parties (police and other law-enforcement agencies, insurance companies, government officials or agencies, private agencies, and ethnic individuals or organizations) in the interracial conflict. Most cases of intergroup conflict in major American cities thus emerge as highly sensitive local events with the involvement of various individuals and organizations of Korean Americans, African Americans, and the white dominant group.

Second, Korean merchants and minority customers involved in interpersonal disputes can easily become emotional, and, in the charged atmosphere, both merchants and customers define their situation based on their personal past experiences and their current interests. This means that emotionally charged judgments on relationships and definitions of the situation play a critical role in the development of an interpersonal dispute. In this situation, it often is not clear who actually initiates or escalates interpersonal conflict, as painfully demonstrated by the Soon Ja Du–Latasha Harlins case.

In this respect, the two major forms of intergroup conflict—boycott and mass violence—are sharply distinguished from interpersonal conflict. Since it is against their interests to start or to escalate either a boycott or mass violence, Korean merchants are not likely to initiate any form of intergroup conflict. Rather, they attempt to prevent and contain the development of such conflict. Once intergroup conflict breaks out, Korean merchants try to minimize the damage of the boycott or mass violence. This suggests that it is usually African American residents and their supporters who attempt to start or to escalate some form of intergroup conflict.

Among African Americans, who would then be the likely initiators or escalators of the intergroup conflict? The incidents of intergroup conflict observed in the three cities demonstrate that the motivations leading to boycotts and mass violence differ in three ways. First, as clearly demonstrated in both New York City and Chicago, boycotts are usually initiated or pushed by boycott leaders based on their own definition of the situation and their calculations of both personal and collective interests. When boycott leaders decide to start or to escalate a boycott, a critical factor is their ability to mobilize people and other resources in order to force Korean merchants to yield to their demands. In contrast, mass violence is often a people-initiated movement. Mass violence is a collective event started by people who believe that their sufferings result from an unfair relationship with the dominant group or any target group and are stimulated by some conspicuous precipitating incident of interpersonal dispute.

Second, since a boycott is a calculated act, leaders' demands in the boycott situation are more or less specific and attainable ones, although some leaders also occasionally express certain idealistic or unrealistic demands for purposes of public consumption. In this context, it is possible that leaders of the two contending parties can negotiate and come to terms in order to end a boycott, as demonstrated by the Chicago case. A boycott may also end in an ambiguous or unsatisfactory way, however, if the confrontation is prolonged by the multiple interests of boycott leaders (Chap. 6). The New York City boycott eventually ended when Korean owners of the targeted stores sold their stores to other Koreans and moved away. In mass violence, on the other hand, people protest their deprived living conditions and demand the restructuring or improvement of their life conditions, but they do not usually articulate their demands. Mass violence does not have a negotiated resolution, but rather ends when peoples' spontaneous course of action is exhausted or is forcefully contained by law enforcement. This explains why mass violence is usually a short-lived event. In Los Angeles, rioting lasted for three days, while outbreaks in Chicago usually lasted one night or less. The damage caused by mass violence depends on the intensity of the violence and the effectiveness of police response. In South Central Los Angeles, the intensity of mass violence was very high and police were ineffective for three days. This is in sharp contrast to the Chicago case, in which the intensity of mass violence was rather limited and police response was quick and firm.

Third, although both kinds of conflict inspire the aid and solidarity of other ethnic members, timing of this support varies depending on the conflict's severity and nature. In times of an acute intergroup conflict, even many Korean Americans who are not directly related to self-employed business are greatly concerned with the interracial conflict. Certain ethnic members, organizations, and their resources are thus inevitably involved to alleviate the intensity of the interracial conflict, to minimize the damage of boycott or mass violence, and to help Korean merchants and other victims. There is, however, a great deal of variation in which ethnic members and organizations are involved, with what resources, for what specific event, and with what outcome or effectiveness. In Chicago, various ethnic members and organizations were actively engaged before the anticipated mass violence (Chap. 9). In Los Angeles, however, Korean ethnic personnel and resources were heavily involved only after the three-day mass violence had occurred, though some store owners and volunteers defended Korean stores during the riots (Min 1996).

Both Chicago and New York City experiences show that in the case of boycotts, ethnic personnel and resources were involved during the boycott to encourage its settlement or to influence its course. One reason why the New York City boycott lasted for such a long period of time was that Korean owners of the targeted stores were under heavy pressure from other Korean merchants to keep the originally boycotted stores open. Many Korean merchants suspected that if those stores were closed down as the boycott leaders demanded, other Korean stores would become the targets of future boycotts. In order to keep the targeted stores open, many Korean merchants and their organizations regularly offered financial assistance to the owners to make up for business losses due to the boycott (Chap. 6; Min 1996). In contrast to this active involvement during boycotts, the experiences in these three cities reveal that certain ethnic members, organizations, and resources are heavily involved before or after mass violence, but rarely during the time of violence itself.

In sum, the comparison of the three forms of Korean and African American conflict that occurred in Los Angeles, New York, and Chicago demonstrates that many overt activities of Korean and African American conflict take place in an atmosphere of unpredictability, uncertainty, and explosiveness. Although they share common features, the major forms of conflict are found to be different in their timing, the issues they raised, their influencing factors, their public visibility, the initiators of the conflict, the types of actors and resources involved, the conflict process, and the outcomes or consequences. For a systematic understanding or effective handling of the overt activities of Korean and African American conflict, it is necessary first to identify the specific form of interracial conflict in question and then to review each identified form in terms of its distinct features.

A great majority of the Korean immigrants in the United States today came to this country in the 1970s and 1980s. The second half of the 1980s was the peak of Korean immigration to the United States; during this time, more than 34,000 Korean immigrants arrived each year. The number of immigrants from Korea has been steadily declining since the early 1990s, however (U.S. Department of Justice, 1970–94). Furthermore, immigrants who recently came from Korea are quite different from those who came in the 1970s and 1980s. These recent immigrants are generally not interested in business opportunities in urban poor minority communities. This implies that there will be fewer and fewer Korean merchants who open a business in urban poor minority communities. Many Korean merchants who have done business for many years in urban minority markets are now getting older, without any prospect of their children taking over the business. Some Korean merchants are currently not doing well in business management or are no longer able to run their business due to their health or other personal or family problems. Furthermore, a high proportion of Korean stores destroyed during the 1992 Los Angeles riots are unable to reopen (Park 1995–96). In short, the amount of Korean business in urban poor minority communities has been gradually decreasing. (*New York Times* January 6, 1997; Park and Kim 1998).

As the amount of Korean business dwindles, how will this trend affect the nature of Korean and African American conflict in urban poor minority communities? If more Korean businesses in urban poor minority communities means more antagonistic Korean and African American conflict, will fewer Korean businesses mean less antagonistic Korean and African American conflict? The past conflict between Jewish merchants and African American residents in urban African American communities was resolved by the withdrawal of Jewish merchants from the minority communities (Chang 1993). Will Korean merchants follow the same pattern of conflict resolution through gradual business withdrawal? Even though this answer is beyond the purview of this book, this trend in Korean business must be reviewed with a consideration of the structural position of Korean merchants and the major forms of Korean and African American conflict. Intercity comparison alerts us to numerous possible avenues of research and amplifies a need for a closer and more detailed investigation of the conflict. This book is preliminary and tentative, and yet it represents a significant first step in this direction.

REFERENCES

Chang, Edward T. 1993. Jewish and Korean merchants in African American neighborhoods: a comparative perspective. *Amerasia Journal* 19:5–21.

Kriesberg, Louis. 1982. *Social conflict*, 2d ed. Englewood Cliffs, N.J.: Prentice-Hall.

Min, Pyong Gap. 1996. *Caught in the middle*. Berkeley and Los Angeles: University of California Press.

Park, Kyeyoung. 1995–96. The morality of a commodity: A case study of rebuilding L.A. without liquor stores. *Amerasia Journal* 21:1–24.

Park, Siyoung, and Kwang Chung Kim. 1998. Intrametropolitan location of Korean businesses: the case of Chicago. *Urban Geography* 19: 613–31.

U.S. Department of Justice. 1970–94. *Statistical yearbook of the immigration and naturalization*. Washington, D.C.: U.S. Government Printing Office.

Contributors

NANCY ABELMANN
Associate Professor
Department of Anthropology
University of Illinois, Champaign-
    Urbana

EDWARD T. CHANG
Assistant Professor
Department of Ethnic Studies
University of California, Riverside

INCHUL CHOI
Director, Korean American Community
    Service of Chicago
Ph. D. candidate
Department of Sociology
University of Chicago

KWANG CHUNG KIM
Professor
Department of Sociology and
    Anthropology
Western Illinois University

SHIN KIM
Ph. D. candidate
School of Social Service Administration
University of Chicago

ANDREW KOLODNY
Medical student
Temple University

HEON CHEOL LEE
Assistant Professor
Department of Sociology
University of North Carolina, Asheville

JOHN LIE
Associate Professor
Department of Sociology
University of Illinois, Champaign-
    Urbana

PYONG GAP MIN
Professor
Department of Sociology
Queens College, CUNY

JUNG SUN PARK
Assistant Professor
Department of Anthropology
Earlham College

KYEYOUNG PARK
Assistant Professor
Department of Anthropology
University of California, Los Angelos

Index

Library of Congress Cataloging-in-Publication Data

Koreans in the hood : conflict with African Americans / edited by
    Kwang Chung Kim.
            p.   cm.
        Includes bibliographical references (p.   ) and index.
        ISBN 0-8018-6103-9 (alk. paper). — ISBN 0-8018-6104-7 (pbk. : alk. paper)
        1. Korean Americans—Social conditions—Case studies.   2. Korean
    Americans—Race identity—Case studies.   3. Afro-Americans–Relations with
    Korean Americans—Case studies.   4. Social conflict—United States—Case
    studies.   5. United States—Race relations—Case studies.   6. Los Angeles
    (Calif.)—Race relations.   7. New York (N.Y.)—Race relations.   8. Chicago (Ill.)—
    Race relations.   I. Kim, Kwang Chung, 1937–   .
    E184.K6K6555   1999
    305.895'7073—dc21   98-32012
                                                                          CIP